THE
KILLING
OF
JULIA
WALLACE

THE
KILLING
OF
JULIA
WALLACE

THE DEVIL IN THE DETAIL

JOHN GANNON

AMBERLEY

This book is dedicated to my wife Lynne with my eternal gratitude for her faith,
encouragement and love. Also to my four wonderful and talented sons,
Allan, Dean, John and Sean with all my love.
LAMYA

First published 2012

Amberley Publishing
The Hill, Stroud
Gloucestershire, GL5 4EP

www.amberleybooks.com

Copyright © John Gannon, 2012

The right of John Gannon to be identified as the Author
of this work has been asserted in accordance with the
Copyrights, Designs and Patents Act 1988.

British Library Cataloguing in Publication Data.
A catalogue record for this book is available from the British Library.

ISBN 978-1-4456-0506-7

Typesetting and Origination by Amberley Publishing.
Printed in Great Britain.

Contents

'So perhaps my sufferings have somehow been worth while? At least I have made history!'

William Herbert Wallace, 'The Life Story of William Herbert Wallace' – draft copy of the *John Bull* series of magazine articles entitled 'The Man They Did Not Hang', published during the summer of 1932.

Preface

At the end of the trial of William Herbert Wallace for the murder of his wife, Julia, the presiding judge, the Right Honourable Mr Justice Wright, said in his summing up, 'It is your duty to decide on the evidence which has been given before you … and whatever your verdict is, that is the acid test which you must apply.' Justice Wright was well aware, in a case of this magnitude, of the dire consequences of subjectivity and selectivity on the part of the jury: you could be sending the wrong man to the gallows.

In examining the circumstances of any unsolved crime (especially one as old as this), the investigator must stand back and take an objective view of *all* the evidence to hand; only then can a proposed solution to the crime be justified. Once a solution is reached, *all evidence must be presented* in justifying that result.

It was with this in mind that I decided to take up the mantle of two previous writers on this subject: Jonathan Goodman and Roger Wilkes. In undertaking this case, Jonathan Goodman had not ventured out on a witch-hunt: going into the subject with an open mind, he simply wanted to find out who killed Julia Wallace based upon the evidence available to him at that time – which he then presented fully. Goodman's book, *The Killing of Julia Wallace*, published in 1969, is a sublime piece of thorough investigative journalism, imparted with skill and wit. Despite the lack of official documentation, he made thorough use of what was available and, with it being only 1966 when he began his researches, many of the people involved in the case were still able to furnish him with first-hand accounts, allowing Goodman to verify, deny or elucidate on the many rumours and conjectures that have surrounded the crime since its perpetration: one encounter involved a face-to-face confrontation on the doorstep of the person who became his 'Mr X' in the subsequent book. Unable, at the time, to furnish readers with this suspect's name due to the likelihood of being sued for libel, Goodman was forced to suppress it.

In 1979, Roger Wilkes was news editor at Liverpool's independent radio station, Radio City, when he began researching the case for a fiftieth anniversary reappraisal, *Who Killed Julia?* to be aired by the station on 20 January 1981. During November 1979, Jonathan Goodman became consultant to the programme and opened up his archives to Wilkes. Between them, they managed to further the investigation by unveiling a new and very important witness, John Parkes, a Liverpool garage hand who claimed he had been forced to hose down Mr X's car on the night of the murder. It was during this programme that the name of Goodman's Mr X could finally be revealed as Richard Gordon Parry (the reading

of the announcement being given by Goodman himself); Parry had died the previous April
of a heart attack at his home in Wales, thus eliminating the chance of a libel suit being
lodged.

Even at this point, fifty years after Julia Wallace's savage murder, Wilkes could still not gain
access to any of the official police files concerning the case. Upon applying to Merseyside
Police for access to the Wallace case files, Wilkes was told that the files had gone missing
and that the police were unable to co-operate in the making of the programme. However,
on the night of the airing of the second programme, at the end of the debate and phone-in
that followed, Roger Wilkes announced that the Merseyside Police had just telephoned the
studio to say that the Wallace case files had just been found. The following morning, Wilkes
renewed his request for the files; this time, he was refused by the then Chief Constable,
Kenneth Oxford. After the recording of the interview with John Parkes that was to be
used in the radio broadcast, the request to view the files was renewed again. The Deputy
Chief Constable wrote back and confirmed that Kenneth Oxford would not release the
files and added, 'In view of the controversy aroused by your previous programme, it would
be inappropriate for Police records to be released as a basis for further public debate.' On
9 March 1981, a Liverpool MP, Bob Parry (no relation to Richard Gordon Parry), issued a
request in the House of Commons to the then Home Secretary, William Whitelaw, asking
him to explain the reasons why the Wallace files could not be examined: his request was
turned down. And so, if it had not been for Goodman's assistance, Wilkes would have had
to rely upon what little official evidence was available and the first-hand accounts of the
remaining contemporary witnesses. In 1984, Wilkes published his own account of the Wallace
case, *Wallace: The Final Verdict* – a gripping, thorough piece of investigative journalism based
upon the research undertaken whilst making the Radio City programme.

On the outstanding work of Jonathan Goodman, augmented and excelled by Roger
Wilkes, I have based my own effort. Unavailable to the latter and the former, the Wallace
files, as such, are now open to examination; both Merseyside Police and the Director of
Public Prosecution files are available to those who wish to form their own opinions. Given
also the overwhelming generosity of Hill Dickinson LLP in allowing this writer exclusive
access to the personal files of William Herbert Wallace's solicitor, Hector Munro – added to
the present climate conducive to family research and the ever-growing digital availability
and ease of access of such files – my task has been rendered a lot easier than theirs. Despite
this, my efforts would have been fruitless had it not been for the solid grounding given to
me by both Goodman's *The Killing of Julia Wallace* and Wilkes's *Wallace: The Final Verdict*. In
addition, I have also been aided by the generosity and encouragement of the latter author,
allowing me to add to the accumulation of evidence established by the former. It was from
among all of this accumulated information that I managed to find the devil in the detail.

In the following pages, I will reveal for the very first time the identities of the mysterious
'R. M. Qualtrough' and the long elusive 'Marsden' with irrefutable evidence. I will show
how integral these names are to solving the murder of Julia Wallace, and prove that the
police knew both the identity and the whereabouts of both these people, and yet no official
statements appear to have been taken from them, nor their names included in statements
taken from any person associated with them. I will also reveal not only why these people

were 'airbrushed' out of the investigation, but why it was so crucial that *both* of these names disappeared, Richard Gordon Parry be kept out of the dock and William Herbert Wallace be quickly ushered onto the end of a hangman's rope.

Along with these startling revelations I will reveal, with proof, how the one single drop of blood to be found outside the scene of the murder found its way onto the lavatory pan in the bathroom; I will show proof of exactly why, on the night of the murder, the Wallaces' front bedroom was found in a state of disorder – and who did it; and I will offer a new, more logical, reassessment of the crime scene. Finally, in the hope of bringing closure to what has been one of the most baffling cases in recent British history, I will offer a viable motive for the perpetration of this most horrific of crimes.

John Gannon
Liverpool, 2012

Prologue

On Monday 19 January 1931, at about 7.20 p.m., a phone call was received at Cottle's City Café in the basement of 24 North John Street, Liverpool – a call that heralded one of Liverpool's most enduring and intriguing mysteries. The call was for a Mr William Herbert Wallace, an agent for the Prudential Assurance Company of Dale Street, Liverpool, and a member of the Central Chess Club which, during the winter months, met at the café every Monday and Thursday night.

Mr Wallace not having arrived, the call was taken by the Chess Club's captain, Mr Samuel Beattie. The caller, a Mr R. M. Qualtrough, wished to speak to Mr Wallace concerning an insurance matter he wanted him to deal with. Mr Qualtrough explained that his daughter was about to have her 21st birthday and he wanted to make her a gift by way of some business to be dealt with by Mr Wallace *specifically*. Wallace not being available, and Mr Qualtrough being too busy to call on him personally because of his daughter's birthday arrangements, he left his details with Mr Beattie and asked him to ask Mr Wallace to call on him at his home, 25 Menlove Gardens East, Mossley Hill, Liverpool, the following night, 20 January 1931, at 7.30 p.m. When Mr Wallace eventually arrived at the Chess Club, Mr Beattie duly passed the message on.

Given the possibility of Mr Qualtrough wanting an annuity or an endowment for his daughter (the commission from such a transaction being sizeable enough to warrant him making the four-mile journey to Mossley Hill), the following night Mr Wallace gathered some documents he felt he might need, left his home at 29 Wolverton Street, Anfield, at about 6.45 p.m., and made his way to the Mossley Hill area of Liverpool, and his appointment with Mr Qualtrough.

After traversing the Menlove Gardens area of Mossley Hill for around 40 minutes, asking numerous people for directions and not having been able to locate 25 Menlove Gardens East, nor Mr Qualtrough, Wallace began his journey back to Wolverton Street at 8.00 p.m. At 8.40 p.m., he entered his home to find his wife's dead body sprawled across the parlour floor; she had been battered to death in a brutal frenzy with a heavy, blunt object.

Initially, the police were working on the assumption that the assailant had been a thief who, having broken into the house, had encountered Mrs Wallace and had beaten her to death to prevent her from giving evidence against him. This assumption came about when Wallace, upon examining a money box into which he usually placed his collection money for the Prudential, noticed that about £4 was missing.

From the outset, the police were baffled. Mrs Wallace had obviously been violently assaulted: there was a huge, gaping hole through her skull, exposing the brain; the floor of the room was dotted with large pools of congealing blood; the walls, furniture, pictures and ornaments in the room were spattered with blood – obviously, there had been a very violent attack – yet every piece of furniture and every ornament in the room seemed to be in its rightful place. In examining the house, no fingerprints could be found; the only other trace of blood that could be found, outside of the parlour, was a tiny blood clot on the rim of the upstairs toilet and a smear on a pound note in an upstairs bedroom – no obvious weapon could be traced. As police investigations proceeded, Wallace volunteered a series of four statements, one of which – his second – produced a list of seventeen people Mrs Wallace would allow into the house when he was absent. Upon investigating this list, the police seemed satisfied that none of the people listed had been instrumental in the commission of this terrible crime. It was not long before suspicion began to fall upon Wallace himself. Having, apparently, exhausted all other lines of enquiry, William Herbert Wallace was arrested on 2 February 1931 and charged with the murder of his wife.

On 25 April 1931, William Herbert Wallace was found guilty of the wilful murder of his wife at the Spring Assizes, held at St George's Hall, Liverpool, and sentenced to death. The following month, on 19 May, Wallace's sentence was overturned at the Court of Appeal. Since that day, no one has been charged with the brutal murder of Mrs Julia Wallace, leaving unanswered the question, 'Who killed Julia Wallace?'

Since that time, an abundance of books and articles have been written about the case; Raymond Chandler called it 'the impossible murder', and said that it was 'the nonpareil of all murder mysteries'. Ever since 1969, when Jonathan Goodman introduced the world to his 'Mr X', who was then revealed to be Richard Gordon Parry (a young acquaintance of Mr and Mrs Wallace) by Roger Wilkes in his 1981 series of radio programmes, in all re-evaluations of the case that have followed, an either/or situation arose, where only two names have stood prominent as possible suspects: William Herbert Wallace and Richard Gordon Parry. Despite the fact that, on the night of the murder, each of these men has a seemingly unshakeable alibi, in all attempts to solve the case, the circumstances surrounding the murder have been pushed and pulled almost out of recognition in an attempt to reconcile the timings of their alibis with the then prescribed circumstances of the murder. One of the biggest distractions in these attempts has been the excessive importance placed upon the Medical Examiner Professor John Edward Whitley MacFall's estimation that Julia had died at around 6 p.m.

Yet, with the simple addition of a third man, not only do these square pegs slide smoothly into the correct holes – *all* the pegs fit into the board.

1

Beginnings

Julia Dennis

Despite the inscription on grave 4837 in section 17 of the Church of England Division of Anfield Cemetery reading 'IN LOVING MEMORY AND AFFECTIONATE REMEMBRANCE OF JULIA, BELOVED WIFE OF W. H. WALLACE, WHO DIED 20TH JANUARY 1931 AGED 52 YEARS', Julia Wallace was, in fact, born on 28 April 1861 and not 1878 as the memorial would have us believe. The second child of seven children – Annie Maria (1860), Julia (1861), Rhoda (1863), Amy (1864), George Smith (1867), John Henry (1869) and Herbert William (1871) – Julia Dennis was born to William George Dennis and Anne Teresa Smith at Bruntcliffe House, a 250-acre farm in East Harlsey, North Yorkshire. In 1856, Bruntcliffe House was tenanted by William's older brother, John. William, then 22 years of age, was working on their father's 322-acre neighbouring farm, Morton Lodge, when their father died. As he was the eldest son, it fell upon John to take over the running of his father's much larger holding, and so he transferred the tenancy of Bruntcliffe House over to William.

After eight years of successful husbandry at Bruntcliffe House, during 1864, whilst his wife was pregnant with their fourth child, William moved his family to No. 5 Farm House, West Harlsey, a slightly smaller holding at 230 acres. Situated across the neighbouring fields to Bruntcliffe House, close to Harlsey Castle, the farm was nestled in the heart of Smith country – home to Julia's mother's family. The Smith family had been tenant farmers in the district since as far back as the sixteenth century, and within this close community Anne Teresa's brother, John Jonathan Smith, was running a 170-acre farm at West Harlsey Grange, and her cousins the 220-acre Harlsey Castle Farm and the 120-acre holdings of No. 2 Farm House. Whilst here, as in many other farming communities, Julia's parents employed the services of a governess, Frances M. Robinson, to give their young family, especially Julia and her three sisters, the chance of better opportunities in their future lives. Tragically, a week before Julia's tenth birthday, on 19 April 1871, Anne Teresa died giving birth to her seventh child, Herbert William. Anne Teresa's death must have hit William very hard; with a farm to run and a large family to look after, it appears that William saw his health go into decline. Only two years after his wife's death, William was forced to give up farming altogether and, in 1873, took up the more salubrious position as innkeeper of the Railway Inn, Romanby, Northallerton. His stay here was only brief, however; in February 1875, he died of liver disease.

Shortly after the death of their father, it would appear that the young Julia Dennis and her sisters, Rhoda and Amy, had aspirations of becoming governesses themselves: Julia's strengths lay in French, music and painting. One of the main attractions of becoming a governess at that time would have been the free board and lodgings usually provided – even if the salary was a pittance, or non-existent. By 1881, aged only 19, Julia was working as assistant governess at Keswick House Ladies School, Keswick Road, Wandsworth, London: the home of Robert Smith, a 44-year-old banker's clerk, and his 38-year-old wife Charlotte, herself a governess. Here, along with their mother, Julia tended to the needs of three of the Smith's four children (Maude, Matilda and Rose) and three female boarders. At this time, Rhoda was also a school governess, living with their older sister, Annie Maria, in Ash Grove, Harrogate, Yorkshire. At the beginning of the 1890s, Julia had returned to Yorkshire and was then residing at Elm House in Woodlesford – the home of 38-year-old Robert John Smith, a clerk to an architect and land and mineral agent, and his 40-year-old wife, Sophia. Here, Julia was governess to their four children, Sarah, Sophia, Claude and Robert.

According to James Murphy in his book *The Murder of Julia Wallace*, in 1855 William George Dennis became leaseholder for a property in East Rounton, North Yorkshire, called the Black Horse Inn; this included, besides all of the associated outbuildings, 17 acres of land. The lease was for 1,000 years. In 1872, a year after Julia's mother had died, the lease on this property was amended to include William's mother, Ann, and appears to have been sold to Isaac Lowthian Bell. In 1892, ten years after Ann Dennis's death, through a Deed of Assignment, the lease on the property was then transferred to her grandchildren. According to Murphy, the lease states that Julia was living in the care of her tutor, Charles Henry Robinson, at 22 Cliffe (*sic*) Road in the Hyde Park district of Leeds. Murphy goes on to speculate that the then 31-year-old Julia may have been living with Mr Robinson as 'man and wife'. This, in fact, was not the case; Charles Henry Robinson had merely acted as Julia's signatory witness on the document. The address given, 22 Cliff Road, was that of Walter Forrester, a barrister's clerk, and his family – possibly a clerk to Robinson's own lawyer.

Charles Henry Robinson was born in 1850 in Headingly, Yorkshire, and was a schoolmaster throughout most of his life. In 1892, he was a private tutor living with his wife, Maria, a confectioner, at 1 Claremont (now Claremont Drive), Headingly, Leeds, with their three sons, George (18), Bertram (15) and Henry (11). As Julia was a governess residing at Elm House (a private house), it is more likely that, as a private teacher, Charles Henry Robinson was also working at Elm House and was a colleague of Julia's. At the turn of the last century Charles Henry Robinson was a secondary-school master living with his wife at 46 Brudenall Road, Headingly, whilst Julia had returned to London, and was living at 182 Stroud Green Road, Hornsey, in a flat above a shop – Taylor's Drug Co. Ltd – listed as 'Living on own means'. It was whilst living here that the first sign of Julia's unease with her identity can be clearly seen: on the census of the time she gives her age as 30, when in fact she was 40. According to Julia's grandnephew, Douglas Birch, Julia had returned to Yorkshire by 1908 and was living at 5 Dragon Parade, Harrogate, when his mother, Annie Teresa, then around 12 years old, went to live with her. Considering Julia her favourite aunt, she stayed with her until 1910.

William Herbert Wallace

Three years after Julia's father's death – when she was 17 years old – a hundred miles west of Romanby, at 44 Newton Street, Millom, Cumbria, William Herbert Wallace was born to

Benjamin Wallace and Margery Hall on 29 August 1878, the first of three children. Along with his brother, Joseph Edwin (born 1880), and young sister, Jessie (born 1883), William revelled in the breathtaking beauty of their Lake District surroundings. He was an introverted and reticent child, and his passions leant more toward science and music; he attributed this to his father and mother respectively. His father, he says, was an ardent geologist, and his mother from a musical family. Despite these early academic and artistic leanings, and an unwanted promotion to the 'big boys school' for becoming top of his infant class at only 5 years of age, Wallace's reticent and sensitive nature rendered the whole experience so fearful he could barely recall it.

Benjamin Wallace, a part-time agent for the Prudential Assurance Company, was a printer and a stationer by trade and, as soon as his eldest child was able, he set him to work in the family business. Wallace said of his own young accomplishment in the trade that 'I was the very "printer's devil"' – a term used to not only denote an apprentice who fetched, carried, mixed, washed and cleaned, but who was also the recipient (and, more often than not, the deserved recipient) of blame when mistakes occurred.

In 1888, when William was 10 years old, the Wallaces began a number of moves – the first of which took them to Blackpool, Lancashire. Almost immediately upon their arrival, William contracted typhoid fever, from which, it was thought, he was unlikely to recover. Wallace fondly attributed his survival to his mother, saying that 'my mother's care and devotion proved, as often such love and tenderness does, that a nurse has more healing power than a doctor'. This most serious of ailments, caused by the *Salmonella Typhi* bacterium, is usually contracted by consuming food or water that has been contaminated with infected sewage, being touched by an infected person, or being exposed to flies that have fed on infected faeces. It would appear, from Wallace's own account, that his condition went unnoticed and, therefore, untreated for some time – hence the near fatal severity of its progress. If this was the case, one of the common complications of late diagnosis and treatment of typhoid fever is kidney failure. It was most likely, therefore, at this young age, that Wallace developed the condition that was to become the bane of his future life.

By 1890, when Wallace was 12 years old, the family were living at 151 Chapel Street, Dalton-in-Furness – close neighbours of the Blackwell family, who lived at 88 Chapel Street. William Blackwell, a one-time blacksmith, was a machine and hammer smith at the local Elliscale iron mine until his death in 1885; both he and his wife Ellen Jenkin had originated from Cornwall – William from White Stile Down, Crowan, Ellen from St Austell. By the time William Blackwell was 20 years old he had left Cornwall and moved to Urswick Much, 3 miles east of Dalton-in-Furness, where he was a blacksmith. In 1854, during a brief return to Cornwall, he married Ellen Jenkin in St Austell, the couple returning to Cumbria almost immediately and settling in Dalton-in-Furness, where the first of their nine children – Mary Ann (1856), Emma (1858), Josiah James (1861), Annie (1862), William James (1865), Richard Arthur (1868), Edmund (1870), Ellen Maud (1874) and Amy Margaret (1878) – was born. At the time of the Wallaces' arrival in the town, Ellen was widowed and living with four of her children – William James, a steam-engine maker; Edmund, a stationary engine driver; Amy Margaret, at only 13 years of age, a pupil at the Dalton Board Girls School in Chapel Street; and her married daughter, Annie, and Annie's husband Joseph Backhouse, an engine fitter at the Elliscale iron mine. A bond must have formed between the two families. Some years later, Joseph Edwin

Wallace would marry their youngest daughter, Amy Margaret. It was whilst living in Dalton-in-Furness that Wallace's introversion was overcome. In contrast to the scholastic amnesia of his time at Millom, his school days at Dalton Board Boys School, Broughton Road, were 'treasured in my memory, dew-starred with happiness'. Ransomesquely, he recalled being leader of a gang of adventure-seeking youths, who would swim in ponds, climb trees and negotiate fields and hedges with firewood tomahawks, scalping make-believe enemies.

In 1892, when 14 years of age, Wallace took up a five-year apprenticeship in the drapery trade with master draper Thomas H. Tenant in Cavendish Street, Barrow, for the weekly sum of 3 shillings, with an annual rise of 2 shillings. By this time, Benjamin Wallace had given up the printing trade and had become a full-time agent for the Prudential Assurance Company. Upon completion of his apprenticeship, Wallace took up the position of assistant draper in several towns, including Manchester, where he took up the position at Messrs Whiteway, Laidlaw & Company, outfitters to Her Majesty's Armed Forces.

By 1901, Wallace was back in the bosom of his family in Dalton-in-Furness, living at 19 Victoria Street. By this time, his brother Joseph was a compositor at a printing firm and his sister Jesse, like Wallace, was a draper's assistant. Wallace, however, had itchy feet; as he noted in his own words, 'wanderlust which had obsessed me in earlier years grew to fever heat and at the age of twenty three I sailed for India, there to take up a position as salesman in a drapery business in Calcutta'. It would appear that a vacancy had arisen at a branch of Whiteway, Laidlaw & Company in Calcutta's main thoroughfare, the Chowringhee, and Wallace had been accepted for it.

Arriving in Calcutta at the end of 1902, Wallace was there to witness the preparations being made for the Durbar (a formal imperial assembly called to mark a state occasion) in Delhi on 1 January 1903, commemorating the coronation of King Edward VII and Queen Alexandra as Emperor and Empress of India on 9 August 1902. At the time of the devastating Kangra earthquake on 4 April 1905, in which 20,000 lives were lost, Wallace was seriously ill in a Calcutta hospital, receiving treatment for his ever-worsening kidney trouble. Not having responded well to the treatment and in terrible pain, Wallace desired a fairer climate and so left Calcutta, moving to Shanghai, where he took up a position as an advertising manager at a general store. His brother Joseph had been here for some time, working as a printer for the British government. Wallace's most vivid recollection of his time in Shanghai was of the various forms of torture and execution that the inhabitants would inflict upon each other. A common sight was the use of cangues on petty criminals, who would be seen wandering about the streets, their arms and necks encased in these heavy wooden collars. Occasionally, he would happen upon a criminal who had been placed upon a pile of rocks, his arms tied to a stake above his head. Each day a rock would be removed until, eventually, the miscreant would be hanging from the stake by his arms alone. One of the more gruesome experiences Wallace encountered was the public execution of six criminals, describing it as 'grimly humorous'. He recounted that

six condemned men knelt in a row awaiting the sword of the executioner, the fellow struck an awkward blow and failed to decapitate the first man. The other five took this as a great joke and roared with laughter though a few moments later their own heads were rolling in the dust.

In 1906, not long after his arrival in Shanghai, Wallace was, once again, admitted to hospital for an operation on his left kidney; three weeks later, he developed an abscess on his right kidney, and three weeks after this his left kidney was operated on once again because of a urinary fistula (an abnormal passage between two organs). Not having received the anticipated relief, he hastily returned to England, confined to a hospital bed on the North German Lloyd Line's *Gneisenau*.

Wallace arrived back in Britain at 2.35 p.m. on 19 March 1907, entering Guy's Hospital, London. On 7 April, he finally had his left kidney removed. Unable to work for eighteen months, funds began to run low. After attempting to re-establish himself at his old job at Whiteway, Laidlaw & Company in Manchester and finding the work too arduous, he reluctantly had to leave. During this time, he had developed an interest in politics – he spoke for the Liberal Party at meetings held in the North Lonsdale constituency. Two years after Wallace's return to Britain, Joseph Wallace also returned and married childhood sweetheart Amy Margaret Blackwell during the autumn of 1909. The couple soon moved to London, where on 6 June 1911 their only child, Edwin Herbert Wallace, was born. Shortly after, Joseph and his family returned to the Malay provinces.

In 1910, whilst living at 9 Belmont Road, Harrogate (by now a guesthouse accommodating four boarders), with his parents and his sister Jessie, Wallace became Liberal Registration Agent for the Ripon Division, West Riding of Yorkshire. Meanwhile, by the beginning of April 1911, Julia Dennis had moved into 11 St Mary's Avenue – a ten-room guesthouse (though at this time Julia lived alone), only two streets away from Belmont Road; it was at this same time that the progression of Julia's unease with her identity became startlingly evident. The census of 1911 was like no other; previously, all censuses had been taken by an official enumerator who would call at each individual house within his given area and complete the schedules himself. The census for 1911, however, was sent to each address to be completed and signed by the occupants themselves. The 1911 census return for 11 St Mary's Avenue, Harrogate, shows only one resident – Jane Dennis, aged 32 (born in 1879); describing herself as 'single' and an 'apartment keeper' living on her 'own account' (being neither an employer nor employed), she also claimed to have been born in 'Hexham, Sussex'. The form is signed 'J Dennis'. How certain can we be that the person who completed this census schedule was, in fact, not Jane Dennis, but Julia Dennis? Given the fact that Julia's name is listed upon the 1911 Burgess Roll for 11 St Mary's Avenue as 'Dennis, Julia ... from 5 Dragon Parade' and given that Julia proves this herself when giving her address as 11 St Mary's Avenue upon her marriage certificate, in comparing the signature within the census schedule with Julia's handwriting from the Wallaces' original marriage certificate (signed on the day of their marriage), it can clearly be seen that there is an unmistakable similarity between the two. There can be very little doubt that it was Julia Dennis who was living at 11 St Mary's Avenue, Harrogate, Yorkshire, at the time of the 1911 census – and that she knowingly falsified her personal details within the census schedule: she changed her Christian name, she decreased her age by eighteen years, and she falsified the place of her birth. In confirmation of this, a 'Jane Dennis' was not registered as being born in the county of Sussex during the years 1878 or 1879.

Mr and Mrs William Herbert Wallace

It was whilst she was living at 11 St Mary's Avenue that Julia and Wallace's destinies crossed. In Wallace's own words, 'Dark haired, dark eyed, full of energy and vivaciousness, she filled in every corner of the picture I had dreamed of "that one woman in all the world" most men enshrine in their hearts.' On 24 March 1914, they married at St Mary's church, Harrogate (a temporary church, known locally as the 'tin tabernacle'). Wallace's mother having died in 1913, both Wallace and his father left Belmont Road, and moved into St Mary's Avenue with Julia.

Close examination of the couple's marriage certificate reveals that Wallace states his age correctly as 36 years old and describes himself as a secretary (most likely for the Liberal Party). Julia, apparently, had no occupation at this time; her age, however, is given as 37 – now sixteen years younger than her true age of 53. In the same document, she augments the deception by describing her father as a 'Veterinary Surgeon'. Julia had also been known to describe her mother as 'Aimee', a lady of French origin. These fabrications may simply have originated as a requirement for Julia to have pursued her career as a governess. At the end of the nineteenth century, governesses were ostensibly single girls from middle-class families with a middle-class education. Julia's family having been undeniably working-class, she may have felt it necessary to manufacture a family background fitting for her position in order to gain employment. However, what might have begun as a necessity had now turned into a blatant deception. Given the information provided by Julia on the 1911 census and the information she supplied on her marriage certificate, how much did Wallace really know about the woman he married? If Julia had maintained this deception, Wallace would have been led to believe that Julia Dennis was born (according to her age on the marriage certificate) in 1877 in Sussex to middle-class parents, veterinary surgeon William George Dennis and a lady of French origin, Aimee Dennis. If this was the case, the only truths he actually knew about his wife were her real name and her present address. Despite three of her siblings still being alive – Rhoda, Amy and George Smith Dennis – on the day of their wedding, Julia's bridesmaid was Wallace's sister, Jessie; Wallace's best man (his brother Joseph being in the Far East at the time) was 53-year-old John Smith Allanson, a store manager from Hartlepool, Durham. At the time of the wedding, Allanson was living with his wife Hannah two doors away from Julia at 15 St Mary's Avenue; he too had boarders staying at his house – one of whom was 35-year-old Ella Warwick, who, like Wallace, was a draper's assistant. Might it have been through Wallace's association with John Smith Allanson or Ella Warwick that, in calling at 15 St Mary's Avenue, he had met Julia? Could Julia's deception have been the reason none of her own siblings had attended her wedding – unwilling to become party to a blatant lie unknown to Wallace? On the other hand, might Julia have not informed any of her siblings about the wedding for fear her deception would be exposed?

At the outbreak of the First World War, Wallace's thoughts on politics soured and, after giving up his office with the Ripon Liberal Party, he attempted to join the Army. After six failed attempts due to his single kidney, he sought another occupation. Because of his father's influence with the Prudential Assurance, Wallace secured a position as a district agent with the company in Clubmoor, Liverpool, with an annual income of £260–270 a year, a bonus every March dependent upon how much new business was introduced and the successes of his weekly collections, and a commission on any life insurance (20 per cent of the first year's premium) or motor insurance (15 per cent on each renewal premium) he introduced. What had brought about this dramatic change of location? Why would the couple not have preferred to remain in that locale? Wallace's father was seriously ill at this time; his sister Jessie was a nurse at a local hospital. According to a funding appeal drawn up by the Prudential Staff Union at the time of Wallace's arrest, it was through the assistance of a Mr N. Allsop (according to Goodman, 'through the good offices of Norman Allsop … a native of Barrow-in-Furness and a close friend of his father') that Wallace had managed to gain his agency in Clubmoor, Liverpool; this might indicate that Wallace had specifically asked for an agency in Liverpool. At this time, Julia had no ties to Harrogate: her sister Annie had died in 1908; Rhoda was a lodging housekeeper in Bridlington; Amy was a schoolteacher in Brighton; and George Smith was a chemist's assistant in Leeds. Might it have been Julia, needing to escape the possible demands of St Mary's church to furnish them with her birth certificate (not provided at the time of the couple's wedding), who had persuaded Wallace to move away from Harrogate? In ensconcing themselves such a distance away, this problem would have been resolved. But why Liverpool? As will be detailed later, a childhood friend of Wallace's from Dalton-in-Furness, Frederick William Jenkinson, had become a teacher, moving to Liverpool in 1909 – might it have been through this connection that the Wallaces found themselves arriving in Liverpool just a year after their marriage?

2

Liverpool

For four months after their arrival in Liverpool in March 1915, the Wallaces lived at 26 Pennsylvania Road, Clubmoor, the district within which Wallace had his agency (at some point during October 1928 and October 1929, this house would be so badly damaged by fire it was pulled down, never to be rebuilt). In July 1915, the couple moved into 29 Wolverton Street, Anfield, paying a weekly rent of around 14 shillings and sixpence to their landlord, Mr Samuel Evans. Here, according to Wallace, his and Julia's lives were 'filled with complete enjoyment … with all the happiness of quietude and mutual interest and affection'. Having previously gained qualifications in electricity and chemistry, Wallace took up researches in chemistry at the Liverpool Technical College, William Brown Street. After two years here, he was appointed assistant part-time demonstrator and lecturer in chemistry, a position he held for five years. To assist him in preparing his lectures and demonstrations, he converted the back bedroom of their home into a laboratory/ workroom where he would spend many happy hours engrossed in his interests. Having played chess since he was a young man, he formed the Central Chess Club, some time around 1922, with a local friend, James Caird.[1] The club's meetings were held at Cottle's City Café, in the basement of 24 North John Street in Liverpool's city centre. Years later, at the committal trial, James Caird was questioned about this by Sidney Scholefield Allen, Wallace's defence counsel: 'Was Mr Wallace well liked at the Chess Club?' Caird replied, 'Yes. We formed it together.' During the wintertime, meetings were held at lunchtime and every Monday and Thursday evening. Wallace's visits, however, were not regular – he generally attended once a week on the Monday and only on a Thursday if a match were being played.

The Wallace Diaries

On 21 January 1931 – the day after Julia's murder – the police took possession of, amongst other items, seven diaries belonging to Wallace: two of these were business diaries; one was the diary taken from Wallace in which he had written Qualtrough's name and address upon having had the message relayed to him by Samuel Beattie on Monday 19 January; the rest were personal diaries covering the period 1 January 1928 to 18 January 1931 (two days before Julia's murder). After their acquisition, these were scrutinised by the police and notes were taken of any *relevant* entries. On 4 March 1931, at Wallace's committal trial, whilst being questioned by prosecution council, Inspector Herbert Gold had produced from his pocket the small, complimentary Prudential diary in which Wallace had written Qualtrough's name and address upon it being relayed to him by Beattie at the Chess Club. However, nothing was mentioned of the other diaries – particularly the four personal diaries. Scholefield Allen had also noticed that none of the other police witnesses had been asked about them either. Feeling that the prosecution were attempting to withhold evidence that may have been of benefit to Wallace, and being fully aware the diaries were in the possession of the police, Scholefield Allen asked, whilst cross-examining Gold, 'Are the police in possession of other diaries belonging to the accused?'

Gold, apparently shocked at the question, brought two small diaries out of one of his pockets: 'There are these business diaries.'

'Are there other diaries – of events, thoughts and opinions?' Scholefield Allen quickly retorted. Fumbling back through his pockets, Gold produced four larger diaries and laid them in front of him. Taking up the top diary, Gold began to recite a potted version of the events Wallace had noted for 5 December 1930 concerning Julia's late arrival home after a visit to Southport earlier that day. Unsatisfied with this, Scholefield Allen asked to be handed the diaries and, after leafing through them, began to recite the entry in full – showing that, up to this point, the diaries had remained solely in the possession of the police.

After being sent to trial at the end of the committal proceedings, Wallace had retained the services of Hector Alfred Munro. On 10 March 1931, Hector Munro approached the prosecuting solicitor, Mr J. R. Bishop, asking him to arrange with the police for the defence to view the diaries. On 16 March, Munro received word from the Town Clerk, Walter Moon, that these arrangements had been made. On 31 March, Munro wrote back to Moon informing him that, a few days previously, he had asked Inspector Gold to inquire whether it would be possible for the defence to have the diaries in their possession for a few days in order for them to be thoroughly inspected. At some point, this had to have occurred; in the bill of costs sent from Hector Munro to Wallace after his success at the Court of Appeal, he lists 'attending Criminal Investigation Department obtaining diaries and later perusing same very carefully and making notes thereon'. On 8 June 1931 (after Wallace's successful appeal), Hector Munro wrote to Chief Constable Lionel Everett, asking that all of Wallace's belongings in the possession of the police be handed over. On 10 June, the Chief Constable informed Munro that these could '*be collected from the Central Property Office by your representative*'; presumably, it would have been around this time that Wallace finally got the diaries back in his own possession. After Wallace's death in 1933, all of his possessions were bequeathed to his brother Joseph. Presumably, this is where the diaries eventually ended up. Consequently, all that has remained of them are the notes taken by the police. It is these that have been used throughout all investigations from W. F. Wyndham Brown's *The Trial of William Herbert Wallace* to this writer's own efforts.

From the start of 1928 through to the beginning of 1931, the Wallace household went through a plethora of ailments, with both Wallace and Julia suffering some form of malady. Wallace's were more concerned with headaches, depression and his constant kidney trouble; Julia's with constant bouts of flu, gastritis and bronchitis. At the beginning of May 1928, after a bout of kidney trouble, Wallace notes in his diary on the 17th: 'Christian service – what is it all about?' At the beginning of the following month, 5 June, he references a newspaper feature, 'Where are the dead?' On Friday 8 June, he references a follow-up feature, 'Where are the dead? Scientists Views.' Wallace's keen mind was, seemingly, preoccupied with questions of mortality and the fate of the soul – could this have been due to his depressions? On Monday 10 September, there was another cutting, 'Sir Oliver Lodge on the Hereafter'. (Sir Oliver Lodge was a physicist and a writer. During the late 1880s, he had begun to study psychical phenomena, largely in the area of telepathy. After the death of his son, Raymond, during the First World War, he became more interested, eventually writing over forty books on the subject.) Again, on 12 September, Wallace refers to another cutting entitled 'Science of Creation'; on 20 September he notes, 'Volunteers for Psychical Research experiments.' If the references to newspaper cuttings are anything to go by, Wallace seemed to have been gaining more and more interest in the fate of man in the great hereafter – so much so, he either took part, or was contemplating taking part, in some form of experimentation concerned with it. As a staunch atheist, was he seeking solace in confirmation of man's perpetuity down other avenues? However, as a stoic, how could Wallace have ever become reconciled to the existence of a hereafter he could never see unless he was already in it? This raises a question: what was Wallace chasing?

At some point during 1928, Wallace mentioned to his supervisor at the Prudential, Joseph Crewe, about wanting to play the violin. Crewe, a musician himself, went with Wallace to purchase an instrument and offered to give him a few lessons until he managed to find a professional teacher. In all, Crewe gave Wallace five lessons over as many weeks. Giving evidence at Wallace's trial, Crewe was asked by Roland Oliver KC, Wallace's defence counsel, 'With regard to the violin lessons, were they five weeks running?' Crewe replied, 'Yes, five weeks running.' On Wednesday 28 November, Wallace notes in his diary that he visited Mr Crewe's house for the first of his violin lessons. The following Wednesday, 5 December, he visited Mr Crewe again; after his lesson, the pair went to the Plaza Cinema in Allerton, where the silent movie *Dancing Vienna*, starring Ben Lyon and Latvian actress Lya Mara, was playing, and had a coffee in a café inside the cinema, Wallace getting home around 11 p.m.

In a diary entry for 19 December 1928, Wallace notes the comments of another Prudential colleague, Assistant Superintendent Joseph Bamber, concerning a young colleague, Richard Gordon Parry: 'Bamber points out how Parry wants watching in insurance work'; and if anyone should have known, the Assistant Superintendent should. In his second statement to police, Wallace elucidates upon this diary entry: 'Although nothing was known officially to the company detrimental to his financial affairs, it was known that he [Richard Gordon Parry] had collected premiums which he did not pay in and his superintendent, Mr Crewe, of Green Lane, Allerton, told me that he went to Parry's parents who paid about £30 to cover the deficiency.' In giving evidence at the trial, when questioned by Roland Oliver, Joseph Crewe qualified this:

Which part is true? The £30 is a little bit exaggerated.
It is not so much as that? Not so much as that, not from his parents.
But there were deficiencies and there were payments by the parents? Yes.

The Parrys

Richard Gordon Parry, born 12 January 1909 at 7 Woburn Hill, Stoneycroft, West Derby, Liverpool, was the oldest child of six children – Richard Gordon (1909), Ada Muriel (1911), Dorothy May (1913), Ailsa Lilian (1916), Frederick Ronald (1918) and Joan Margaret (1927) – born to William John Parry, a treasury official with Liverpool Corporation, and Lillian Jane Evans, daughter of seaman Richard Evans and cigar maker Sarah Jane Ley. His paternal grandfather, John Parry – born in Connagh's Quay, Flintshire, North Wales, in 1864 – arrived in Liverpool around the age of 17. He began working for David Jones, a linen draper, at 100 Mill Street as a shop man. At the end of 1887, John Parry married Elizabeth Morris Owen, daughter of William Owen, a hosier, who also had his shop in Mill Street. During early 1888, William John Parry was born, the eldest child of four children: William John (1888), Lilian Elizabeth (1891), Doris Rebecca (1893) and Norman Ewart (1899). By the early 1890s, John Parry had his own drapery shop at 59 Lodge Lane, Liverpool, and was doing well enough for him to employ two servants. Eventually, the family moved to 36 Hartington Road, a street away from their shop on Lodge Lane. John Parry, by all accounts, appears to have been a staunch Methodist – at one time J. Ferrier Jones, a Calvinistic minister from Crickhowell, Cardiganshire, stayed at his home. This situation would usually occur when a guest speaker or preacher was invited to attend a church to give a lecture or sermon; it would then fall upon one of the trustees of the church to both accommodate and entertain their guest.

This had a strong influence on the young William John Parry, who was to become a Primitive Methodist lay preacher himself. Educated at Liverpool College, he went on to the University of Liverpool, studying at the School of Social Sciences. In 1904, William began working as a junior clerk at Liverpool City Council Transport Department. There for only eight months, he transferred to the Treasury Department, where he remained, until his retirement in 1950, as assistant city treasurer for administration. Before his death on 12 May 1966, William John Parry had led an active and accomplished life. During the First World War, he had served with the Royal Air Force in France and Italy; he was a founder member of North West Students' Society of the Institute of Municipal Treasurers and Accountants; treasurer of the National Vigilance Association; treasurer of the Gordon Smith Institute for Seamen; chairman of the governors for Holly Lodge Girls School, Liverpool; co-opted member of the Liverpool Education Committee; member of the governing committee of Shrewsbury School; senior circuit steward of Liverpool Methodist Church; and chairman of Liverpool Workshops for the Blind. During the Second World War, he was seconded to the Ministry of Food, where he organised the first issue of ration books to the citizens of Liverpool. It has been suggested that William John Parry was related to another distinguished Liverpudlian of the time, George Henry Parry, Chief Librarian of Liverpool; having undertaken thorough researches, however, I find this to be unfounded and untrue. Despite the fact that a 'W. J. Parry', described as George Henry Parry's cousin, was one of the many family members and dignitaries who attended his funeral, this was, in fact, William John Parry, son of Edwin Parry – George Henry Parry's uncle – a coal merchant's manager living in Poulton, Wallasey, at the time.

William John Parry's eldest child, Richard Gordon, however, was never destined to rise to the heights of his distinguished father. Possibly rebelling against his father's strong Methodist principles and the fact that he knew he had no hopes of ever bettering (or even equalling) his father's accomplishments, Richard Gordon Parry apparently gained the attention of the law from a very early age. Court clerk Henry Harris, in an interview with Jonathan Goodman in the 1960s, claimed that whilst Parry was attending Lister Drive School, Stoneycroft, he was convicted at the juvenile court of damaging property:

> Each day on his way to and from school, he pulled down a boundary wall at the front of houses in the course of erection. It was done so regularly that the builders decided to keep watch, and Parry was caught in the act. I think the damage was considerable … I do know that, thereafter, he was a great source of sorrow and anxiety to his parents because of his evil tendencies.

It must be noted that, despite this author's thorough and extensive researches, no documentary evidence of this incident, nor the ensuing legal consequences, could be found. In an interview with Roger Wilkes, a friend of Parry's from his younger days, James Tattersall, confirmed that, despite this apparent brush with the law, Parry's ardour never ceased: 'I admit, he and I were a couple of bad lads; but there's a difference between pinching money out of phone boxes and pinching cars and killing someone.'

It was whilst in his youth, attending Lister Drive School, Stoneycroft, that Parry first met his future girlfriend Lily Lloyd; the two were both amateur actors in the school's dramatic society. Lilian Josephine Moss Lloyd was the eldest of three children of Evan Reginald Lloyd, a clerk for an insurance company, and Josephine Ward Hewitt. The couple were married at the end of 1909. Around the same time the following year, their first child, Lilian, was born, soon to be followed by Daphne Victorine (1912) and Stanley Reginald (1915). On 16 September 1935, Daphne, a one-time dancer with the Ziegfeld Follies in New York, married musician Salvatore Mario Carminita, at St Mary's church, West Derby – their glamorous wedding was given front-page coverage in the *Daily Mirror* at the time. Subsequent to their Liverpool wedding, the couple flew to their new home in Paris, on the Boulevard Berthier, to be married again at the Italian Embassy. Sadly, aged only 36, Daphne was to die at her parents' home – 50 Almond's Green, West Derby, Liverpool – on 2 June 1949 whilst her husband was in Milan.[2]

Parry left Lister Drive School in 1923. In the September of 1926, he joined the Prudential Assurance Company as an apprentice insurance salesman. According to his police statement, this is when he first met Mr and Mrs Wallace, having had to call at their house on several occasions on business for his superintendent, Joseph Crewe.

On 26 December 1928, Wallace had his last violin lesson with Mr Crewe. Sometime between the next day, Thursday 27 December, and Monday 31 December, Wallace was, apparently, stricken with bronchitis and had to take to his bed. For some inexplicable reason, the agent who took over Wallace's collections during his illness was, of all people, Richard Gordon Parry. Surely, when Wallace informed the Prudential of his condition (either when he took in his collection money on the 27th, or via a phone call) knowing of Parry's untrustworthiness, none of his superiors would have sent him out to take over Wallace's collections. Did Wallace, despite having been warned about Parry's 'unreliability', ask him personally?

Another entry in Wallace's diary, for 31 December 1928, states: 'Off with bronchitis. Parry does work for a fortnight but is not methodical enough.' (It can only be assumed that the reference to Parry must have been written in retrospect.) In confirmation of this, Parry also stated that he was working for Wallace for about two weeks and, during that time, called at the Wallaces' home only twice to hand over cash: on the Thursday morning of the first week, and the Wednesday evening of the second week. According to Wallace, he did his own collections (gathering payments from approximately 560 clients) on a Saturday morning, all day Monday and all day Tuesday before paying in his collection money at the Prudential offices on the Thursday. This would mean that Parry would have kept to the same schedule. As New Year's Day was not designated as a bank holiday until 1974, Parry would have begun his work for Wallace on the Monday morning of 31 December, collecting all day on Tuesday 1 January 1929 and possibly on Wednesday 2 January (if Wallace had been unable to do his round on the previous Saturday because of his illness); hence his taking the collection money to Wallace on the Thursday morning during the first week of assisting him. In taking the following week's collection money to Wallace on the evening of Wednesday 9 January, would this have meant that Wallace had recovered enough from his illness to be taking the collected monies down to the Prudential offices on the usual Thursday? At some point during these collections, Wallace found discrepancies in the amounts Parry was handing over to him and those entered in the account book. Wallace confronted him, but Parry dismissed it as a simple mistake. As part of a Prudential agent's collections, Joseph Crewe stated that besides collecting the weekly premium, on one day a month the agent also collected a monthly premium. The week of this collection was called a 'monthly week'. The takings for this week were considerably larger than a normal week due to the amalgamation of monies from those who paid their premiums weekly and those who paid them monthly. The monthly week for January 1929 fell on Monday 7 January, and Parry did the collection. This may have been where the discrepancies occurred.

It was also during this period of illness, according to Wallace, that Parry recommended a friend of his who had worked for the Prudential, but was out of work at that time – a man Wallace could only name as 'Marsden'. In relation to Marsden, Wallace stated in his second police statement:

There was another man named Marsden who also did part of the work for me while I was ill in December 1928. I do not know his address. He was an agent for the Prudential Company for two or three years and had left before he did my work. I gave him the job because he was out of work. Parry recommended him. I have heard that Marsden left the Prudential on account of financial irregularities. While he was working for me, he often came to my house to see me on business. He also knew the interior arrangements of my house. I have seen Marsden several times since he worked for me. I do not know if he is working now and I do not know anything about his private affairs. If he had called at my house, my wife would have asked him in. Both Parry and Marsden knew the arrangements of my business with regard the system of paying in money collected to the Head Office, Dale Street … Parry and Marsden knew I kept the money in the box because while they worked for me, I always put the money into it when they called to pay over to me their collections. They had both seen me take it down and put it back to the top of the bookcase in the kitchen often. Marsden is about 28 years of age, about 5 foot 6/7 inches, brown hair and fairly well dressed.

When one examines more closely this reference to Marsden, the facts concerning Wallace's illness, Wallace's diary entries, Parry's statement and the system used for the collection of the Prudential money, they do not seem to corroborate Marsden ever having been required to assist during Wallace's illness. Wallace said he was incapacitated due to bronchitis, an ailment that generally has a recovery rate of about two weeks. Both Parry and Wallace's diary entry state that Parry was working for Wallace for only two weeks (the recovery period); during that time, Parry called at Wallace's home twice to hand over the collection money. In the police notes on Wallace's diaries, no mention of Marsden is made, but the notes do mention Parry:

> December 19 Tues [*sic*]: Bamber points out how 'Parry' wants watching in Insurance work. Interval to Dec 31 off with Bronchitis. Parry does work for a fortnight but is not methodical enough. End of 1928. 1929. January 1st: Wallace ill with Bronchitis. 16th: Cutting from the 'Listener' referring to Evolution, Intelligence and Consciousness.

Surely, Wallace would have made a note of this stranger having to do work for him? Parry makes no mention of Marsden in his police statement, in relation to doing work for Wallace or in any other capacity. Referring to Marsden, in his police statement, Wallace stated:

> While he was working for me, he often came to my house to see me on business ... Parry and Marsden knew I kept the money in the box because while they worked for me, I always put the money into it when they called to pay over to me their collections. They had both seen me take it down and put it back to the top of the bookcase in the kitchen often.

If we give Wallace the benefit of the doubt, and say that Marsden did do some work for him, this could have only been on an occasion when Parry, for whatever reason, could not undertake a number of collections himself during the two weeks he worked for Wallace. As Parry handed over the collection money to Wallace on 3 January and 9 January, Marsden would have had to have worked for Wallace at some time during the period between these two dates. If this were so, at most, Marsden could have made only two collections: on the morning of Saturday the 5th and Monday the 7th. The fact that Parry took collection money to Wallace on Wednesday the 9th would have required him to have made the collection on Tuesday the 8th himself. If, after collecting on Wallace's round, Marsden was unable to hand the money over to Parry, given that he was not a Prudential agent and was an apparent stranger to Wallace, surely he would not have been allowed to have taken the money home with him, and would have had to have taken the collection money to Wallace's house each night. This would, to some extent, justify the statement that 'he often came to my house to see me on business' and the fact that both Parry and Marsden would have witnessed, on more than one occasion, where the cash box was located. However, Marsden's only calling at 29 Wolverton Street on the afternoon of the 5th and the evening of the 7th can hardly be termed 'often'.

The fact, however, remains that, despite attaining only a vague description of Marsden and a surname from Wallace, knowing he knew the location of the cash box and knowing that Julia would allow Marsden into the house in Wallace's absence, it would appear that, in taking a statement from Parry (the one man who could have given them all the information they needed in order to locate him) the police never asked him a single question concerning Marsden, and he never volunteered any information – or the police forgot to include any references to Marsden when they typed up Parry's statement. Having gained only scant information from Wallace – and Parry, seemingly, having made no reference to him at all – would not the police's next port of call have been the Prudential Assurance Company? Wallace had stated that Marsden had worked for the company before working for him: surely, they would have retained information pertaining to him? Sadly, if this report ever existed, it is no longer contained within the remaining police files. The only official mention of Marsden to be found is his surname and description in Wallace's second statement.

If Wallace did employ these apparent ne'er-do-wells, this does not sound like the actions of the upright, methodical, stalwart jobsworth that Wallace was considered to be. To employ the services of Parry, a young colleague, one could forgive Wallace in possibly wanting to show him the error of his ways and instil in him the virtues of honesty and decency required in his position at the Prudential. However, to employ two men – one of whom he *knew* to be a thief, and the other, it would appear, he knew little of but by reputation *as a thief* – might lead one to consider that there was more to this collaboration than met the eye.

The diary entries for 1929 followed much the same pattern as 1928 with regard to the Wallaces' illnesses – Wallace with his depressions and complaints about pain behind his eye and Julia occasionally bedridden with her coughs and colds. On Wednesday 13 February, he notes that, whilst on his way home (Wednesday not being a collection day, a paying-in day nor a chess night, he must have been somewhere else) he had a discussion with someone concerning religion, during which both he and his companion agreed that 'if there is a hereafter, the man without any so-called religious beliefs, and a non-church attender, but who lives a decent life, and who abstains from telling lies, or cheating, or acts of meanness, and who honestly tries to do good, has as much chance of getting there as the professed Christian who attends his place of worship regularly'. It would appear from this that no thoughts of murdering Julia had entered his head at this point.

On Good Friday, 29 March, he and Julia had listened to a radio adaptation of *The Master Builder*, a play by the Norwegian dramatist and poet Henrik Ibsen. Wallace commended the play for its clarity in depicting how, in eschewing love and the deeper meaning of life in order to become a great success in his career, a man eventually realises that his life has, in fact, been an utter failure. Commenting upon Julia's reaction to the play, he notes, 'Curious that Julia did not appreciate this play! I feel sure she did not grasp the inner significance and real meaning of the play.' Seemingly indignant at Julia's reaction, and in finding it 'curious', could Wallace have been shocked at Julia's lack of compassion? Could this have been how she truly felt about their own relationship? Would she sooner have given up their love for success? Could this simple observation of Wallace's actually underline certain comments given by various witnesses as to Julia's disappointment with her life? At the time of the murder, one of the officers on the case, Inspector Herbert Gold, wrote up a report concerning Wallace's background. Within this report are comments by various people who had been associated with the Wallaces, regarding their opinion of the couple. A Mrs Florence Mary Wilson (at the time of the murder, a matron at a Police Remand Home at 31 Derwent Road, Stoneycroft), who had visited 29 Wolverton Street for three weeks during 1923 to nurse Wallace through a bout of pneumonia, said – even at this early stage – the Wallaces were 'a very peculiar couple … their attitude toward each other appeared to be strained [and] the feeling of sympathy and confidence which one usually found existing between man and wife appeared to be entirely absent'. Mrs Wilson went on to describe Wallace as 'a man who appeared to have suffered a keen disappointment in life'. She said of Julia, 'Mrs Wallace was peculiar in her manner and dirty. During her husband's illness she slept on the sofa in the kitchen although the front bedroom was vacant … the house itself was dirty and Mrs Wallace did not seem to have any desire to keep it clean. She did not appear to have any enthusiasm for anything.' In Mrs Wilson's opinion, 'relations between them were not those of a normal couple, and they were certainly not the "happy and devoted couple" as described by other people'. An ex-Prudential agent and friend of Wallace's, a Mr Jones (deceased at the time of the murder) described Julia to another Prudential agent as 'a proud and peculiar woman who thought she had lowered herself by marrying an insurance agent. She hated the business and would give not give assistance to her husband. She would keep clients standing at the door when they called to see him on business, and she would not take premiums which clients brought during her husband's absence.' Even the Wallaces' family doctor, Dr Louis Curwen, was noted to have 'attended both the accused and his wife at their home fairly often during the past five years. Since the death of Mrs Wallace he had considered their attitude towards each other and had come to the conclusion, from his observations, that they did not lead the happy and harmonious life that outsiders supposed they did.'

On Monday 9 September 1929, the Wallaces had taken a trip to Settle in Yorkshire. Wallace notes of the journey home:

> At four o'clock Julia and I left for home, but getting lost we had to return to Settle, so that it was five o'clock before we really got away. The roads were crowded with cars, and at Clitherow all cars were being held up for inspection of licenses [*sic*]. Probably the police were trying to comb out in order to get some line on the motorist who ran down a police constable on the previous Thursday, leaving him to die in the road. If they get him, I hope he gets ten years hard labour for his callousness.

It would appear, even at this time, that Wallace had no thoughts of murder.

The year 1930 continues in the same vein regarding the many illnesses of the Wallaces. However, there are also seven occasions mysteriously labelled 'Reference to Mr Crewe'. On Friday 24 October, the police noted a 'Reference to mental trouble'. Then, on Sunday the 26th, Wallace once again contemplates the possibility of a life beyond death:

No one has ever had any knowledge of a previous existence. If I previously existed as a thinking organism, I probably argued much as I do now, and now that I am here, I recognized clearly that immortality means absolutely nothing to me. Any individuality I possessed formerly has gone. So, too, when I pass out of this existence, individual immortality is meaningless, unless I am able to retain something of my present, and the fact that my previous existence has also no meaning for me. So why worry about a life hereafter which for me has no meaning.

Could these moments of self-doubt and despair be linked to his bouts of depression?

On Monday 15 December, Wallace relates an incident where Julia had visited Southport, Lancashire, but had not returned until the early hours of the morning:

On arriving home, found that Julia had not returned. I waited until nearly 1 a.m., then thinking something surely must have happened, went off to the Anfield Road police station to see if there was any report of any accident to hand. None. So went back home and found that her ladyship [this is as it was read out directly from Wallace's diary by Scholefield Allen during the committal hearing – the police notes of the diary entries have the phrase 'her ladyship' replaced by the word 'she'] had just turned up. It seems a laundry van had been smashed up on the railway line, the train derailed, and the line blocked. Julia waited at Southport Station until after ten o'clock and she had apparently no hope of getting a train she decided to take a bus. She arrived in Liverpool at 12.30 and reached home at 1. It was a relief to know she was safe and sound, for I was getting apprehensive, feeling she might have been run over by a motor car or something.

The accident had occurred at 6 p.m. at a level crossing known as 'Roy's Crossing', approximately 600 yards from Ainsdale station, Lancashire. It was dark, and a thick fog had covered the area when Percy Bennett, aged about 18, was driving an Ainsdale Laundry Company van back over the crossing after visiting Mr Roy. His young passenger, 15-year-old Geoffrey Bond, jumped out of the van to close the crossing gate after them as Bennett continued on over the line. As Bond closed the gate, through the heavy fog, he saw a train heading toward the van at around 50 mph. Before he had time to call out, the train bulldozed straight through the van, flinging Bennett onto the track and dragging him 60 yards down the line before derailing a hundred yards further on. When they found the poor youth, he had a hole smashed through his head. The accident short-circuited the line to Southport, leaving trains stranded at almost every station. A breakdown van was sent from Sandhills station, Liverpool; but, having to wait until all the trains were cleared off the track, it did not arrive in Ainsdale until around 9 p.m., leaving trains running about an hour late, with normal train services resuming at around 10.30 p.m.

The train accident had happened at 6 p.m. Julia, therefore, had to have arrived at Southport before this. She had to have left the house during the afternoon whilst Wallace was out in Clubmoor on his rounds. In his diary entry, Wallace states that upon his arrival home that night, Julia had not yet returned; with it being a Monday, though not marked down for a game on the fixtures pinned to the Chess Club notice board (at meetings where there were an odd number of players, one of the members would have to sit it out), he may have been at the Chess Club and would have arrived home at around 10.30 p.m. Whilst anxiously awaiting Julia's return, had this been the pivotal and defining moment when Wallace had contemplated what his life would be like if Julia did not return? What if she had been struck by a car – would this have been so great a loss? In a statement given to Hector Munro by Wallace's Assistant Prudential Superintendent, Albert Wood, he states that he had seen Julia three weeks before the murder when he had called at the house and handed an envelope to her at the front door. On this occasion, she had told him how upset Wallace had been upon her arriving home late after the train accident. Mr Wood's visit would have been around 30 December 1930, over two weeks after the train accident. Why, upon his flying visit, had Julia felt the need to relate Wallace's upset over the incident? As Wallace's Assistant Superintendent, had Albert Wood noticed a marked change in Wallace's demeanour over the weeks since the incident and thought it might have been an escalation in his ongoing health problems, and so asked Julia if he was well?

Of the seven diary entries listed by the police for January 1931 (1st, 2nd, 4th, 7th, 14th, 17th and 18th), probably the most noteworthy (though slightly incoherent) is that of Sunday the 4th: 'Work out some definite scheme of study of properly planned and rigorously adhered to each particular difficulty consistently tackled and overcome.' According to Wallace's nephew, Edwin Herbert Wallace, 'During the last two years, my uncle became very keen on music and developed the violin so as to accompany his wife on the piano, which she played very well. My uncle took a great deal of trouble with the violin, and had lessons. This interest in the violin superseded my uncle's interest in the laboratory.' It could simply be that the diary entry refers to Wallace's determination to become more proficient in playing his violin; it could also mark his determination to plan the perfect murder. A diary entry for Sunday 18 January reads, 'Have not touched fiddle all day. It is unusual to let Sunday go by without some practice.' However, according to Wallace's nephew Edwin, who had visited Wolverton Street with his mother Amy on 18 January, Wallace had played his violin: 'Looking back on the evening, I can see nothing whatever abnormal about it. They played to us in the usual way, and there was a good deal of conversation.'

3

The Instigation

On Monday 19 January 1931, the inhabitants of Liverpool had woken to turbulent weather. Strong winds were whipping across the city. According to a statement given by Wallace to Hector Munro, at around 8.45 a.m. Wallace and Julia had risen and, as Julia prepared breakfast, he readied himself for a morning's collection in Clubmoor. His working routine was so arranged as to allow him a Monday afternoon off every other week and this was his week off. Having caught the tram to Clubmoor at 10 a.m., he was home again by 2.30 p.m., when the couple had lunch. That afternoon he spent working on his books and getting his papers in order. At 5 p.m., Wallace and Julia sat down to tea. Between 5.30 and 7.00 p.m., as Wallace practised his violin in the kitchen, Julia read. According to Wallace, having been persuaded by Julia earlier that day, he had decided to visit the Chess Club at the City Café that night: 'I discussed with my wife whether I should go or not, and she eventually said "Oh, you had better go, as you have got a match game to play, but don't stand about talking outside when you've finished."' After putting away his violin, Wallace went upstairs to wash. He stated that, between 7.15 and 7.20 p.m., he had left via the back door and walked along Richmond Park and up to the junction of Breck Road and Belmont Road to catch a No. 14 tram.

At approximately this same time, a switchboard operator at the Anfield Telephone Exchange, Miss Louisa Alfreds, was alerted by a signal from her board telling her that someone had put two pennies into a payphone and required assistance. She quickly responded by inserting the appropriate plug into a socket in the switchboard that would enable her to speak to the caller. The caller, a man, asked to be put through to 'Bank 3581', the telephone number of Cottle's City Café, home of the Central Chess Club – the very place Wallace was making his way towards. Satisfied that the correct money had been placed into the box for the call, Miss Alfreds pulled the plug and inserted it into the appropriate jack to connect the caller to Bank 3581; she then carried on with her work. After a couple of minutes had passed (at about 7.17 p.m.) the same indicator on the switchboard lit up. This time Miss Alfreds' colleague (sitting directly to her right), Lilian Martha Kelly, responded to the call. It was the same caller Miss Alfreds had just been speaking to: 'Operator, I pressed button "A" and haven't had my correspondent yet!' Miss Kelly asked the man what number he had asked for and was told: 'Bank 3581'. After conferring with Miss Alfreds, Miss Kelly instructed the caller, 'Press button "B" and regain your two pennies', and asked, 'Do you think there ought to be a reply from this number?' To which she received the answer, 'Yes, it's a restaurant.

There ought to be plenty of people there.' After failing in her attempt to receive a reply from Bank 3581, Miss Kelly informed her supervisor, Miss Annie Robertson, who succeeded in making the connection. She instructed Miss Kelly to put the call through. According the recipient of the call at the City Café, waitress Miss Gladys Harley, Miss Robertson had enquired, 'Bank 3581?' Miss Harley confirmed this and, after a little delay, Miss Harley asked, 'Do you require this number?' Whereupon, Miss Robertson replied, 'Yes – Anfield is calling you; hold the line.' Miss Harley states that Annie Robertson then asked the caller to insert his pennies into the telephone box in order to pay for the call. At this point, Lillian Martha Kelly plugged the caller through. A man's voice then said, 'Is that the Central Chess Club?' To which Gladys Harley replied, 'Yes.'

To confirm that the caller had now reached the correspondent he was asking for, Miss Kelly listened in on the line: 'I listened on the line for a moment with a view to ascertaining if he got the right people. I heard him say, "Is that the City Café?" and received the reply, "Yes". I then went off line.' In putting the caller through, Annie Robertson logged the two telephone numbers, including the number of the caller, 'Anfield 1627', the time the call was put through, 7.20 p.m., and 'NR' (No Reply) in the margin. In Miss Lillian Kelly's own words, 'By reason of the complaint of his not having had his conversation with the person he wanted when he first asked for his number, a record was made of his second call.' What could have gone wrong with the initial connection to Bank 3581?

It has long been speculated by many authors that in having the call put through by a supervisor – and thus having the call logged – the caller at Anfield 1627 was employing a ruse, by which it could be later established exactly what time the call was placed, and thus assist in eliminating the suspicion that Wallace had placed the call. In a statement, given to Hector Munro, City Café waitress Gladys Harley said:

> I am absolutely positive that our line had not been used by anyone for the previous half hour. The box is in full view of the part of the café where I am accustomed to be, and the ringing of the bell is clearly audible. I had not seen anyone enter or leave the box, and usually when there is a call I answer it in the first place.

On the night of 19 January 1931, from the time Gladys Harley had arrived at the City Café, until she had responded to Annie Robertson's call from the Anfield Telephone Exchange, nobody had used the phone at the City Café, and the phone had not rung. This being the case, when Louisa Alfreds had initially connected the caller to Bank 3581, that particular phone did not ring. Upon Miss Kelly attempting a reconnection, once again, the telephone did not ring; only when Miss Robertson attempted the connection did it ring. This had to be a technical fault and nothing at all to do with the caller at Anfield 1627.

In 1931, the procedure for using a payphone differed from that of today. Because the phones had no dial, a call had to be put through via a telephone exchange. To accomplish this, the caller would unhook the earpiece from the left side of the telephone and place two pennies into the slot at the top of the telephone box. This would then light up an indicator at the telephone exchange and alert the operator that a call was waiting to be put through. The operator would then plug a wire into the appropriate socket on the switchboard to enable her to speak to the caller and request the number the caller was wishing to contact. If this was a local number, the wire would be connected to the appropriate socket on the switchboard for that number. Upon the recipient of the call answering the phone, the caller would hear a series of tones, whereupon he would have to press a button labelled 'A' on the front of the payphone. This would cause the money inserted into the slot to drop into the box and the call would then proceed. If, however, no answer was gained from the recipient's telephone, the caller would then press a button labelled 'B' on the right side of payphone, and retrieve the money. If the caller had encountered any problem during the making of the telephone call, there was also an 'Emergency' button that, upon being pressed, would light up an 'Emergency' indicator on the switchboard at the telephone exchange. Neither Louisa Alfreds, Lillian Martha Kelly, nor Annie Robertson stated that upon receiving the second call from Anfield 1627 they had been responding to an emergency call. Lillian Martha Kelly said simply, 'At about 7.17 p.m. I received a call from the Call Box Anfield 1627.' Having been told by the caller, 'Operator, I pressed button "A" and haven't had my correspondent yet!', the caller had to have deposited his original two pennies in the phone box. Without pressing the emergency button, the only way to garner the attention of the telephone operator was to reinsert another two pennies. Upon receiving the call, Miss Kelly appears to have been satisfied that this had been accomplished. If this was, indeed, the case, then the sequence of events after the caller had entered the phone kiosk, Anfield 1627, would most likely have been as follows:

- The caller unhooks the earpiece hanging at the side of the box and puts two pennies into the slot.
- An indicator on the switchboard at Anfield Telephone Exchange lights up, informing the telephone operators that a call is waiting to be plugged through.
- Louisa Alfreds responds to the indicator, plugs into the caller and asks the number required.
- Upon being given the required number and being satisfied that the correct amount of money had been paid for the call, she plugs the caller through to the number required and carries on with her work.
- Knowing for certain that there will be someone there to answer his call, the caller at Anfield 1627 pushes button 'A' before the call is answered, thus depositing his two pennies into the box. Because of what must have been a fault, the call is not connected to Bank 3581 and so is not answered.
- The caller replaces the earpiece, disengaging the call and losing the two pennies.
- The caller picks up the earpiece once again, and inserts another two pennies into the slot.
- Once again, the indicator on the switchboard lights up to inform the operators that a call is waiting to be put through. This time, Lillian Martha Kelly takes the call.
- The caller tells her, 'Operator, I pressed button "A" and haven't had my correspondent yet!'
- Miss Kelly asks for the number and instructs the caller to press button 'B' and retrieve his coins whilst she attempts the connection herself. In making the connection manually, this

overrides the automatic connection of the call once button 'A' is pressed; the caller would have to put his pennies in the slot upon the operator's instruction should the connection be successful.

- Upon not being able to connect to Bank 3581 (the fact that the telephone did not ring at the City Café shows a fault had to have been present), Miss Kelly asks her supervisor for assistance.
- Miss Annie Robertson attempts the connection and speaks with Gladys Harley at Bank 3581.
- The caller is then asked to reinsert the two pennies and the call is then connected.
- The caller at Anfield 1627 had *not* used a ruse either to obtain a free call or to have the call logged in order to have a record of the time it had been made. A simple fault on the line had caused this disruption and the subsequent record taken of the call was to enable Post Office engineers to check the line for possible repairs.

At the time of Julia's murder, in all official reports and maps, the roads at the corner of which the telephone kiosk stood are given as Breck Road and Rochester Road (the Cabbage Hall Cinema also stood on this road), a continuation of Lower Breck Road leading to Breck Road. This, however, is incorrect. Rochester Road actually ceased to exist – becoming part of Lower Breck Road – in 1927. Despite that fact that the nameplate on Rochester Road had been changed to 'Lower Breck Road' and was clearly visible, upon investigating the area of the Anfield 1627 telephone kiosk, officials (police and surveyors) appear to have been guided by incorrectly labelled plans and maps (even recent maps).

On the opposite side of the road from the telephone kiosk, there was a tram stop (at the corner of Lower Breck Road and Townsend Lane) that Wallace, as it was later suggested at his trial, could quite easily have used to catch the tram to take him to the City Café if it had been him who had made the call. Wallace, however, maintained that at the time of the phone call, he had left his home via the back door and ambled down the back entry into Richmond Park, before making his way *up* Breck Road to the junction of Breck Road and Belmont Road to catch the tram to the City Café – in the opposite direction to the telephone kiosk. Of the two routes Wallace could have taken to catch his tram, the one to the tram stop at the corner of Lower Breck Road and Townsend Lane was the most convoluted. After leaving his front door, Wallace would have had to have crossed Wolverton Street, gone through an entry between Nos 12 and 14 to the top of Redbourn Street, turned left, passing the top of Redbrook Street, gone through a narrow entry to the top of Redcar Street, gone down Redcar Street to Lower Breck Road, then crossed over onto Lower Breck Road and turned down Townsend Lane – a distance of about 420 yards. The Breck Road route, however, gave Wallace a choice of three stops: one at the end of Richmond Park, 243 yards from his back door; a short walk of 157 yards further up Breck Road was another stop at the end of Newcombe Street; and then there was the Breck Road/Belmont Road junction stop, 400 yards from Wallace's back door.

At Bank 3581, after City Café waitress Gladys Harley had confirmed to the caller from Anfield 1627 that he had at last reached his desired correspondent, the caller asked, 'Is Mr Wallace there?' Only knowing Wallace by sight, Miss Harley approached Chess Club

Captain Samuel Beattie to take the call. Beattie had not seen Wallace since sometime before Christmas. The caller, once again, enquired after Wallace and asked if he would be there.

'No,' Beattie replied.

'Can you give me the address?'

'I'm afraid I can't.'

'But he will be there?'

'I can't say. He may or may not. If he is coming, he will be here shortly. I suggest you ring up later.'

'Oh no, I can't, I am too busy; I have got my girl's twenty-first birthday party on and I want to do something for her in the way of his business. I want to see him particularly. Will you ask him to call around to my place tomorrow evening at 7.30?'

'I will if I see him, but he may not be here tonight. However, there is a friend of his, perhaps you know him? Mr Caird, who is fairly certain to be here tonight, I will try to get the message delivered through him. But I can't promise that Mr Wallace will get the message; but you had better give me your address again so that I can pass it on.'

The caller then gave Beattie the name 'R. M. Qualtrough'. Beattie duly noted it down on an envelope he had in his pocket and spelt it back to him. Mr Qualtrough then gave him the address: '25 Menlove Gardens East, Mossley Hill'. This Beattie also wrote down and repeated back to him. Qualtrough hung up the receiver and Beattie went back to his game.

If, as police would later suspect, it was Wallace on the end of that phone using the pseudonym of R. M. Qualtrough and he had wanted to create a credible marker by which the time of the call could be established, a much simpler and more effective method could have been employed during this conversation with Beattie. After being told that Wallace had not yet arrived, Qualtrough could simply have asked what time Wallace would be likely to appear. Naturally, this would then force the receiver of the call to check the time. Alternatively, after Beattie had suggested he ring up later, Mr Qualtrough could have stated the time himself: 'It's already twenty-five past seven; I'm far too busy at the moment …'

At about 7.35 p.m., James Caird, a long-time friend of the Wallaces, arrived at the club. At around 7.45 p.m., he noticed Wallace arrive and, before he had time to hang up his hat and coat, Caird asked him if he would like to play him in a game. Wallace declined, telling Caird he was behind in his tournament games and wanted to catch up (he was, in fact, behind on two tournament games; he had missed a game with a Mr T. Moore on 8 December 1930 and one with a Mr J. Walsh on 5 January). Wallace asked Caird if his tournament opponent for that night had arrived, a Mr F. C. Chandler. As he had not, and as Wallace was unable to play Caird because the rules of the game did not allow members of different classes to play in tournament games (Caird was one of the first-class players, while Wallace was in the second class, having only moved up from being a third-class player in November 1930), Wallace settled down to a game with a Mr McCartney, who was also a second-class player. To bide his time, Caird wandered from table to table, watching other people play when, upon arriving at Beattie's table, Beattie asked him for Wallace's address and Caird informed him Wallace was already in the café. Beattie approached Wallace and explained about the phone call and the message. Wallace was mystified: he had never heard the name Qualtrough, had no idea who he could be, and had no idea where Menlove Gardens East was. After he noted down

Qualtrough's details in an old diary he kept with him, a discussion ensued within the group about the location of Menlove Gardens East. Although Samuel Beattie and another member of the club, Egbert Bertram Deyes, lived within half a mile of the estate, all those who were present could give no assistance.

There is no doubt at all that R. M. Qualtrough's telephone call that night was a ruse to get Wallace out of the house the following evening in order that his wife should be left alone; at least that is what it would eventually be perceived to have been. The phone call itself, and the conversation held between Samuel Beattie and R. M. Qualtrough, contain important clues to the true identity of the caller and, possibly, the identity of Julia Wallace's killer. In placing the call to Cottle's City Café and asking if Mr Wallace was there, Qualtrough had to have been armed with a range of important information, all of which Wallace would have been able to supply — some of which *only* Wallace could have supplied. Qualtrough would have had to have known that Wallace was a member of the Liverpool Central Chess Club and that it was based at Cottle's City Café, met there on a Monday night and that it was a rule of the club that all games had to begin by 7.45 p.m. – by which time, all members who were attending would be present. Whilst cross-examining Samuel Beattie at the Assize trial, it was suggested by Wallace's defence counsel, Roland Oliver KC, that any random customer to the City Café could quite readily have known that the Central Chess Club held its meetings there and when Wallace would be likely to attend. This information was readily available from a large noticeboard, prominently titled 'Liverpool Central Chess Club', on which a notice had been placed.

Was this a notice concerning the second-class championship that was going on during those months? Yes.

I find Mr McCartney and Mr Wallace were both in it and a Mr Chandler. Yes.

According to this, was not Mr Wallace posted on that board as being due to appear on 19 January? Yes.

What does the cross mean opposite the name? Does that mean he is not expected? No, that is a blank date. When there is an odd number of players, there is a blank date on which he does not play.

So far as the notice is concerned, for the month of December, he was not due to appear after the 15th, but he was due to appear on 5 January and again on the 19th? Yes.

Any person using the Café who was interested in that information could see it? Yes.

This board is quite near the door, is it not? Yes, quite public.

Plain for anybody who comes to the Café to see it? Yes, it is plain for the ordinary customer to see it.

In order for Qualtrough's ploy to work, it was most important that Wallace should not be present when the call was received — nor should anyone who would be able to furnish Qualtrough with Wallace's address. Wallace's friend at the Chess Club, James Caird, was a grocer who lived yards from Wallace's house, at 3 Letchworth Street, and had a shop at 113 Stanley Road. He and Wallace had been friends for around fifteen years and he had visited the Wallaces at their home on many occasions to play chess with Wallace and on social visits, so he knew exactly where Wallace lived. In his police statement, Caird, in describing his whereabouts on the night of the murder, said, 'I was in my shop, 113 Stanley Road, until about 7.15 p.m. I then took a tram from Great Mersey Street to Castlewood Road and then walked home, arriving there about 7.45 p.m.' If it was Caird's usual practice to close up his shop and leave at around 7.15 p.m., Qualtrough must have known this. The distance from Caird's shop to his home is approximately 2 miles; this journey took him about 30 minutes to accomplish. The distance from Caird's shop to the City Café was also about 2 miles. If on the Monday night he, as usual, left his shop at 7.15 p.m., he would not arrive at the City Café until approximately 7.45 p.m. In fact, he arrived there at approximately 7.35 p.m. If Qualtrough wanted to make absolutely sure that, when his call was received, Caird was not present, he would have had to have called prior to 7.30 p.m., otherwise he would be cutting it very fine and heightening the odds that Caird would indeed be there. How would it be possible for Qualtrough to have known that the only person who could have furnished him with Wallace's address was not already there unless Wallace had told him? He knew for an absolute certainty that whoever picked up the phone would not have this information – including the captain of the Chess Club himself. Upon becoming a member of any club or society, forms are filled, details taken; members usually meet up privately, outside of club hours, to pursue their interest. Yet, Qualtrough knew it was perfectly safe to ask for Wallace's address – and only Wallace would have known that there would be no one present who was able to supply it. If Wallace had been there and taken the call, or James Caird had been there to pass Wallace's address on to Beattie and thence to Qualtrough, the plan would have failed immediately. Qualtrough would have obtained the information he sought and that would have been an end of it. When Qualtrough asked if Beattie could get in touch with Wallace, Beattie told him that 'there is a friend of his, perhaps you know him? Mr Caird, who is fairly certain to be here tonight, I will try to get the message delivered through him', proving that everyone present when the call was taken did not know Wallace's address, otherwise Beattie would have asked one of them.

Samuel Beattie stated that he arrived at the City Café on Monday 19 January at 6 p.m. Qualtrough had made his first attempt at calling the City Café at about 7.15 p.m. If he was so anxious to contact Wallace and avoid anybody present who knew Wallace's address, why had he not called any earlier? It appears that the only answer would be to make absolutely certain that Wallace could not be accused of making the call. The call was made at the approximate time that both Wallace and Caird had begun their journeys to the City Café: 7.15 p.m. In fact, all three events appear to have been as good as synchronised. Qualtrough had to have known that it would take both men approximately 30 minutes to arrive there. The timing of the call and the time of Wallace's arrival at the café would have to be such that Wallace would not have had time to make the call and be at the Chess Club at the time he arrived. The fact that Wallace did not elicit any attention (and therefore witnesses) on his tram journey to the Chess Club as he subsequently did on his tram journeys to Menlove Gardens has been used as an argument for Wallace's innocence. However, to use the same ruse twice, on consecutive nights, would surely have been folly; suspicion as to his guilt would certainly have been aroused. Wallace was seen to have arrived at the Chess Club at 7.45 p.m. This would have allowed him only 25 minutes to have made the journey once the call had been put through. If we take into account the time taken in speaking to Gladys Harley, waiting for Beattie to get to the phone, conversing with Beattie – not only saying one's name and address, but repeating them whilst they were being spelt out and taken down – and estimate that this took a minimum of 5 minutes, Wallace would, in all, have had only 20 minutes to complete the journey.

Given the failure of the police to test the two debated routes – the route Wallace said he took from the corner of Breck Road and Belmont Road and the route Edward George Hemmerde (prosecuting counsel at the trial) said Wallace could have taken after making the phone call from a tram stop at the corner of Lower Breck Road and Townsend Lane – on 16 April 1931, Hector Munro, Wallace's solicitor, commissioned a report to be made by P. Julian Maddock, a civil and consulting engineer, whereby the two routes were both rigorously tested. In investigating the route described by Wallace, beginning at his back entry door, Maddock came to the conclusion that the shortest time this could be accomplished would be 23½ minutes. This would mean that Wallace's suggestion is quite valid: he arrived at 7.45 p.m., so would have begun his journey at about 7.20 p.m. In testing the route from the tram stop near the telephone box, Maddock came to the conclusion that (assuming Wallace had stepped directly onto the tram upon arriving at the stop and not waited for a tram to arrive) the shortest time it would take would be 26 minutes. Add to this around 5 minutes spent talking on the phone to the City Café and this becomes 31 minutes. Therefore, if Wallace had phoned the City Café, his call having been put through at 7.20 p.m., he could not have arrived at the café until 7.51 p.m. at the absolute minimum. Wallace did not make that call. I will, however, later introduce another reason – a more significant reason – as to why Mr Qualtrough may have placed his call to the City Café at 7.20 p.m.

Regarding the appointment made by Qualtrough to be held at 25 Menlove Gardens East, if the journey to Mossley Hill and Wallace's fruitless endeavours to locate 25 Menlove Gardens East were simply a device by which Wallace could furnish himself with an alibi for the murder of his wife, why had he chosen that particular area of Liverpool? Why not Bootle, Aintree or Fazakerley? Instead of putting himself though all the trouble, could he not have simply located himself within a closed environment around people he knew, who could then have verified that he was in their company within a significant time frame? Why had he not simply made arrangements with his friend of fifteen years, James Caird, to call at his house for a game of chess? Why had he not visited childhood friend Frederick William Jenkinson? The answer to this question is quite simple. If he had done so, this would have been so out of character as to make it suspicious in the light of future events. According to Wallace's diaries and testimony, the Wallaces were not a very sociable couple; as a couple, the only visits they were likely to make were to Wallace's sister-in-law, Amy Wallace, who lived at 83 Ullet Road, Liverpool, and Frederick and Alice Jenkinson of 112 Moscow Drive. As for Wallace personally, he is only noted as visiting his Prudential Superintendent, Joseph Crewe, for violin lessons, and his violin teacher, Mr Davis. James Caird said of his friendship with Wallace:

During the time I knew him, I can hardly tell how often I visited him; sometimes I would go to the house two or three times a month, and then it might be seven or eight months before I went there again. My wife never visited the house, but she knew Mrs Wallace very well. They used to meet while in the roads in the district or when shopping. So far as I know Mrs Wallace never came to our house and Mr Wallace had not visited us for some years.

Therefore, a visit to James Caird's house would have been out of the question. The only option Wallace would have had so that he could be seen to be going about his usual business and to place himself before as many witnesses as possible so that they could then verify his presence, would be to seek out a potential client some distance away from the murder scene. The main drawback with this, however, would be the fact that one would need a constant supply of witnesses to verify that you had remained in the vicinity for the whole of a given time frame. To this end, Wallace hampered and pestered everyone he could possibly see. But why Mossley Hill – and 25 Menlove Gardens East?

As far as the primary function of the exercise is concerned – the manufacturing of an alibi – this address could have been anywhere in Liverpool that was some distance away. One of the prime factors of the alibi is distance. Anybody wanting to dissociate himself or herself from a murder could do no better than to be as far as they possibly could be from the scene of that murder at the time the murder was committed. Regarding the address, 25 Menlove Gardens East, as Roger Wilkes pointed out in his book *Wallace: The Final Verdict*, 'In 1931, the houses in Menlove Gardens were little more than five years old. Some were still being built.' Given that the erection of the Menlove Gardens estate was so recent and that there was a North, South and West, anyone not familiar with the area would assume there would, of course, be an East – as was proven when he related his predicament to around ten people during his journey to, and his traversing of, the Menlove Gardens area on the night of the murder. Of the eight witnesses the police were able to trace, five did not know there was no Menlove Gardens East. These included a tram driver, a tram conductor, a tram inspector and two women who actually *lived* in Menlove Gardens. Wallace had noted in his diaries that on 5 August 1928, he and Julia had gone to Woolton Woods and, during the May and August of 1929, they had made two trips to Calderstones Park. At the Assize court, Crown Prosecutor Edward Hemmerde questioned Wallace about these trips:

Now another question. You used to go to Calderstones very often or fairly often? My wife and I might have gone possibly once a year.

Rarely, was it not? No, I do not think so. We generally went about twice a year – the time the roses were out.

How used you to get there? Take a car to Lodge Lane and change over.

The only route is off Menlove Avenue, is it not? I could not really tell you that.

Could you not? No.

I put it to you; you can only get to Calderstones by tramcar via Menlove Avenue? No, I could not say that definitely. There may be two routes, I cannot really tell you. I do not know.

When you went to Calderstones, as your diary shows, used not you to go up Menlove Avenue? We probably did, but I did not know whether there was any other route or not.

Did you not know Menlove Avenue quite well? No, I did not.

I see here twice, 22 May 1929 and 30 August you go to Calderstones; that is twice in a few months. Yes, quite possible.

You did not know Menlove Avenue well? I did not.

How did you go to Woolton Woods with your wife? Took the car to Smithdown Road corner. I probably enquired of some driver of a car which car would take us there and get on that one.

You would find yourself then at the Penny Lane junction? Possibly.

In undertaking these journeys, the most direct route to both Calderstones Park and Woolton Woods would have taken them on the same tram route that Wallace had taken on the night of 20 January 1931 (possibly on the same tram). This route had two tram stops at the Menlove Gardens estate: one at the bottom of Menlove Gardens West, and the other further on, at the bottom of Menlove Gardens North; it is then only two or three stops to Calderstones Park, Woolton Park being further on, at the end of Menlove Avenue. It is quite feasible that, whilst on their way to these destinations, when the tram stopped at each of these roads, Wallace had noted the street names. There being a West and a North, he too may have assumed that there would naturally be a South and an East. Could it have been mere coincidence that Qualtrough's address was within sight of a tram stop? Mossley Hill, and specifically the Menlove Gardens area, however, had something no other destination possessed: a safe house. Wallace's Prudential Superintendent, Joseph Crewe, lived at 34 Green Lane – directly opposite Menlove Gardens North. Throughout all of the hours and days Wallace spent at the Detective Office being questioned by police – and throughout his making of all four police statements – he never once mentioned the fact that he had called at Crewe's house on the night of the murder. The first time the matter had been mentioned was when Crewe was being questioned by Wallace's defence counsel, Scholefield Allen, at the committal trial:

Do you recollect 20 January? Were you in or out that night? I was out of my house.

After Crewe's reply, no more was asked about the incident. Obviously, Wallace had still said nothing. In fact, Wallace had only confided this information in his statement to Hector Munro. It was not until Wallace's trial at the Assizes court that this fact came out whilst he was being questioned by Roland Oliver:

Where did you find yourself then? In Menlove Avenue at the tram stop.

Where did you go next? Down Green Lane.

What did you know about Green Lane? I knew that my Superintendent lived there.

You had been there before? I had.

Was that when you had the violin lessons two years ago? It was.

When you went there on those occasions how did you get there. What tram route did you take? I cannot exactly describe it but I think possibly I would take a car which would branch off in the other direction and come down to what I now know to be Allerton Road. I would get off at a big cinema there, I think it is called the 'Plaza', and walk up to his house.

That does not take you anywhere near Menlove Gardens East? No.

In fact, have you ever seen Menlove Gardens East? No.

Finding yourself in Green Lane, did you do anything with regard to Mr Crewe's house? Yes, I rang the bell or knocked, I do not remember which, and could not get an answer and walked down to the bottom end of Green Lane and somewhere round about the bottom there was a policeman coming across the road, the policeman who has given evidence here. I stepped into the road and asked him could he tell me where Menlove Gardens East was.

If this fact had not come to light, as far as the jury – and everyone else – would have been concerned, Wallace's trip to seek Mr Qualtrough at the Menlove estate would have been a truly random event, having no other association with his personal or business life whatsoever. Had Oliver deemed it necessary to reveal this fact in fear that if it had come to light that Wallace had never mentioned it, the jury would feel he was hiding something, thus prejudicing the jury against Wallace even further? Later, whilst being cross-examined by Edward Hemmerde, this point was indeed raised:

Do you say that you stated somewhere that you called on Mr Crewe that night, that you ever stated it to anyone till you gave it in evidence today that you called on Mr Crewe? I think that is in evidence in one of my statements to the police. I will not be positive about it, but I think so. I think Inspector Gold would probably have that information.

I will find out if it is there. I have got Exhibit 44 when you went and gave all the names [Wallace's second statement]. *'When I was at Allerton looking for the address, 25 Menlove Gardens East, in addition to the people I have already mentioned, I enquired from a woman in Menlove Gardens North. She came out of a house near the end by Menlove Gardens West. She told me it might be further up in the continuation of Menlove Gardens West. I went along as suggested by her and came to a crossroad, I think it was Dudlow Road, and I met a young man about 25 years, tall and fair and I enquired from him but he could not inform me. I walked back down the West Gardens to the South Gardens and found all even numbers. I did not knock and came out on to Menlove Avenue itself where I saw a man waiting for a tram by a stop where there was a shelter. I went up to him and asked him if he could tell me where Menlove Gardens East was. He said he was a stranger and did not know. I think these are all the people I spoke to that night at Allerton.' Did you in any statement that you made – I will go through them if necessary – ever state that you called that night and knocked at Mr Crewe's?* Yes, I think I did.

What statement? I cannot tell you, but I think I volunteered that information on some statement.

I have looked through them and I cannot find it. I put it to you; you never have said so until today. Of course, you realise now the importance of that point, that you were quite near the Superintendent who would know the district well, and yet you were walking round asking of everybody else where it was.

At this point, Oliver interjects and effectively diverts Hemmerde from pursing his line of questioning:

Mr Roland Oliver: I am sure my friend does not want to do the witness injustices. This was put to Mr Crewe at the Police Court, and I am sorry I did not put it to Mr Crewe here, but it was put to Mr Crewe there in fact and it was ascertained he was out. [As shown previously, this was true, but only in as much as it established Crewe was not at home on the night of the murder – not that Wallace had admitted he had called to his home.]

Mr Hemmerde: My learned friend does not see my point as to whether he was out or not. I first got the point from the witness that he did not know he was out.

Mr Justice Wright: I do not remember Mr Oliver, it may or may not be important, as one goes along any statement in which the witness said he had gone to Mr Crewe's.

Mr Roland Oliver: I am not suggesting it occurs in any of his statements. What I mean is, it was in the notes of his defending counsel as early as the 20th January and put to Mr Crewe. [This statement cannot be true; Wallace retained the services of Hector Munro on the day after his arrest, 3 February 1931. It could only have been after this date when he gave a statement to Hector Munro.]

Mr Hemmerde: My learned friend does not quite see my point.

Mr Justice Wright: It is a matter for argument. Your point is it is not in any of the voluntary statements.

Mr Hemmerde: Yes, my Lord, that he has never stated so at all himself in any of the statements that he went there.

Mr Justice Wright: If you are passing away from that, I want to ask Mr Oliver something for my own information. I may have misheard it, but I thought you mentioned about the question of the coins being all right by Mr Johnston.

Mr Roland Oliver: My recollection of the evidence was that before the police officer arrived Mr Johnston, or one of them, had said something to the effect: 'Is it all right upstairs?'

Mr Hemmerde: That is so.

Julia Wallace (as I will proffer later) was probably murdered at some time between 7.30 and 8.30 p.m. Wallace may have thought that forensic science (such as it was at that time) would almost certainly establish this and, therefore, an *absolute* alibi would be needed to cover him for the time of death. What could possibly be better than to be sitting at the fireside of not only a friend, but also your superior, relating the night's exploits at the time the police determine that your wife had been brutally murdered. Wallace did, in fact, call at Joseph Crewe's house after wandering around Menlove Gardens; unfortunately, Mr and Mrs Crewe had decided to take themselves off to the Plaza cinema in Allerton Road – where *The Second Wife*, starring Conrad Nagel and Lila Lee, had been due to begin at 7.15 p.m. – and were not in at the time. Had he been at home, in giving his evidence, Crewe would then not only have given Wallace a cast-iron alibi, but would also have added a glowing character reference into the bargain.

With regard to the actual address itself, 25 Menlove Gardens East, was it important that this was a fictional address? Absolutely not: whilst being questioned by Roland Oliver at his trial, Wallace was quizzed on the subject on the address:

When you had discovered this name and address was non-existent that you had been searching for, what passed through your mind about that? I think I came to the conclusion that a mistake had been made in the telephone message, either that Mr Beattie had got it down wrong or in some way, the wrong message had been conveyed to me. I could not account of it in any other way.

This could equally have applied if the address had been real; Wallace would have found that Mr Qualtrough did not live at 25 Menlove Gardens East and then have proceeded in exactly the same manner – traversing the area, knocking on doors and asking people if they knew of a Mr Qualtrough living in the area. The fact still remains that his journey to Mossley Hill was well witnessed. He still could have enquired at four addresses at the least: 25 Menlove Gardens West, 24 Menlove Gardens South, 24 Menlove Gardens North and 25 Menlove Avenue – ultimately, he would still have had (he thought) his rendezvous at Joseph Crewe's house.

Another piece of information given by the caller that could possibly identify who he may have been was the fact that he wanted to see Wallace in order that he might put some business his way with regard to his daughter's 21st birthday. In accounting for his whereabouts on the night of the murder, Parry stated, 'On Tuesday the 20th instant [I went] to Mrs Williamsons [*sic*], 49, Lisburn Lane, and saw her. We had a chat about a 21st birthday party for about 10 minutes …' In corroborating Parry's statement, Lily Lloyd stated, 'On Tuesday the 20th inst Parry called between 8.30 p.m. and 9 p.m. but I think it was nearer 9 than 8.30 p.m. He told me in answer to my question as to where he had been that he had been to a Mrs Williamsons [*sic*], 49, Lisburn Lane. I know Mrs Williamson, she is a friend of mine. He told me that he had got an invitation for myself and him to Leslie Williamson's 21st birthday party in April.'

As can be seen, Parry also refers to a 21st birthday party both he and Lily were to attend – could this have been a mere coincidence? Regarding his whereabouts for the night and time of the phone call to the City Café, Parry stated:

On Monday evening the 19th instant, I called for my young lady, Miss Lillian [*sic*] Lloyd, of 7, Missouri Road, at some address where she had been teaching, the address I cannot for the moment remember, and went home with her to 7, Missouri Road at about 5.30 p.m. and remained there until about 11.30 p.m. when I went home.

When questioned about this, Lily Lloyd stated:

I am a music teacher … On Monday the 19th inst I had an appointment at my home with a pupil named Rita Price, 14a Clifton Road at 7 p.m. I cannot remember properly but either Rita Price was late or I was late. It was not more than 10 minutes. I gave my pupil a full ¾ of an hour lesson and about 20 minutes before I finished Parry called. That would be about 7.35 p.m. I did not see him and when I finished the lesson he had gone. I know he called because I heard his car and his knock at the door and I heard his voice at the door. I do not know who answered the door. He returned between 8.30 and 9 p.m. and remained until about 11 p.m. He told me he had been to, I think he said, Park Lane.

Lily's mother stated:

> On Monday the 19th of January 1931 Mr Parry called at my house at about 7.15 p.m. because my daughter has a pupil named Rita Price, of Clifton Road, who is due for a music lesson at 7 p.m. or a bit earlier every Monday. Last Monday (19th inst) she was a few minutes late and she had started her lesson when Parry arrived in his car. He stayed about 15 minutes and then left because he said he was going to make a call at Lark Lane. He came back in his car at about 9 to 9.15 p.m. and stayed until about 11 p.m. when he left.

In accounting for his whereabouts on the night of 19 January 1931, Parry obviously had something to hide and had blatantly lied to the police to cover it up. Both Lily Lloyd's statement and her mother's statement corroborate each other – but neither corroborate Parry's. If Parry was truly innocent of complicity in this most serious of crimes, why, facing a possible murder charge that carried the possible sentence of death by hanging, would he make up such a barefaced lie? Surely, any other misdemeanour he may have had to admit being involved in on that night would have paled into insignificance. If, as it would appear, Parry was lying to police because it was he who had made the phone call to the City Café, might it have been Leslie Williamson's 21st birthday party he was referring to when, posing as Qualtrough, he told Samuel Beattie it was his daughter's? The police had these statements, knew Parry was lying through his teeth and, seemingly, did absolutely nothing about it.

Leslie Williamson was born at 129 Lisburn Lane, Liverpool, on 2 April 1910, the only child of Joseph Lawrence Williamson, a clerk, and Annie Wilson, a one-time schoolmistress's assistant. During the live debate and phone-in that was aired after the second episode of Roger Wilkes's *Who Killed Julia?* radio programme, the first of the callers was Leslie Williamson himself. Both Roger Wilkes and Jonathan Goodman, not having had access to the Merseyside Police Wallace case files and consequently none of the prosecution statements, had no idea that in his police statement Parry had claimed to have called at Williamson's house on the night of the murder and had spoken to his mother about his 21st birthday party. Had they known, this would have been a prime opportunity to tackle Williamson over the police statement.

During his phone call, Williamson related the fact that his mother, like Lily Lloyd, was a piano teacher; could this have been where the friendship between the Williamsons and Lily had developed? Had Mrs Williamson given Lily piano lessons? Leslie Williamson went on to say that both he and his mother knew Parry only too well:

> While I was away at sea, he conned my mother into handing over my … insurance cards for some reason or other … [B]ecause of his vicious character – and I knew he had a dual personality and he could fight – I took another chappy along with me to his home off Green Lane in case there was any fisty-cuffs, so I could get my insurance cards back – which I did do.

Of Lily Lloyd, he said:

All I knew about her was that she was such a wonderful pianist. And he [Parry] at that particular time, if I remember rightly, he'd conned her mother into an insurance policy, and he'd also conned her into handing over her engagement ring.

This shows that, if Lily Lloyd and Parry had been invited to Leslie Williamson's 21st birthday party, it would have only been through Lily's relationship with Leslie's mother – Parry only being invited because of his association with Lily Lloyd. Leslie Williamson also related the fact that

on the week of the murder, I was at home, on leave from sea ... [Parry] called at our house ... about four or five o'clock or something like that, one evening, and I answered the door. He wanted to see my mother – my mother was a music teacher, and she had a pupil in at the time, and it was a sacrilege to break into the lesson ... he was most adamant ... he got in through the vestibule, in Lisburn Lane, and he wanted to see my mother about a song: he wanted some music. Well this is funny ... Anyway, he did see my mother; my mother came out after I'd asked her, and I can always remember them going to the music stool and asking the student to get up off the music stool, and he chose a song out of this particular stool ...

Throughout Williamson's telephone call, in which he vehemently underlined his loathing of Parry, he neither mentioned the fact that Parry had called to his mother's house on the night of the murder (surely a memorable occasion), nor the fact that the police had questioned either him or his mother about Parry's statement concerning the night of the murder. It would appear as though the police had never approached the Williamsons for a statement. However, I will later relate the circumstances of another birthday party that may have played a more significant role in the murder of Julia Wallace – not a 21st birthday party, but a birthday party on the 21st.

Giving evidence at Wallace's trial, Beattie was asked by Prosecution Council Edward George Hemmerde what sort of voice Qualtrough presented: 'a gruffish voice but of a man sure of himself, a strong-voiced man'. In asking if he thought it was Wallace's voice, Beattie replied, 'Certainly not ... It would be a great stretch of the imagination for me to say it was anything like that.' Beattie had known Wallace for about as long as the Central Chess Club had been in existence – eight years. For at least three hours a week, almost every week, Beattie had heard Wallace's voice through a range of emotions and situations and categorically stated that, as far as he was concerned, it was not Wallace on the telephone that night. The telephonists at the Anfield Telephone Exchange concurred in their descriptions of the caller. Louisa Alfreds stated, 'The voice was quite an ordinary one and appeared to me to be that of a man used to using telephones. It was decidedly not gruff.' Lilian Martha Kelly stated, 'The man spoke with an ordinary voice, certainly not a gruff voice and appeared to be a person accustomed to using the telephone.' Both were amused at the way the caller had stressed the word 'café'; in fact, Louisa Alfreds remarked to her colleague, 'What a funny thing to say, "caf-ay".' City Café waitress Gladys Harley, however, said Qualtrough's voice was 'deep', that he 'spoke very quickly', and that it 'seemed the voice of an elderly gentleman'.

One point stands out above all else: whoever made that call felt as though he *needed* to disguise his voice – ergo, whoever telephoned that night was not a stranger to the City Café, nor to the members of the Central Chess Club. If he were, why would he have to disguise his voice?

Tim Costello, scriptwriter, filmmaker and an ex-director for Ireland's RTE Television service, and also a long-time aficionado of the Wallace case, undertook a number of experiments to either prove or disprove Hemmerde's assertion that it may have been Wallace on the telephone that night and that Beattie simply had not recognised his voice. Costello said:

> I decided to replicate that phone call with the help of a few friends. It was important for us to speak to other people who were both well-known and only casual acquaintances. We tended to favour people who were known to us less than the eight years mentioned above.
>
> We each in turn phoned a friend with a list of instructions while trying to assume a strange voice. We tried putting slices of apple in our cheeks, muffling the mouthpiece with a scarf but to no avail. Each one of us was rumbled, identified, by the friend sometimes within a few seconds of the phone call starting! Very embarrassing and of course we had to explain what we were doing to all our 'correspondents'!

Parry was an amateur actor – a member of the Mersey Amateur Dramatic Society. On 17 November 1930, the company staged a production of Alfred Sutro's *John Glayde's Honour* at Crane Hall, Hanover Street, Liverpool (recently the Neptune Theatre). Every Tuesday and Thursday, the company would rehearse the production at the City Café. Parry stated, 'It was during these rehearsals that I saw Mr Wallace at the City Café on about three occasions. I did not know previously that he was a member of the Chess Club there.' This being the case, Parry would not have been overly concerned about using his true voice when calling the telephone exchange. In speaking to Gladys Harley and Samuel Beattie at the City Café, however, he may have had reservations. Whilst rehearsing at the City Café on a Thursday night, Parry would know that both Gladys Harley and Samuel Beattie would have heard not only his true voice, but also his voice whilst in character. In speaking to both these people, Parry would not have wanted to take the risk of them recognising him and so would have disguised his voice. If Parry was Qualtrough, he would have had every reason to disguise his voice and was well equipped to have accomplished this.

When making the phone call to the City Café, the caller also gave another vital piece of information – he used the name 'R. M. Qualtrough'.

4

The Qualtrough Connection

The significance of the name 'R. M. Qualtrough' to the caller in phone kiosk Anfield 1627 has remained a mystery ever since the name was uttered to Samuel Beattie through the earpiece of the telephone at Cottle's Café at around 7.20 p.m. on 19 January 1931. It has long been the general consensus that if you found Qualtrough, you would find Julia's killer. That would, of course, only pertain if, in using the name R. M. Qualtrough, the caller was referring to a traceable person who could then be associated with the caller, and not simply a random name picked up from some source. It has been related to me that there existed, within eyesight of the telephone box within which the call was made, a butcher's shop which bore the name of its owner, 'Qualtrough'. It is argued that the caller, glancing through the windows of the phone box, saw the shop sign and so used that name. However, there was no shop in the vicinity of the telephone box, a butcher's or otherwise, owned by anyone named Qualtrough (there was a Thomas John L. Douglas Qualtrough who was a butcher; but he had his shop 3 miles away at 108 Country Road, Walton. If, indeed, it was the case that the name was a random thought, the identity of Qualtrough was, and forever more would be, the exclusive knowledge of the orchestrators of Julia Wallace's murder, and that line of investigation would have to be closed. In just a few minutes' time, however, you too will know exactly what the caller in the telephone kiosk knew on the night of the call to the Chess Club eighty years ago: the true identity of the man whose name was appropriated to initiate this most terrible of crimes and his importance in finding the killer of Julia Wallace. In order to accomplish this, I must first introduce you to the more significant, but equally mysterious, 'Marsden'.

Like Qualtrough, the identity of Marsden has been long debated. Marsden was named by Wallace in the same statement that referred to Parry – indeed, in connection with Parry – as the man who was introduced to Wallace *by* Parry in December 1928, when Wallace was ill with bronchitis, and as a man whom Julia would have allowed access to 29 Wolverton Street in her husband's absence, had Marsden called.

In his statement to Inspector Herbert Gold, given on 22 January 1931, Wallace describes Marsden thus:

> He was an agent for the Prudential Company for two or three years and had left before he did my work. I gave him the job because he was out of work … Marsden is about 28 years of age, about 5 foot 6/7 inches, brown hair and fairly well dressed.

Wallace estimated that Marsden was born sometime around 1903. During the time Wallace maintained he had worked for him, December 1928 and the beginning of January 1929, he was out of work, but had worked for the Prudential for two or three years previously. If Marsden had left the Prudential by 1928, Wallace estimated he had started working for them sometime in 1925 or 1926. In searching through the reams and reams of official documentation in Merseyside Police files, Director of Public Prosecution files and those of Wallace's solicitor, Hector Munro, I was hoping there would be at least a fragment of a statement from Marsden or possibly his inclusion in Parry's statement, thus showing that, in interviewing Parry, the police had at least done their job and asked for more detail on his unnamed friend. Contained in what remains of the files held by Merseyside Police, I noticed a single document pertaining to investigations carried out at the time into the names given in Wallace's second statement of people Julia would allow into the house during his absence. It is headed: 'Copy of handwritten page'. On this piece of paper, amongst other things, is written 'G. R. Parry [*sic*]; 7 Woburn Hill – Seen' and 'Mr Marsden (was an agent for the Prudential 23 years ago) – Seen'. This was John Wilfred Marsden, who was living at 55 Knoclaid Road. Although an insurance agent at the time, he was 45 years old when he was interviewed by police, and was too old to have been Wallace's Marsden. At the bottom of the page it read, 'J. C. Marsden; 24 Adelaide Road, Kensington; Works at Bernard Murphy, 2 Kings Street'.

Sifting through more documentation, I came across three sheets of paper, all headed in a similar fashion to the other: 'Copy of hand written page'. These were the notes taken by Sergeant Harry Bailey upon trudging around Liverpool and interviewing as many of the residents named Qualtrough as he could find. Bailey put so much effort into the initial stages of the case that he had to be sent home on two occasions 'owing to his haggard appearance'. After Wallace was arrested, Bailey was placed on the sick list by the Police Medical Officer. Examining these sheets in the light of the previous document, I was amazed to find this particular note:

> Richard James Qualtrough; 8 Northumberland Terrace, joiner. At home all evening Monday 19/1/31. Does not know Wallace. Insured with the Prudential, agent Mr Sutton, 74 Queen's Drive Walton. Has son, William 25yrs. s/a with Miss Thompson, 20 Orient Street, at her house from 8.00 p.m. to 12; at home until about 7.55 p.m. Mr Marsden, Adelaide Road, collected for Prudential for about 3 or 4 years, up to about 3 or 4 years, when Sutton took it over.

If, according to Goodman and Wilkes, Bailey undertook his investigations of the Qualtrough families present in Liverpool on 21 January 1931, this would have meant that the police already knew of Marsden and his connections to both Wallace and R. M. Qualtrough the day before Wallace named him in his second statement. This cannot have been the case. Despite this, these documents show that at the time Bailey undertook his Qualtrough investigations, Marsden (and probably Parry) were strong suspects. This also shows that when this information was gained from Richard James Qualtrough, the police not only knew where to contact the 'mysterious' Marsden, but also knew of his close connection to the

Qualtrough name, making him a very strong suspect, and effectively placing him at the top of the list of people who Julia was likely to allow into the house in her husband's absence (until Parry's inept statement regarding the night of the phone call would put him in the same position as Marsden). When one reads through Bailey's notes, it appears that, upon confronting each Qualtrough household, he had a set regime of questioning: where were you on the night of Monday, 19 January? Do you know William Herbert Wallace? Are you insured with the Prudential Assurance? If so, who is your agent? Do you know anybody by the name of Marsden? It is clear from these documents that, at the time of this investigation, Bailey did not know Marsden's first name. Of the Qualtroughs interviewed, he received only two positive responses – each calling Marsden 'Mr Marsden' – and these were noted down. In these documents there is no mention whatsoever of Parry. Either the Qualtrough families were never asked if they knew of a Richard Gordon Parry (which is unlikely) or any other names contained within Wallace's second statement, or they had answered negatively and their response was not then noted. If they had been asked, and they had never heard of him, this gives further proof that it was highly unlikely to have been Parry or Wallace who came up with the name R. M. Qualtrough.

Richard James Qualtrough, the eldest of ten children, was born in West Derby, Liverpool, in 1872, though, like most Qualtrough families in Liverpool, he had his roots in the Isle of Man. His father, Richard Qualtrough, a joiner, was born in Arbory, Isle of Man, in 1847. By the end of 1870, he had left Arbory and was living in Ormskirk, Lancashire, and was married to Elizabeth Trehearne. After a move to 19 Kilshaw Street, Everton, Liverpool, Richard James was born. Like William John Parry, the Qualtroughs were members of the Primitive Methodist Church. After the closure of their own church in Kilshaw Street and the opening of Jubilee Drive Primitive Methodist Church, Liverpool, in 1890, the family soon became active members, Richard and his two sons, Richard James and William, becoming long-time trustees. Like his father and his grandfather (also named Richard), Richard James became a joiner; in 1896, he married Ellen Davies in Upton, Wirral, in Cheshire. Moving back to Liverpool soon after their marriage, the couple moved into 17 Martensen Street, Edge Hill, where they welcomed the birth of the first of their seven children: Mary Elizabeth (1899), Richard Henry (1905), William John (1906), Mona Kathleen (1908), Richard George (1910), James Trahearne (1912) and Annie (1914). On 18 May 1913, at a meeting of the Chapel Committee and Trustees of the Zion Primitive Methodist Church, Northumberland Terrace, Everton, a motion was carried that the then caretaker, James Peden, have his letter of resignation accepted and a new caretaker be sought. The lucky applicant would not only have a job – he and his family would also have tenancy of the church's adjoining house at 8 Northumberland Terrace. A motion was passed at the committee meeting that the vacancy be 'announced from the pulpit of the Everton Road, Jubilee Drive and Zion Churches'. It was from the pulpit of the Jubilee Drive Methodist Church that Richard James Qualtrough heard of the vacancy. At a later meeting of the Zion Chapel Committee, it was resolved to 'appoint Mr Richard James Qualtrough as caretaker under the usual terms and conditions'. In 1913, Richard James, his wife Ellen, and their two surviving children, Mary Elizabeth and William John, moved into 8 Northumberland Terrace, where, during January 1931, they would be interviewed about the brutal murder of Julia Wallace. During the beginning of the Second World War, on 1 May 1941, a series of German air attacks began throughout Merseyside that would last for four days. Soon after darkness fell on Saturday 3 May, until dawn the following morning, Liverpool suffered a particularly heavy and sustained attack, causing many casualties and substantial damage. Included in this damage were the Zion Primitive Methodist Church and its adjoining house. On 30 May 1941, the church trustees both received and accepted the resignation of their caretaker, Richard James Qualtrough. Having maintained his position for over twenty-eight years, he was now reaching his seventies and his wife Ellen was ill. With the devastation then befalling the country, and now Liverpool itself, Richard James decided it was time to return to his roots. Having bought a cottage in Clifton Terrace, Douglas, Isle of Man, the couple removed themselves there, out of harm's way. However, not long after the war had ended, Richard and Ellen were forced to return to Merseyside to enable their daughter, Mary Elizabeth, to look after her mother, who was gravely ill at this time. Ellen Qualtrough died in Birkenhead, Cheshire, in 1946 aged 75; Richard James Qualtrough, inconsolable after the death of his wife, died three months later aged 74 – some say of a broken heart.

The Marsdens

In 1931 the residents of 24 Adelaide Road, Kensington, Liverpool, were Harold Egbert Marsden, Margaret Elizabeth Marsden and Joseph Caleb Marsden. At this time, Harold Marsden was a fruit warehouseman, whilst his son Joseph Caleb was a clerk employed at Bernard Murphy & Son, a bookmaker at 2 King Street, Tranmere, Birkenhead. Descended from a long line of successful brushmakers originating from Over Darwen, Lancashire, Harold Egbert Marsden's father, Joseph Caleb Marsden (born 31 December 1823), had eschewed the family business to become a watch jeweller.[3] A trade in itself, the craft of the watch jeweller is highly specialised: tiny jewels are ground and shaped to be inserted into a watch mechanism as a pivot, reducing the amount of friction encountered as the cogs turn on their spindles. Married on 23 May 1853 at St Mary's church, Edge Hill, to Betty Arnold, daughter of wheelwright Richard Arnold and Martha Lawton, the couple had ten children – seven boys and three girls. The first four children – Joseph Caleb (1854), Thomas Alfred (1856), George William (1858) and Francis Arnold (1860) – were all given an opportunity of learning the craft of the watch jeweller, being offered apprenticeships by their father.

Unfortunately, only one of the brothers, George William, managed to succeed in making a living from the skills he learned. Specialising in nautical instruments, George turned his hand to various occupations: optician, ship's compass adjuster, brass finisher and nautical instrument maker. Of the others, Francis Arnold Marsden was considered to have been the black sheep of the family. Apparently receiving a good education, he was considered to have squandered it. A story persisted within the family of an incident that occurred whilst he was licensee of The Bishop public house in Beaufort Street, Toxteth, between 5 May 1887 and 14 September 1888. Engaged in a fight with a drunken customer one night, Francis hit him over the head with a bottle. Fearing he had murdered the man, he apparently absconded, hiding out for some years in Australia. Upon his eventual return, he found the man to be fit and well. At the time of the sudden loss of his father to 'apoplexy' (an archaic medical term for a stroke) on 13 March 1880, Harold Egbert Marsden, the couple's fifth child (born 30

March 1863) would have been only 17 years old and so was deprived of the benefits that a watchmaking apprenticeship might have bestowed. Instead, it would appear that his older brother, Joseph Caleb, took him under his wing in the fruit and vegetable trade and Harold became a fruiterer. Of Joseph Caleb Marsden and Betty Arnold's remaining five children, Alice Gertrude Marsden – their ninth child and second daughter – is the most noteworthy. She was married on 2 March 1897 at Christ Church, Kensington, Liverpool, to Robert Duckworth (son of pawnbroker William Duckworth and Eliza Ann Rothwell, daughter of pub landlord William Rothwell); a member of the Liverpool City Police, Robert was one of the officers who escorted Hawley Harvey Crippen (arrested for the murder of his wife, Belle Elmore) from Liverpool to London upon the latter's return to England from Canada on the White Star liner *Megantic*.

On 12 February 1888, Harold Egbert Marsden married Margaret Elizabeth Houghton, daughter of warehouseman James Houghton, at St Emmanuel church, Everton. In all they had eight children: Mary Isabella (1889), Walter James (1891), Harold Egbert (1893), William (1897), Bessie Arnold (1898), Frances Ann (1900), Joseph Caleb (1900) and Constance Irene (1904). The couple's youngest son, and seventh child, Joseph Caleb Marsden, was born on 21 September 1900 along with his twin sister, Frances Ann, who unfortunately died soon after. At the time of his birth, the family were living at 31 Kemble Street, West Derby, Liverpool, where his father was now a fruit warehouseman. Joseph Caleb Marsden was the ex-Prudential agent referred to in Richard James Qualtrough's statement to Sergeant Harry Bailey.

Let us now review the evidence we have. Wallace stated that the Marsden he knew was born sometime around 1903 and had begun working for the Prudential around 1925 or 1926, having lost his employment at some point previous to doing work for him in 1928. Richard James Qualtrough stated that Joseph Caleb Marsden began collecting from him for the Prudential six to eight years prior to 1931 – between 1923 and 1925 – and stopped collecting three to four years before 1931, either 1927 or 1928. Both Wallace's and Mr Qualtrough's facts concerning their own Mr Marsden as good as agree and, as we now know, Joseph Caleb Marsden was born in 1900. So unusual was the Qualtrough name that only fourteen families in the whole of Liverpool possessed it (several of these were related to each other). The likelihood of finding a Qualtrough not only associated with a Marsden, but with a Marsden who was an insurance agent and who had worked for the Prudential for about the same time period, and who was around the same age as that given by Wallace in his second police statement, has to be extremely remote. There can be little doubt that Joseph Caleb Marsden is Wallace's mysterious 'Marsden', friend of Richard Gordon Parry. This being the case, Richard James Qualtrough of 8 Northumberland Terrace has to be the origin of the name 'R. M. Qualtrough', used in the telephone call to the City Café on the night of 19 January 1931. Had it been through complaints put to the Prudential by Mr Qualtrough that Marsden had lost his job? Had it been within the accounts of Mr Qualtrough that the Prudential had found (according to Wallace) discrepancies? Could it be that the result of the complaints had been a lot more serious than a simple dressing down and the loss of his job, causing Marsden to have a good reason to remember Mr Richard James Qualtrough? It has to be noted that, other than Wallace's assertion within his second police statement that

'Marsden' had left the Prudential 'on account of financial irregularities', despite thorough research, no official evidence could be found of Joseph Caleb Marsden having participated in any form of criminal activity whatsoever.

The police were seeking information about, as far as they were concerned, two unconnected names: one, R. M. Qualtrough, in direct association with a brutal killing; the other, 'Marsden', one of seventeen names given by Wallace of people his wife would allow into his home in his absence. The names were given by two different witnesses (Qualtrough given by Captain Beattie, Marsden given by Wallace) in association with two different circumstances. In finding Richard James Qualtrough, the police had the two names linked to each other – and yet they seemingly did absolutely nothing about it: no official statements appear to have been taken from either man. Except, that is, for one tantalising note scribbled on an official document. Included in what remains of the official case files held by Merseyside Police, is a typed copy of Wallace's second police statement. In the margin of this document are two inked annotations; one is adjacent to Wallace's references to his Prudential colleagues, Joseph Crewe, Crewe's assistant Albert Wood and Assistant Superintendent Joseph Bamber. It reads, 'at home at 5.45 p.m. to 7.30 p.m. Then went parent's 26 Cedar Road, Aintree, 20th'. To which of Wallace's colleagues did this refer? The residents of 26 Cedar Road, Aintree, in 1931 were Charles Bamber, Ellen Bamber and John William Bamber – Joseph Bamber's parents and his brother. The other annotation, above this one, is adjacent to Wallace's references to Marsden. It reads, 'in bed with Flu 20th'. Might we now know, at long last, what alibi Marsden used for the night of Julia's murder? If this is so, where is the full official statement? Where are the corroborating statements?

As has been shown, the police knew Marsden's address upon interviewing Richard James Qualtrough. It is plain that the police did go and speak with Marsden: they knew his place of work, Bernard Murphy & Son, and he had apparently told them he was 'in bed with Flu'. What has to be remembered is the important fact that these details were not contained within one particular document – they were annotated on separate documents *after* the police had spoken to Marsden. Somewhere in the police file had to have been a full statement from Joseph Caleb Marsden from which these details were taken. Despite the most thorough research by this author, this document cannot now be located. Why are the only remaining official references to both Qualtrough and Marsden scribbled notes on scraps of paper?

Where was Joseph Caleb Marsden on the night of the murder? During their investigation of the case, it would appear the police had not questioned Richard Gordon Parry about his association with Marsden – thus neglecting the only person they knew of who could readily have given them all the information they required. In interviewing Parry, they should have found his alibi for the night of the telephone call to be extremely suspicious and yet failed to pursue these blatant inconsistencies. Joseph Caleb Marsden, like Parry, was named in Wallace's second statement as someone of dubious character who knew where to locate the cash box containing the Prudential collection money and who was someone Julia would allow into the house in his absence. How could Joseph Caleb Marsden and Richard James Qualtrough have been simply airbrushed out of the case, their identities left to remain a complete mystery for over eight decades? The police had to have known that in revealing the identity of Qualtrough, it would be possible to discover the identity of Marsden and the link between them. Could this be the reason why Richard Gordon Parry's statement was never questioned? If he had taken the witness stand, he would undoubtedly have been asked, in open court, about his relationship with Joseph Caleb Marsden. Would this then have revealed Marsden's link to Richard James Qualtrough and possibly his connection to the murder of Julia Wallace?

5

Tuesday 20 January 1931

Sunrise on the morning of Tuesday 20 January 1931 was at 8.16 a.m. Fourteen-year-old Douglas Metcalf, a local paperboy for Yates' Stationers in Breck Road who regularly delivered a newspaper every morning, and a copy of *Armchair Science* magazine every month, had already pushed a copy of the *Financial Times* through the Wallaces' letterbox half an hour previously. At 8.30 a.m., as the sun attempted to break through a curtain of low cloud that hung over Liverpool, Mr and Mrs Wallace yawned their way downstairs to breakfast. Nosing through the kitchen curtains, Wallace suspected rain. Around 10.15 a.m., equipped with mackintosh and bowler hat, Wallace boarded a tram on his way to Clubmoor to begin his collections.

After seeing her husband off, Julia had tidied away the breakfast dishes and at 11.00 a.m. was called to the front door. It was her window cleaners, Arthur and Emily Hoer. Arthur Hoer was a Labour member of the city council and would regularly have to attend to council business. On the odd occasion when he was falling behind with his window-cleaning round, his wife would often help out. This morning they had knocked for some water for their bucket; Julia gladly helped them out. Sometime during that morning, according to Russell Johnston (grandson of the Wallaces' next-door neighbours at No. 31, John Sharp Johnston and his wife Florence Sarah), his mother (Amy Beatrice Towers, married to the Johnstons' third child and youngest son, Robert Leslie Russell Johnston) was cleaning the front bedroom windows at No. 31 when she saw Julia in her front bedroom window and waved to her. Around two o'clock that afternoon, the weather finally having turned for the better, Wallace had just left 177 Lisburn Lane, the last call on his morning round, and was heading down Maiden Lane to catch a tram to Holy Trinity church and home. Arriving at about 2.10 p.m., he and Julia had lunch and at 3.15 p.m., having left his mackintosh drying on the hanger in the hallway, he changed into his lighter overcoat and went on his way again to begin his afternoon collections.

At 3.30 p.m. Wallace's sister-in-law, Amy Margaret Wallace, arrived for a flying visit with Julia. Julia had not been too well when Amy had last called on the previous Sunday with her 20-year-old son, Edwin Herbert, and she wanted to see if Julia would be well enough to attend a pantomime with her that coming Friday. During the visit, Amy was told about the mysterious phone call Mr Wallace had received at the Chess Club:

> Mrs Wallace told me that her husband had been down to chess the night before and
> had had a phone message to go to see someone and as far as I can remember, it was

someone in the Calderstones district; but Mrs Wallace did not know of anyone in that district, but she stated it was for business.

Meanwhile, about this time Constable 296G James Edward Rothwell claimed he was cycling down Maiden Lane, Clubmoor, on his way to Anfield police station from his home at 30 Craigs Road, Clubmoor, to sign on for his afternoon revolving point duty, when he saw Wallace rushing up Maiden Lane. Of the encounter, Rothwell said:

> I saw Mr Wallace walking at a very fast pace going south along the foot walk, alongside a small brook which runs on the other side of the wall. He did not speak to me or recognise me and would be about 30 yards from Townsend Lane, and was looking on the ground and appeared to me as if he was crying. He was dressed in a tweed suit, a light fawn overcoat – a mackintosh; he had his hands in his pockets of his overcoat. His face was haggard and drawn and he was very distressed – unusually distressed; he was dabbing his eye with his coat sleeve and he appeared to me as if he had been crying. I noticed his eyes were on the ground and I failed to attract his attention. He gave me that impression, as if he had suffered from some bereavement.

Wallace had been Rothwell's Prudential agent for about two years, so the pair were not complete strangers. Yet Rothwell maintained that, although he was in full uniform and only feet from him, Wallace did not seem to notice him. Whilst being cross-examined at the Assize trial, Roland Oliver asked Rothwell, 'About his being distressed, you do not think you could be mistaken?' Rothwell denied this. Oliver was confused: 'Although you never spoke to him?' Rothwell replied, 'He gave me that impression; as if he had suffered from some bereavement.' In the light of the events of the night ahead, Rothwell seemed to be implying that Wallace was already aware of them, and possibly regretting them. Roland Oliver was less than impressed by this witness: 'If I were to call about 25 people who saw him that afternoon about that time or round about that time and they said he was just as usual, would you say you had made a mistake?' Rothwell was adamant: 'No. I should stick to my opinion.' It is noteworthy that whilst PC Rothwell gave his official police statement at the Anfield police station on Friday 30 January 1931, on 20 February, at the committal trial, he stated, 'I made a report to my superior officer on the evening of the murder.'

The witnesses Roland Oliver was referring to were the very clients Wallace was about to visit during the afternoons collections. Wallace's first call, minutes after the alleged encounter with PC Rothwell, was at 5 Worcester Drive, the home of Mrs McPailin, who said of him, 'He was his usual self, pleasant and nice.' Mrs Jane Elizabeth Harbord of 15 Worcester Drive said of him, 'I have always found him very pleasant and jolly … he was his usual self and I noticed no change in his manner whatever.' Suffice to say, PC James Edward Rothwell's evidence was not referred to again.

At 4.30 p.m., Amy Wallace had just left 29 Wolverton Street when Neil Norbury, the local baker's boy, arrived with Julia's bread. He noticed she did not look too well and was wearing 'a kind of scarf, a bit of sort of material'. Julia had reassured him it was just a touch of bronchitis and closed the door. Around the same time, Charlie Bliss, brother-in-law of

Arthur Hoer, had just cleaned the upstairs back windows at 29 Wolverton Street and was about to make a start on No. 31, the home of the Johnstons, when Julia appeared at the back kitchen door and paid him the twopence charge. By the time Emily Hoer arrived to clean the downstairs back windows, it was dark, the house was quiet, and the back kitchen door was closed. Through the blinds of the middle kitchen, she could see a light. She also noticed a light in the back bedroom.

At 5.45 p.m., Wallace had made the last call of his round to a Miss Ann Miller at 4 Brookbridge Road. She remembered him asking the time and, though her clock said six o'clock, she stated that it was 15 minutes fast. From here, Wallace had to make a special call on Mrs Margaret Martin of 19 Eastman Road to see her about the surrendering of a policy. She remembered him arriving about 5.50 p.m. Leaving her a form to sign, he made an appointment to call on her the next day at 5 p.m. to pay her the value of the policy.

By 6.05 p.m., when Wallace arrived back at Wolverton Street, the streets of Anfield were in darkness. In anticipation of him having to leave not long after his arrival in order to keep his appointment at 7.30 p.m. with Mr Qualtrough, Julia had tea and scones ready and the couple sat down to tea. At around 6.30 p.m., Wallace gathered together a sheaf of documents he felt he might need when interviewing Qualtrough and went upstairs for a quick wash and brush up in the upstairs bathroom. About this time, paperboy David Jones pushed the *Liverpool Echo* through the letterbox. In his statement to the police, given on Thursday 22 January, Jones had said he had put it through the letterbox at 'about 6.30 p.m.' In his statement to Hector Munro, he maintained he had 'delivered there between 6.25 and 6.35 p.m. I thrust it though the letterbox.' At around 6.45 p.m. there was a knock on the front door; when Julia opened it, milkboy Alan Croxton Close had left a can of milk on the doorstep and was standing on the doorstep of No. 31 pouring milk into Mrs Johnston's milk jug, which had been left just inside her lobby. Julia took the can from the step and brought into in the house to fill her own milk jug. Pulling the Johnston's door to, Close waited on the doorstep of No. 29 for Julia to return the empty milk can. As he was waiting, James Allison Wildman, a paperboy, passed him on his way to Mr and Mrs Holmes' house, No. 27, to deliver their *Liverpool Echo* and noticed Wildman was wearing a Liverpool Collegiate School cap. Returning to the door with the milk can, Julia told Close to hurry on home out of the cold. Wallace, having readied himself by this time, left the house accompanied by Julia as far as the backyard door and began his journey to Menlove Gardens East. It was, apparently, both his and Julia's practice to leave and enter by the back door during the day, using the front door only at night (though at 6.45 p.m., with the winter night having well drawn in and settled, should not Wallace, by his own admission, have left by the front door?). When questioned by Inspector Gold, Wallace retraced his steps to catch the tram at St Margaret's church on the corner of Belmont Road and Rocky Lane, West Derby, to begin his journey to Menlove Gardens East:

> I left by the back door and up the entry to Richmond Park and across and up the entry by the new Institute to Sedley Street and then to Newcombe Street to Castlewood Road, and to Belmont Road and St Margaret's Church, where I got on a tram to Allerton and back.

After alighting from the No. 26 tram from Belmont Road, Wallace had boarded a No. 4 tram at the junction of Lodge Lane and Smithdown Road. The tram conductor of the No. 4, Thomas Charles Phillips, throughout his statements (two police statements and his testimony at both the committal proceedings and the Assize trial) could not decide whether his tram had left Smithdown Lane bound for Penny Lane at 7.06 p.m. or 7.10 p.m. Upon arriving at the Penny Lane junction, Wallace boarded a No. 5A tram that, according to its conductor, Arthur Thompson, began its journey at 7.15 p.m. In his report, commissioned by Hector Munro, into the timings of the journey Wallace had taken to the City Café on 19 January and Wallace's journey to Menlove Avenue on 20 January, civil and consulting engineer P. Julian Maddock states, 'Tram conductor Thompson says Mr Wallace got on his No. 5A ... car at Penny Lane at 7.15. If Phillips did not leave Smithdown lane until 7.10 this is manifestly impossible as it only allows 5 minutes for the journey to Penny Lane.' After carrying out three tests of the journey from Smithdown Lane to Penny Lane junction, Maddock found that the average travelling time was 9 minutes 38 seconds. This would have meant that if Phillips was correct in his assumption that he had left at 7.10 p.m., he would not have arrived at Penny Lane until 7.20 p.m. However, using Phillips's earlier time of 7.06 p.m., this would have meant the No. 4 tram would have arrived at Penny Lane at 7.15 p.m. There can be no doubt that when Wallace boarded the No. 4 tram at Smithdown Lane, the tram had to have left at 7.06 p.m.

Thomas Charles Arthur Phillips recalled his encounter with Wallace in his second statement to police, given on 3 February 1931 (the day after Wallace's arrest):

> When my tram stopped at the corner of Tunnel Road and Smithdown Lane on the 20th January at 7.06 p.m. there was a fair crowd waiting to board the car, and about the last to get on was the man who asked me if the car went to Menlove Gardens East. I told him 'No' that a 7 or a 5W would take him, but then I changed my mind and told him I could give him a transfer ticket or a penny fare and he could change. He got on and took his seat inside. I went in for the fares and he said he was a stranger in the district and that he had an urgent 'call' or 'business' at Menlove Gardens East and emphasized the word 'East'. I gave him a penny ticket and he then said 'You won't forget Guard; I want to get to Menlove Gardens East'. I collected my fares inside and outside and when I got back to the platform he turned his head and said 'How far is it now and where do I have to change?' I told him he would have to change at Penny Lane and when we got there, I saw a No. 7 car waiting and I told him to get that. He hurried away and I saw he was going towards a No. 5 car which was also waiting, and I shouted 'Not that one, a No. 7 in the out loop' and he went towards the No. 7 car but I cannot say if he boarded it or not.

In fact, Wallace had not boarded the No. 7 tram. Instead, he had boarded the No. 5A tram to Calderstones Park. According to the conductor of the No. 5A tram, Arthur Thompson:

> I boarded a No. 5A car coming towards Calderstones at 7.15 p.m. A gentleman, I think it was the accused, was sitting on the left-hand side of the car. He asked me to put him

off at Menlove Gardens East. I said I would. When the car arrived at Menlove Gardens West I beckoned to the gentleman and he came to the platform of the car. I said 'This is Menlove Gardens West. Menlove Gardens is a triangular affair, three roads. There are two roundabouts off on the right. You will probably find it is one of them.' He said 'Thank you, I am a complete stranger around here'. He then left the car.

Wallace had been pestering Thomas Phillips ever since he had got onto his tram; Phillips told him he needed to take the No. 7. Yet, in his statements to both the police and Hector Munro, and, in contradiction to Phillips's statements, Wallace had insisted that Phillips had told him to take the 5A:

> The conductor pointed to a tram, a 5A which was standing there and told me that would take me to Menlove Gardens, I boarded it … The car arrived at Penny Lane, and the conductor told me there was a 5A car standing on the other side of the road, which would take me to Menlove Gardens. I alighted and at once boarded the 5A car.

Upon alighting from the No. 4 tram, despite being told to take the No. 7 tram, he headed straight for the No. 5A. Even when Phillips called after him and redirected him toward the No. 7 – according to the evidence of Arthur Thompson – Wallace still boarded the No. 5A tram: Wallace appears to have known exactly how to get to where he was going. Had this, in fact, been the route he had taken with Julia whilst travelling to Calderstones Park? Could this also have been the actual route he had taken when visiting Joseph Crewe for his violin lessons? In fact, it appears that Wallace had been to Crewe's house many more times than either Crewe or Wallace were admitting. During the committal trial, whilst being questioned by prosecution solicitor J. R. Bishop in an attempt to ascertain how well Wallace knew the district, Crewe was asked how often Wallace had called at his house:

> I went to live in Green Lane three and a half years ago … and Mr Wallace has visited me there perhaps four or five times. He really came more as a friend than anything else, and it came about in this way. About two years ago, Mr Wallace asked me if I knew anything about the violin. I suggested I should go with him to buy one, which I did. I then asked him who was going to teach him to play it, and he said he did not know anyone. I suggested I should give him a few lessons until such time as he found someone to teach him. That is how he came to call at my house. That was the only reason he came to see me, and it covered a period of five weeks.

He reiterated this whilst being examined by prosecution counsel Edward Hemmerde at the Assize trial:

> *Did you go and live at your present address some three and half years ago?* Yes.
> *Had the accused visited you there?* Yes.
> *Often?* Yes.
> *How many times altogether?* Five times?

Some time ago, did he suggest anything to you about music? Yes.

What was it? Well, he suggested he would like to play the violin and asked me if I knew anything about it and I said I knew a little bit.

Did you play yourself? Yes, I did and I went with him to buy one. I asked him who was going to teach him and he said he did not know, but he was going to get one and I said I would give him a few lessons till he got one.

You undertook or suggested you should give him a few lessons? That is right.

How many lessons altogether did you give him? Five.

Apart from those lessons, did he come at any other time? No.

Wallace himself, upon being questioned by Roland Oliver, qualified the vagueness of his memory about his visits to Crewe's house (and, therefore, the district) due to the length of time since he had been there and the very limited number of times he had called in order to have his violin lessons:

Was that when you had the violin lessons two years ago? It was.

When you went there on those occasions how did you get there. What tram route did you take? I cannot exactly describe it but I think possibly I would take a car which would branch off in the other direction and come down to what I now know to be Allerton Road. I would get off at a big cinema there, I think it is called the 'Plaza', and walk up to his house.

However, in Joseph Crewe's first statement, given to police on 5 February 1931 – two weeks before the start of the committal trial – he had stated that Wallace had been to his house on *more* than the five occasions he had called for violin lessons. Contrary to his testimony at the committal trial where he said, 'I suggested I should give him a few lessons until such time as he found someone to teach him. That is how he came to call at my house. That was the only reason he came to see me, and it covered a period of five weeks', he admits that Wallace had been to his home for more than violin lessons: 'I went to live at my present address about 3½ years ago and since then Mr Wallace has visited me on business at my home on many occasions, and for a period of about 2 months, about 18 months ago, he visited me once a week.' At what point did Crewe decide to confine his evidence to only the five violin lessons – and why? He had to have realised that in admitting that Wallace had 'visited me on business on many occasions', he would be playing into the prosecution's hands and condemning Wallace. Wallace himself also had to have been warned to admit to having been to visit Crewe's house for only the five violin lessons. Having been there on business on 'many occasions', how could he have possibly been so vague as to how he had got there? Might the fact of the matter be that, in travelling to Crewe's house on these occasions, Wallace had travelled the same route he had on the night of Julia's murder and used the tram stop at Menlove Gardens West as a prompt to remind him to alight at the next stop, Menlove Gardens North? Could this prove that, in having travelled to the Mossley Hill area so often, Wallace had no need whatsoever to pester the tram staff and this was, indeed, a ploy by which he could manufacture an alibi?

According to all of the information given by Wallace in his police statements, his statement to Hector Munro and his testimony at the Assize trial, after alighting from the 5A tram at 7.20 p.m. at the beginning of Menlove Gardens West, he had walked up Menlove Gardens West on the right-hand side of the road – next to a triangular garden area. Reaching the junction with Menlove Gardens North, he turned down the road and walked (still on the right-hand side next to the gardens) as far down as either No. 8 (home of John McSwigin, Margaret Jane McSwigin and Albert Edward Bloomfield) or No. 10 (home of Robert Monteith McKenzie and Christina Tivendale McKenzie). Seeing a woman leaving No. 8 or No. 10, Wallace crossed into the middle of the road and asked for directions to Menlove Gardens East. Having no idea where this was, the lady told him, 'It might be further up in continuation of Menlove Gardens West.' Retracing his steps to the junction of Menlove Gardens North and Menlove Gardens West, he turned to the right and continued on up Menlove Gardens West until he came to Dudlow Lane (ironically, the very road where the major partner in the legal firm he would employ for his defence lived – Herbert J. Davis lived at Sanford Lodge in Dudlow Lane). Crossing the road, he continued along the upper part of Menlove Gardens West until he reached a road to his right – Dudlow Gardens. Retracing his steps, he arrived back at the junction of Dudlow Lane and the top of the lower part of Menlove Gardens West. Here, Wallace approached a young man, Sidney Hubert Green. In a statement given to police on 22 January 1931, Green said of the incident:

> I am a Clerk and reside at 16 Towers Road, Woolton Road, Wavertree. About 7.15 p.m. on Tuesday 20th January 1931, I was walking down Menlove Gardens West, when a man about 50 to 60 years, thin build, 5 feet 10 inches, wearing a trilby and what appeared to be a dark overcoat, stopped me and said, 'Do you know where Menlove Gardens East is?' I told him there was no such place to the best of my knowledge and he replied, I have been told to call at, either 16 or 26 Menlove Gardens [sic], and can only find Menlove Gardens North and South. I told him that there was a Menlove Gardens West and he said 'I know'. He then said I will call at 16 or 26 Menlove Gardens West and see if that is the place and 'Goodnight' and left me. I noticed the collar he wore was a Gladstone collar shape.

At both the committal trail and the Assize trial, Green stated he had had an appointment to keep that night and had left his house at 7.10 p.m. in order to reach Penny Lane to catch a tram. In all of Green's testimonies he states that he had talked to Wallace at 7.15 p.m. This, however, is an impossibility: Wallace had only just left the Penny Lane junction on the No. 5A tram at 7.15 p.m. and he would not alight at the bottom of Menlove Gardens West until 7.20 p.m. From this point, to the point where he met Green, Wallace had walked approximately 680 yards. Walking at an average speed of 3 miles per hour, this would have taken him 10 minutes. Wallace could not have met Sidney Hubert Green until approximately 7.30 p.m.

Apparently concerned that either he or Beattie had made a mistake in taking down the address, Wallace decided to knock at 25 Menlove Gardens West – the home of Richard Mather, his wife Katie and their daughter Marjorie. However, this must have proved more of a task than Wallace had realised: 25 Menlove Gardens West had no number on the gate – it was simply named 'Brierley'. No. 19 was quite legible, though Nos 21 ('Barholme') and 23 ('Halliwell') also had no number. No. 27 ('Dalkieth') had its number in brass raised figures the same colour as the gate and was practically illegible.

Upon eventually arriving at 25 Menlove Gardens West, Wallace knocked and asked Mrs Mather if a Mr Qualtrough lived there. Mrs Mather explained there was no one of that name there. After Wallace had once again explained his dilemma over 25 Menlove Gardens East, Mrs Mather told him she didn't know the name. In attempting to extend these enquiries to Menlove Gardens South and North, Wallace found both roads contained only even numbers. He continued on down Menlove Gardens North, arriving at the junction with Menlove Avenue itself, where he saw another young man at a sheltered tram stop: he too was a stranger to the area and could not help Wallace.

Having now found himself at the top of Green Lane, it was, according to Wallace, at this point that he had recognised where he was and, knowing he was close to Joseph Crewe's house, had decided to call in on him and ask if he knew where his destination was to be found. Unfortunately, Mr Crewe had gone to the Plaza cinema that night with his wife and so Wallace got no answer. This was a few minutes before 7.45 p.m. What would have happened if Crewe had been at home? To begin with, Wallace would have been assured of two reliable witnesses to both the time and his presence in the Mossley Hill area. Most likely, he would have had a cup of tea and regaled Mr and Mrs Crewe with the whole Qualtrough saga. After voicing his concerns about not being able to locate either 25 Menlove Gardens East or Mr Qualtrough, he could have then left the house in time to catch the 8 p.m. tram back to Belmont Road. Instead, ambling down Green Lane, he saw a policeman crossing over the road from a police station at the junction with Allerton Road: PC 220F James Edward Serjeant. Upon stopping the constable, Wallace was once again told there was no Menlove Gardens East and that Serjeant had never heard of the name Qualtrough in the district. Then, for no apparent reason, other than 'The policeman was of a friendly type', Wallace regaled him with the story of Qualtrough's phone call and the appointment. Serjeant suggested he should try 25 Menlove Avenue. Wallace turned to walk away, then turned back and asked if Serjeant knew where he could see a street directory (the equivalent of a modern-day phone book). Serjeant advised him to try the post office in Allerton Road, or the police station. Wallace said, 'It is not eight o'clock yet' and pulled out his pocket watch. Serjeant reciprocated. 'It is just a quarter to,' Wallace observed. Serjeant agreed and, pointing him in the right direction, Wallace walked off toward a post office close to the Plaza Cinema. Had this confirmation of the time with PC Serjeant been to compensate for the fact that he could not gain entry to Joseph Crewe's house in order to confirm the time of his presence in the Mossley Hill area with him?

At the post office Wallace found there was no directory to be had and so asked the counter clerk if he knew either Qualtrough or 25 Menlove Gardens East. The clerk knew of neither, but suggested that Wallace might try a paper shop on the other side of the road. Glancing at the post office clock, Wallace noticed that 'it was now 6 or 7 minutes to 8'. When Wallace called in at the newsagent's shop, 130 Allerton Road, shop assistant Nancy Collins handed him a directory. Whilst he was browsing through it at the cigarette counter, manageress Lily

Pinches approached him to see if she could be of any assistance. Wallace asked if she knew what he was looking for and (once again) went on to explain the reasons behind his journey. Lily Pinches told him there was no Menlove Gardens East – only North, South and West – and even looked for the address in the shop's account book in case a Mr Qualtrough or the inhabitants of 25 Menlove Gardens East might have had an account: they did not. With that, Wallace left the shop and, at about 8 p.m., took a No. 8 tram, at the corner of Allerton Road and Queen's Drive (close to the Plaza Cinema), to the junction of Tunnel Road and Smithdown Lane; he then took a No. 27 tram back to Belmont Road. Alighting from the tram at St Margaret's church at approximately 8.30 p.m. (the very time that Parry would claim he had left Mrs Brine's house at 43 Knoclaid Road), Wallace stated that he took a direct route back to his front door at Wolverton Street via the same route he had taken on his outgoing journey and claimed he had not stopped to speak to anybody on the way.

There was, however, a witness who disputed this. Miss Lillian Hall, a 20-year-old typist for commission agents Littlewoods Ltd based in Whitechapel, Liverpool, lived at 9 Letchworth Street – three doors away from Wallace's friend, James Caird. She had known Wallace by sight for three or four years, though had only learned his name about a fortnight prior to this encounter. Lillian Hall was a friend of Wallace's next-door neighbours' son, Robert Leslie Russell Johnston. His wife, Amy Beatrice Towers, had lived across the road from the Halls' house at 8 Letchworth Street before their marriage on 30 August 1930. Whilst visiting the Johnstons at 31 Wolverton Street (where the couple were living), Lily Hall had asked about Wallace. At around 8.35 p.m. on the night of the murder, Miss Hall was making her way home from work. As she was en route, walking down Richmond Park, she claimed to have seen Wallace's unmistakable frame on the opposite side of the road, facing her, wearing 'a trilby hat and a darkish overcoat'. He was standing 'at the bottom of the entry by the Parish Hall … running at right angles to Richmond Park, and parallel with Letchworth Street'. She witnessed Wallace talking to a stocky man wearing an overcoat and cap, who was around 5 feet 7 or 8 inches in height. She went on to say of the encounter:

> I was on the pavement on the opposite side. I passed him before I crossed over to the side on which he was … He and the other man parted as I crossed Richmond Park. One went down the entry and the other down Richmond Park but I do not know whom … The man went down the entry opposite the institute.

This would be the entry between 79 and 81 Richmond Park – the same entry leading from Wallace's back door that he had used on his outgoing journey to Mossley Hill and the same entry he had identified to police in his statement as the entry which he had used upon his return. When tackled by Inspector Gold at the Detective Office about Lily Hall's statement, Wallace denied that he had spoken to anyone: 'I was not so alarmed that I would not raise my hat or speak to anybody, but I did not.' He thought for moment, and then added, 'I am positively certain.'

Wallace's Return

Upon reaching the front door, Wallace tried his key in the lock and found the latch would not turn. He knocked gently and waited. Having had no response, he went around to the back entry and found the back entry door closed, but not locked. Entering the yard, he could see that there was a light in the back kitchen, but none in the kitchen. Trying the handle on the back kitchen door and finding this also locked, he knocked – once again, no response. Next-door neighbour Mrs Johnston at No. 31 stated:

> On the evening of the 20th January 1931, I and my husband were getting ready to go out at about twenty minutes to nine. We were in our living room at the back of our house, and I heard Mr Wallace's usual knock on the back door leading into his house. I think he knocked about three times.

Returning to the front door, Wallace tried his key once again. As before, whilst the key turned, the door would not budge and, after pushing on it, he decided that the door had to be bolted. Alarmed, he rushed back through the entry, where he happened upon next-door neighbours John Sharp Johnston and his wife Florence Sarah Johnston[4] coming out of their back door on their way to visit their daughter Phyllis in Townsend Avenue. The Johnstons had known the Wallaces since they had moved into 31 Wolverton Street with Mrs Johnston's father, Arthur Mills, in 1921.

After spending many years working as an engineering superintendent for the Blue Funnel Line in Hong Kong (being able to return only every couple of years to see his family), John Sharp Johnston returned to his much-missed family in England after the end of the First World War and became an engineer at Cammell Laird shipbuilders in Birkenhead. Arthur Mills had been living at 31 Wolverton Street with this wife, Agnes Lucy Kermode, since their marriage (Arthur's second) in 1902 when, on 5 April 1920, his wife died. Arthur being a ship's steward, the house would have been left empty for much of the time whilst he was working. It would appear from the records that Arthur Mills did not retire from service until after September 1927, when he was a night watchman on the RMS *Baltic*.

It was during 1921 that the Johnstons, along with their four children, Norman Russell, Phyllis Mary Russell, Robert Leslie Russell and Norah Russell, moved into 31 Wolverton Street. Effectively, until Arthur Mills' retirement (before his death in March 1932, aged 74), 31 Wolverton Street had become the Johnstons' home, with Arthur Mills staying only upon his returns to Liverpool. At the time of the murder, the Johnstons were waiting to move in with their eldest daughter Phyllis and her husband Edgar Mann at 358 Townsend Avenue. With their recently married son Robert, his wife Amy, their youngest child (18-year-old Norah) and Mrs Johnston's father all living at the house, things were becoming very cramped. In order to accommodate such a large family in a small, three-bedroom terrace house, the sleeping arrangements may have been such that Mr and Mrs Johnston and their son Robert and his wife Amy would have had the larger front and middle bedrooms, whilst their youngest daughter, Norah, had the smaller back bedroom (at No. 29, Wallace had converted this into a workroom and laboratory). Mrs Johnston's father, Arthur Mills, after a lifetime at sea, may have been infirm or debilitated in some way and, besides living in the parlour, also slept there. Despite having been neighbours for ten years, the Johnstons and the Wallaces were never close enough to be on calling terms; in all this time, Mrs Johnston had been shown into the Wallaces' parlour only on three occasions and Mr Johnston stated that he did not know Mrs Wallace's first name was Julia until the night of the murder. The couple had not seen Mrs Wallace for over three weeks, though both described their neighbours as 'devoted'. Mrs Johnston said, 'I never saw any arguments between them and do not believe that Mr Wallace would have ever thought of doing any harm to his wife.'

Mr Johnston recalled, 'At 8.45 … I and my wife were just stepping out of our back door to go out. As I opened the door, my wife stepped out and at the same time, Mr Wallace passed our door. My wife said "Good Evening, Mr Wallace".' Looking quite anxious, Wallace asked if they 'had heard any unusual noise in my house during the last hour or so'. 'Why, what's happened?' Mrs Johnston asked. Wallace explained that he had been out that night and upon his return had found he was locked out of his house. Having moved to the doorway of Wallace's yard by this time, Mr Johnston asked if he had tried the back kitchen door. Wallace told him he had, but could not open it. 'Try again; if you can't manage it, I'll get my key,' Mr Johnston offered. Walking toward the back kitchen door, Wallace looked back toward the concerned couple standing in the backyard doorway: 'She will not be out; she has such a bad cold,' he uttered. Arriving at the door, Wallace turned the handle; this time the door opened quite easily. 'It opens now,' he exclaimed. 'I'll see if everything is all right.' Mr Johnston reassured him, 'I'll wait a minute.'

In a report written by Inspector Gold on 6 March, two days after the end of the committal trial, he disputes that this is what Mr Johnston had actually said in his initial police statement, stating that at the committal trial all witnesses adhered to their first statements except for Mr and Mrs Johnston:

> The Johnstons in their first statements, which were taken on the night of the murder, say that when they saw Wallace in the entry, he asked them to wait while he went into the house to see if everything was alright. In the witness box they stated that it was Mr Johnston who said he would wait and that Wallace did not ask them to … It is significant that these … witnesses were interviewed by the Defending solicitors, Messrs H. J. Davis, Berthen & Munro, before the committal proceedings commenced.

Inspector Gold, however, is incorrect; in his original police statement John Sharp Johnston claimed he had said, 'I'll stop here while you have a look round.' Florence Sarah Johnston had claimed her husband had said, 'We will wait a minute. See if everything is all right.' Here, police investigating the case give a prime example of the extreme bias they had toward Wallace – a man yet to be tried. This is even more blatantly underlined by the fact that both Mr and Mrs Johnston had *not* changed their statements and Gold as good as accuses Hector Munro of coercing witnesses into giving false evidence. The evidence against Wallace at this juncture in the proceedings was extremely thin. In light of his alibi, there had to have been a stronger case for Wallace's innocence than any circumstantial evidence the police had so far gathered that pointed the finger of blame towards him. Could the police have had information from other, undisclosed sources that had left them in no doubt as to Wallace's guilt, and were they determined to have their man receive the justice he deserved?

Inside the house, the kitchen was in darkness. Upon lighting the gaslight, Wallace claimed to have noticed that a small, home-made cabinet in which he kept his photographic equipment had been broken into and a piece of the door was lying on the floor (the door of this cabinet had been broken in half before the murder and had been temporarily repaired). Thinking Julia may have gone for a lie down, Wallace proceeded upstairs calling her name. In the middle bedroom, the light was still burning, just as he had left it earlier when he had prepared for his appointment with Mr Qualtrough. He turned the gas up, but there was no sign of Julia. Quickly checking the bathroom (where, once again, the light was still burning as he had left it), he struck a match, then, nosing into the back bedroom (his laboratory and workroom), he went to the front bedroom and struck another match. This room was essentially Julia's room, where she kept her coats, handbags and hats. He noticed that the bedclothes at the corner of the bed nearest to the door had been pulled back, exposing the mattress.

After a later police inspection, Constable Fred Williams described the front bedroom as he had found it:

> The front bedroom which was in darkness was in a state of disorder, as follows: the bedclothes were half on the floor and half on the bed, two of the pillows being near the fireplace; the door of the wardrobe and the drawers in the dressing table were shut and apparently in order.

Superintendent Hubert Moore noted that 'two lady's handbags, together with three lady's hats were on the mattress, the bedding being pushed from the side next to the door towards the fireplace'. In a statement given by the Wallaces' cleaning lady, Mrs Sarah Jane Draper, she says, 'I used to clean the front bedroom and the bed was always kept made with blankets, sheets and pillows. Mrs Wallace used to have her hats spread out on it. I have never seen the bed in the state it is now.'

It has long been debated why this room was in such a condition. If it was the result of the killer rummaging through the room, what was he looking for? Could the motive for Julia's murder have lain hidden in that room? Was Julia Wallace murdered in order to enable the killer to gain access to the front bedroom and retrieve something vitally important to him? I feel the answer is far more simple and mundane. The most likely reason the bed was in this state would seem to be that Mrs Wallace had simply pulled the bottom sheet from the bed in order to mend it or utilise it for some other purpose. On 20 January 1981, after Radio City aired the second part of Roger Wilkes's *Who Killed Julia?* programme, there was a phone-in whereby callers could speak to a panel of experts (including Jonathan Goodman). One of the callers turned out to be the Johnstons' grandson, Russell Johnston. He related the fact that, on the morning of the murder (he does not say how late into the morning), his mother (the Johnstons' daughter-in-law, Amy Beatrice Towers) was cleaning the upper bay windows in the front bedroom at No. 31 and could remember waving to Julia, whom she could see through the bay windows of the front bedroom next door – thus proving that on the day of her murder, Julia had spent some time in the front bedroom.

PC Williams statement about 'two of the pillows being near the fireplace' showed that the bed contained more pillows than just those found on the floor: there were most likely another two pillows laid out beneath the blankets, in the sleeping position, near the headboard, the two pillows on the floor being placed on top of the blankets when making up the bed. In having to pull back the blankets far enough to extract the bottom blanket, the two top pillows would have to be removed. Hubert Moore stated that, placed on the exposed mattress, there were two lady's handbags and three lady's hats. If an intruder had been in the room searching the bed, surely the whole contents of the bed would have been thrown to the floor thoughtlessly? The most logical scenario is that Julia, for some reason, had decided to utilise the under-blanket and chose that day to do so. As Mrs Draper stated, Julia would lay out her hats on top of the bed. Therefore, in order to strip out the blanket, Julia would have put the top pillows, the hats and the bags onto the floor, pulled back the top blankets, stripped out the bottom blanket then replaced her hats and bags on the bare mattress. I will show further proof of this later: proof that was in plain view for all to see – and no one to recognise.

Upon leaving the front bedroom, Wallace quickly made his way back downstairs to the parlour. He noticed that the door was ajar so, striking a match and holding it up, he entered:

> I was horrified to see my wife lying across the rug in front of the fireplace. Her head was towards the door, and by the light of the match I could see it was horribly battered. There were big bloodstains on the floor. As far as I can remember I struck a match, stepped round her body and lit the right-hand gas.

Besides the bloodstains on the floor, the walls were spattered with blood, largely to a height of about 4 feet, though the odd spatter or two reached a height of around 7 feet; the majority of the blood was concentrated around a two-seater couch in a corner opposite the doorway. Much has been made of the fact that Wallace, in entering the darkened parlour and stepping around Julia's body, had managed to avoid any contact at all with the pools of congealing blood surrounding the fireside rug. This, in fact, has been used by many as proof that Wallace had to have struck the blows that killed Julia – thus, knowing where the blood was, he avoided it. The fact of the matter is, besides the pool of blood surrounding Julia's head, the rest was to be found behind her body – on the left-hand side of the room. Wallace took a path to the right to light the right-hand gas mantle. There has never been any reporting of blood in front of Julia's body. Besides which, if this was such a difficult task to accomplish, how (as will be shown later) did Mrs Johnston avoid the pools of blood? Upon entering the parlour, not once, but twice, she took up a crouching position behind Julia – where the blood was located – and yet there are no reports of her having stepped in, or been contaminated by, any blood at all.

In the Wallace household, the parlour was reserved for guests (as it was in many households of the time) and for the Wallaces' musical evenings, when Julia would play the piano and Wallace would accompany her on the violin. As the room was kept especially clean and tidy, any guests who were invited into the house were immediately made comfortable in the parlour. The room, however, was cramped to say the least. Approximately 13 feet by 10½ feet (including the recesses and the bay of the window), it contained several articles of large furniture. Moving in a clockwise direction as you enter through the door, in the centre of the left-hand wall was a large sideboard holding photographs, vases, chinaware and a large potted plant; in front of this, at the end nearest to the door, was a wooden straight-backed chair standing close to the left corner of a hearth rug. Next to the sideboard, at an angle, crossing the left-hand corner from the left wall into the left recess of the chimney breast wall, was a two-seater couch that had Wallace's violin case resting across the arms and a large cushion lying flat on the seat. In the centre of the chimney breast was a Sunbeam gas fire, the mantelpiece of which was adorned with photographs and a large vase in the centre. In the right-hand recess of the chimney breast wall, a chaise longue extended outward, parallel to the window. A square table stood at the back of it in the window recess and a small round table in front, near to its end, edging the right-hand corner of the hearthrug: both held large potted plants. Along the wall to the right of the doorway was a piano, in front of which was a music stand and, between the piano and the door, were two more wooden straight-backed chairs, one in front of the other. Each chair held a stack of sheet music upon it, a leg of the front chair standing about 6 inches away from Julia's head. The hearthrug Julia was lying across was 5 feet long by 3 feet wide, bordered by the furniture. Julia Wallace's murderer would only have had a space approximately 6 feet by 4 feet in which to manoeuvre, and yet he managed to viciously bludgeon her to death without upsetting a single piece of furniture, ornament or picture in the room. There was obviously no struggle – her murder had to have been premeditated, precise and extremely fast.

The positioning of Julia's body, as found by Wallace, has consistently been given as lying on her stomach, stretched out, almost diagonally, across the fireside rug – her feet together (her toes almost touching the right-hand side of the fender surrounding the fire), heels uppermost. The trunk of her body, slightly bent at the hips, brought her shoulders in line with the long edge of the rug close to the door, her right arm lying on the rug by her side, her left arm extending across the floor toward the window. This description has almost exclusively been taken from two photographs produced by the official police photographer, Harry Hewitt Cooke, taken one after the other at approximately 1 a.m. on the night of the murder. The first of these photographs was taken from the doorway of the parlour (the door actually having to be lifted from its hinges in order to accomplish this); the other from behind the chaise longue in front of the window. If one looks carefully at each image, it can be plainly seen that, even in the time taken to move the camera from the door to the window, Julia's body has been repositioned. By the time these photographs were taken, the police had been allowed to blunder their way around the crime scene without restraint or accountability; the room, at times, had been as busy as Lime Street railway station on a bank holiday. Between Wallace, Mrs Johnston, the police and two medical examiners, the room had been entered and exited innumerable times and Julia's body had been prodded and probed for over four hours. Luckily, in examining Hector Munro's vast archive of files concerning the case, I was more than excited to happen upon two statements given by Mr and Mrs Johnston at the committal trial in February 1931; these, in combination with other evidence, give quite a complete picture of the original positioning of Julia's body when Wallace first entered the parlour and, presumably, when the killer left the house. Julia was lying on her right-hand side, almost diagonally across the rug, her legs slightly parted, her feet lying flat on their sides close to the right-hand end of the fender, toes pointing toward the window. Her right arm was hidden beneath her body; her left arm lying against her body, was bent at the elbow, the forearm resting over her chest, the fingers almost touching the floor. Approximately 18 inches from the open door, Julia's head lay on its right side, her eyes staring out toward the window. Surrounding her head was a 9-inch border of congealing blood, brain tissue and bone. Just above, and in front of her left ear was a huge, cruel opening in her skull, 2 inches wide by 3 inches long, through which what remained of her brain could be seen.

As well as the repositioning of Julia's body, there were other things noticeably different about the positions of other items in the room in comparison to the photographs. In describing the room when she first entered it, Mrs Johnston stated, 'I noticed that the violin stand was immediately behind the deceased's head. It was standing up in position but had no music on it. I did not see anyone move it.' Upon being questioned at Wallace's trial, it was pointed out to Cooke that the two crime scene photographs themselves had discrepancies: in the photograph taken from the doorway, the chair by the sideboard on the left of the room was in front of the sideboard, whereas the same chair in the photograph taken from behind the settee had moved to the side of the sideboard, in front of the door, a position it could never realistically occupy. As the door (when on its hinges) opened inward towards the sideboard, the chair would jam the door and one would never be able to enter the room. As well as the repositioning of Julia's body, another most important and serious difference highlighted by the photographs was the repositioning of a mackintosh, originally found folded and tucked (almost invisibly) next to Julia's neck and right shoulder. As can be plainly seen in the photograph taken from the window, the mackintosh had been unfolded and laid out, almost corpse-like, next to Julia's body. Questioned about this at the Assize trial, Hubert Moore had said by way of explanation, 'The photographer must have caught his foot in it as he went out of the door.'

At the trial, Roland Oliver questioned Cooke about the repositioning of the chair in his photographs:

> *Do you suggest you could not have got out of the room past the chair?* When the photograph no. 7 [the photograph taken from near to the window] was taken it was taken in the dark by flashlight and I had to get over the couch round past the table, over the body and through the small space which was left had the chair been there, but the chair was put by the door so that I could get past in the dark.

If the photographs had to have been taken in the dark, this would mean that, in taking the first photograph from the doorway, after having taken the door off its hinges and positioning the camera, somebody had to have turned off the gaslights. After the gaslights had been turned back on, Cooke then states that, after positioning his camera behind the settee for the second photograph, the lights were again turned off. If it had been done with a bare hand, this would have eliminated a vital piece of evidence – the fingerprint of the last person to have touched the right-hand gas mantle: Julia Wallace's if the gas light was lit when Wallace first entered the room (thus proving he was lying about it having been off when he entered the room), or Wallace's if he had turned it on when he first entered the room. If the tap had been turned off using a handkerchief, this would have eliminated the fingerprint altogether.

Cooke also suggests that, after having taken the photograph from behind the settee, he was left to traverse the crime scene in total darkness carrying his cumbersome camera, tripod and powder flash – yet he seems, from later evidence, to have had no problem at all avoiding Julia's body or the pools of blood, although, as previously stated, Wallace is often condemned for having had the ability to do the same thing, unencumbered, with a lit match and total familiarity with the room. In the few minutes it took to reposition his camera by the window, Cooke claimed that, because the pictures were taken in total darkness, he had no idea who moved the chair or repositioned the mackintosh. Above all else, the police scene-of-crime photographs show the undeniable, utter incompetence of the police, even at that early, most crucial stage of the murder investigation.

Having lit the gaslight, Wallace noticed his mackintosh lying on the floor behind Julia. In his first police statement, he admitted:

> When I discovered my wife lying on the floor I noticed my mackintosh lying on the floor at the back of her. I wore the mackintosh up to noon today but left it off owing to the fine weather. My wife has never worn a mackintosh to my knowledge.

Crouching, he took hold of Julia's left hand, but could find no pulse. Rushing back out of the house, he called to the Johnstons, exclaiming, 'Come and look; she has been killed!' As the Johnstons hurried through the kitchen and into the parlour, Mrs Johnston noticed a spent match by the kitchen doorway. Once in the parlour, Wallace stood in front of Julia, next to the chaise longue by the window. Mr Johnston remained close to the door. As Mrs Johnston moved further into the room, close to the sideboard she noticed two more spent matches near to the doorway, close to Julia's right shoulder, and a box of matches on the table in the window recess. In a statement given to Hector Munro, she claimed that she had asked Wallace if the box of matches was his and he had said they were. On being asked about the matches at the Assize trial, however, she stated, 'I said to Mr Wallace "Are those Mrs Wallace's matches?" and he said "Yes".' Stooping down, all three were silently observing Julia's devastated body when Wallace exclaimed, 'They've finished her! They've finished her!' Reaching down, he took hold of her left hand, murmuring something unintelligible about her rings being missing, and then uttered that 'perhaps she hadn't had them on'. Mrs Johnston reached over and felt Julia's left hand, bemoaning, 'Oh, the poor darling.' Mr Johnston asked his wife if Julia was cold, to which she replied, 'No.' In a report ordered by Hector Munro from the Bidston Observatory, Cheshire, regarding the temperatures for Liverpool on the day of the murder, taken at two-hourly intervals, Mr Bigleston, the Principal Assistant, stated that between the hours of 8 p.m. and 10 p.m. the temperature ranged between 5.4 °C and 6.0 °C. If Julia had been murdered at around 6.45 p.m., she would have been left lying on a draughty floor with the door to the room slightly open, in plunging temperatures for two hours; after this length of time, the body should have cooled dramatically. The body being warm to the touch must surely be a strong indicator that Julia was murdered not very long before Wallace's return. With everyone standing now, Mr Johnston offered to go for the police. Wallace said, 'Yes, and for a doctor, but I don't think it's much use; they've finished her.' Leaving the parlour, all three removed themselves to the kitchen.

Like the parlour, the kitchen was cramped and small, approximately 12 feet by 10 feet, but it was where the Wallaces actually *lived*. When the room was entered from the hallway, it was obvious that the huge, black, iron kitchen range on the opposite wall was the heart of the room – the heart of the house. On the left-hand side of the wall to the hall doorway was the doorway to the smaller back kitchen. In front of this, between the back kitchen doorway and the window looking out onto the backyard was a small cabinet, its top strewn with papers, books and a wooden 12-inch ruler. Slightly above this, on the cabinet's single shelf, was a line of books. On either side of the kitchen range was a recess of about 3 feet in width; the left-hand recess contained a low cupboard, about 2½ feet high with five shelves above it, four of which were filled with books. The top shelf, just over 7 feet from the floor, contained various items of bric-a-brac, a couple of books and, almost at its centre, the small cash box Wallace used to store his Prudential collection money. Between the top of the cupboard and the first shelf was a gap of about 1½ feet containing a microscope Wallace had bought for £70 or £80 (after trying, unsuccessfully, to build his own), a box of chessmen, books and the home-made cabinet containing his photographic equipment – a piece of the door now lying on the floor in front of the cupboard.

The recess to the right of the kitchen range was covered by two glass-panelled doors, under which was another cupboard, its surface, once again, littered with boxes, papers, bric-a-brac and what appear to have been Wallace's radio, accumulator battery and headphones. In front of this, extending along the right-hand wall toward the hall doorway, was a chaise longue similar to the one in front of the window in the parlour.

In the centre of the room, below a low-slung gas mantle, was the kitchen table, covered with a dark, heavy, tasselled tablecloth, surrounded by three mismatched chairs. Tucked under its right-hand corner, near the hallway door, was a wooden straight-backed chair, with Julia's handbag on its seat, slightly hidden by the folds of the tablecloth (when eventually examined by the police, the handbag was found to contain a few letters, a King George half-crown and £1 5s 10½d). Next to this was Julia's chair – a wooden-framed armchair, positioned at the right-hand corner near to the kitchen range. Wallace's chair – a leather-covered wicker armchair – sat opposite Julia's. The surface of the table was strewn with domestic clutter that gave its own testimony of the day's activities. A large white sheet was draped diagonally from the left corner nearest the back kitchen doorway, across the table, around a teapot, cups and a plant pot toward Julia's chair; the contents of Julia's sewing basket were spread out in front of it, a linen swatch roll resting on top of a neatly folded newspaper. Sitting on top of the white cloth was a sugar bowl, two plates stacked one on top the other (the top plate containing crumbs) and a newspaper, placed at the corner nearest the back kitchen door, its edge resting on top of the plates. At the corner nearest to Wallace's chair, the cloth had been pushed back and either a clothes brush or a shoe brush lay in the space.

From the location and arrangement of these objects, a sequence of events might be deduced. At the lowest stratum lay the teapot and cups, the plant pot, the folded newspaper, the white cloth and the sewing basket. The *Financial Times* having been delivered that morning at around 7.45 a.m., as the Wallaces were coming down to breakfast, the newspaper was probably brought in from behind the front door and placed, unread, on the table, where it appears to have remained for the rest of the day. Sometime during that morning, Julia must have decided to fetch the bottom sheet from the front bedroom. In extracting the bottom sheet from the bed, she had to have thrown the pillows in front of the fireplace, moved her handbags and hats, pulled the top blankets over, and then pulled the sheet from the mattress. Once extracted, she must have haphazardly pulled the top blankets over the bed and replaced her hats and handbags. The presence of that sheet lying across the kitchen table must prove that it was Julia herself who caused the mysterious disturbance in the front bedroom. After laying it across the kitchen table, she sat in her chair and spread out the contents of her sewing box (placing the linen swatch roll on top of the *Financial Times*), and began working on the sheet. With all of the comings and goings throughout that day – window cleaners, Wallace returning for lunch, Amy Wallace and the bread boy (she might have even gone out shopping to purchase the scones for Wallace's dinner) – she did not get a chance to finish off whatever she had planned to do with it before Wallace arrived home after finishing his collections.

The middle stratum consists of the sugar bowl and the dirty plates. After Wallace finished his rounds and returned home for a dinner of tea and scones, the sugar bowl was placed on top of the bed sheet (presumably, one or both of the Wallaces took sugar in their tea). Wallace pushed back the sheet in order to place his plate there. Once the meal was over, the plates were moved on top of the sheet out of the way.

The top stratum comprises the clothes brush and the newspaper: when Wallace went upstairs to prepare himself for his meeting with Qualtrough, the *Liverpool Echo* was delivered sometime between 6.30 and 6.45 p.m. Wallace had said that he was unsure if the paperboy had been when he left; therefore, he had not picked up the *Echo* himself or read it. Julia had to have picked it up and placed it at the end of the table, resting on top of the dinner plates – thus indicating that they had finished their meal before the arrival of the *Echo*. Returning to the kitchen after his ablutions, Wallace gave himself, or his shoes, a quick brush down with the brush and went on his way to Menlove Gardens East.

Upon entering the kitchen with the Johnstons, Wallace directed their attention towards the floor near to the cupboard in the left recess of the kitchen range: 'See; they've wrenched that off,' he sighed. Following the direction of his finger, the Johnstons' gaze fell upon the broken door from the photographic equipment box, a piece lying on the floor. Close by were three coins: a half-crown and two separate shillings. 'Is there anything missing?' Mr Johnston asked. Reaching up to the top shelf of the bookshelves above the cupboard, Wallace brought down the small, black cash box he used to store the money he collected for the Prudential. Not being locked, he lifted the lid and peered inside. Turning to Mr Johnston, Wallace said, 'About £4 – but I can't say for certain until I've checked my books.' In later evidence, according to Wallace, there should have been a £1 note; three 10s notes; thirty or forty shillings in silver; a postal order for 4s 6d from a W. P. Stringer of New Road, Tuebrook; a cheque for £5 17s, made payable to Wallace by the Prudential, drawn on the Midland Bank, Castle Street; and four 1d stamps. All that remained were the stamps and an American dollar bill of Wallace's that he had owned for some time. As Wallace replaced the cash box, Mr Johnston asked, 'Is everything all right up stairs, before I go for the police?' Taking himself back up the stairs, Wallace mooched back around the rooms, especially the middle bedroom, where he knew Julia kept their savings. On the mantelpiece in the room, he spotted a jar of banknotes he estimated to contain about £5. Returning to the Johnstons, he told them, 'Everything's all right up there, there's five pounds in a dish they haven't taken.' Whereupon, Mr Johnston left through the back door to fetch a doctor and the police.

Rushing down to Lower Breck Road, Mr Johnston bumped into his youngest daughter's boyfriend (and future husband), Francis George McElroy, on his way to see Norah. Quickly telling him the tale of the night's awful events, Mr Johnston exasperatedly told him, 'Frank, I have to get Florence out of there as quickly as possible!' Rushing on, Mr Johnston called on the nearest doctor he could find, Dr John Dunlop (whose surgery was next door but one to the Cabbage Hall Cinema), only to be advised that this was a job for the police surgeon. Dashing on to Anfield police station, he arrived there at about 9.05 p.m. and informed Constable 99G Saunders that Mrs Wallace of 29 Wolverton Street had been found murdered a short time before. After alerting Constable 191G Frederick Robert Williams, who was on duty in Anfield Road, Saunders telephoned for an ambulance, then immediately tried to contact the Divisional CID.

In the meantime, Wallace and Mrs Johnston had returned to the parlour. Wallace knelt in front of Julia and took her left hand once again. Mrs Johnston, remaining close to the sideboard, did likewise and, in what could have only been minutes, noticed that her hand had cooled. 'They've finished her; look at the brains!' Wallace exclaimed. Bewildered by the utter devastation before her, Mrs Johnston asked, 'I wonder what they've used?' Inexplicably, Wallace began examining the rug, running his fingers just under the edge and patting the top, as if hoping to find something that might have been capable of causing the terrible damage inflicted upon Julia's head. The pair stood and were about to leave the room when Wallace glanced down at the material pushed close to the back of Julia's body: 'Why, what was she doing with her mackintosh; and my mackintosh?' 'Why, is it your mackintosh?' Mrs Johnston asked. Wallace stooped and probed the cloth. 'Yes, it's mine.'

The pair returned, once again, to the kitchen. The gravity and horror of the situation was unbearable, inaction augmenting the already mounting pressure. Mrs Johnston noticed that the fire in the kitchen range was almost out, barring a couple of embers that were still glowing. 'Well, we'll have a fire,' she decided. As Wallace slumped into Julia's chair, Mrs Johnston took some wood chips from out of a side oven in the kitchen range and threw them into the grate. 'See, she hasn't had time to wash up the tea things,' Wallace said glumly as he eyed the dinner plates among the clutter on the kitchen table. Noticing that Mrs Johnston was having difficulty getting the fire going, he joined her. Stirring the few remaining ashes together and throwing on a handful of coal, the flames eventually began to catch. Slumping back into the chair, Wallace covered his face with his hands; Mrs Johnston sat quietly opposite him, not sure what to do next. She asked if he would like a cup of tea. Wallace declined.

During the trial, whilst being cross-examined by Crown Prosecutor Edward Hemmerde, Wallace was asked when he first noticed the mackintosh. He said he was unsure whether it was upon his second or third visit (both in the company of Mrs Johnston), but thought it was the second. He then went on to qualify why he could not have seen it on his first visit to the Parlour: 'I think that was with Mrs Johnston [when he remembered seeing the mackintosh]. The first visit I had not time to see anything at all; I simply saw that she was lying there and I lit the gas and rushed out.' Hemmerde asked if he was sure that he had not noticed it on his first visit to the parlour when he first discovered Julia; Wallace was satisfied that he did not see it then. Hemmerde then played his trump card and read back to him part of his first statement, given to police on the night of the murder: 'On the evening of the 20th when I discovered my wife lying on the floor, I noticed my mackintosh lying on the floor at the back of her.' Confronted with this, Wallace appears not to have missed a beat, and simply replied, 'I cannot remember whether it was my first or second visit.' He eventually had to agree with Hemmerde, that he did, in fact, see and recognise the mackintosh on his first visit to the parlour, after he had lit the gaslight. Hemmerde then put it to Wallace that, when in the parlour with Mrs Johnston during his third visit, in saying, 'Why, whatever was she doing with her mackintosh; and my mackintosh', he was attempting to give the impression that he had only just then discovered it. Wallace did not deny this; he simply said, 'I do not know what impression I made upon her.' However, the impression Wallace was undoubtedly trying to give to the court was that when he first discovered the mackintosh, Mrs Johnston was present and it therefore had to be either his second or third visit; most definitely *not* on his first visit. Therefore, upon saying to Mrs Johnston, 'Why, whatever was she doing with her mackintosh; and my mackintosh', it would appear he *was* attempting to give the impression that he had just discovered it. In a statement given to Hector Munro, Wallace had also lied to him in implying that he first saw the mackintosh upon his third visit to the room, after Mr Johnston had left for the police:

> When we got in [he and Mrs Johnston], I looked more carefully, and saw *something* under her shoulder that *looked like* a piece of mackintosh. *Looking closely*, I thought there were two mackintoshes there, and said to Mrs Johnston 'Why, what was she doing with her mackintosh; and my mackintosh'. We both looked and I touched it, and then saw that there was only one mackintosh, and that it looked like mine. Mrs Johnston said 'why; is it your mackintosh?' I said 'yes'.

In analysing this statement, we find that Wallace was implying that, during this encounter, he noticed something he did not quite recognise tucked under Julia's shoulder. Looking at it more carefully, he thought it could be a piece of mackintosh. From the look of the material, he thought there might be two mackintoshes: his and Julia's. Examining the material, he realised it was only one mackintosh, and it was his – not Julia's.

Unfortunately, there are no definitive pictures, diagrams, photographs (Hubert Moore had the garment lifted from beside the body before the official police photograph could be taken) or statements of the mackintosh in situ to give any clear idea of its actual placement or orientation (collar near the head of the body or near the legs), save a single, naive sketch contained in the archives of Hector Munro. All witnesses who saw it (except Wallace) agree that it was unrecognisable as a mackintosh, and that it was pushed in close to the back of Julia's body, bunched up around her right shoulder and her neck. Wallace considered it was two mackintoshes. Could this mean that it was folded in half, giving the impression of one mackintosh on top of the other? Mrs Johnston said she had simply thought, until Wallace pointed it out, that it was something 'roughed up'. Constable Williams said he had noticed it, but had no idea what it was until his third visit to the room, after Wallace had lit the left-hand gaslight. At the committal trial, Inspector Gold voiced his astonishment when he learnt that Wallace had previously identified the mackintosh as being his – whilst still in position at the back of Julia's body:

> I was very much surprised when I did learn that it had previously been identified by him, because in the position it was when I first saw it by the body it seemed to me that it would be almost an impossibility for anyone to have identified it as a particular mackintosh, or as a mackintosh at all. It was in such a crumpled condition that it might have been a cycling cape or an old army ground sheet.

Superintendent Moore could not identify it as a mackintosh until he had closely scrutinised it: 'I made an examination and I found the collar, and from that, I gathered that it was a mackintosh.'

During the trial, Roland Oliver, Wallace's defence counsel, disputed that Wallace ever uttered the phrase 'her mackintosh; and my mackintosh' (though he undoubtedly knew of Wallace's statement to Hector Munro). Oliver insisted that what Wallace more likely said was '*a* mackintosh; and my mackintosh'. Oliver became most insistent that Mrs Johnston change her opinion of what she heard – to the point where, when the judge, Mr Justice Wright, would interject and ask Mrs Johnston to clarify her answers, Oliver would reiterate his previous points, as if he were worried she would forgot where they were up to in the lesson:

> MR ROLAND OLIVER: I ought to put something to you about what you said he said. The words you say he used were 'Why, whatever was she doing with her mackintosh and my mackintosh?'
>
> MRS JOHNSTON: Yes, that is exactly what he said.
>
> MR ROLAND OLIVER: There was only one [mackintosh] across there?
>
> MRS JOHNSTON: Yes, but I take it he possibly thought she had her mackintosh and then he realised it was his – still, I do not know really what he thought.
>
> MR ROLAND OLIVER: It is almost the same thing and it might be you are mistaken – 'Whatever was she doing with *a* mackintosh and my mackintosh?'
>
> MRS JOHNSTON: Yes, it might be a mistake on my part; he might have said 'a mackintosh' but I am almost positive he said 'her mackintosh'.
>
> MR JUSTICE WRIGHT: You think he said 'her mackintosh and my mackintosh?'
>
> MRS JOHNSTON: Yes, because he hesitated after 'her mackintosh', and then said 'and my mackintosh', as though there were two mackintoshes there.
>
> MR ROLAND OLIVER: Yes – 'Whatever was she doing with *a* mackintosh and my mackintosh?'
>
> MR JUSTICE WRIGHT: 'Whatever was she doing with her mackintosh and my mackintosh?'
>
> MRS JOHNSTON: Yes.
>
> MR JUSTICE WRIGHT: He might have been correcting himself and saying 'a mackintosh' – 'and my mackintosh?'
>
> MRS JOHNSTON: Yes.

Why was Oliver so adamant to have this 'confusion' cleared up? Could it be that he feared it would lead Hemmerde to think that Wallace had *expected* it to have been Julia's mackintosh, and question him about it? After all, Mrs Johnston had said that Wallace had hesitated after he said 'her mackintosh'. Had he then realised, to his surprise, that it was not Julia's mackintosh then quickly amended the sentence to include his own mackintosh for fear that it would incriminate him? If that was the case it would suggest that Wallace must have known she would be wearing her mackintosh that night and, therefore, knew she would be leaving the house at some point – in complete contradiction to earlier evidence revealing that, upon entering the house through the back kitchen door, he had said to Mr and Mrs Johnston, 'I know she won't be out, she has had a bad cold.' The fact of the matter is that Wallace himself admitted in his statement to Hector Munro that he had, indeed, said 'her mackintosh; and my mackintosh': 'Looking closely, I thought there were two mackintoshes there, and said to Mrs Johnston "Why, what was she doing with her mackintosh, and my mackintosh?"' Roland Oliver had to have read this statement and known this, and yet he attempted, in open court, to divert the course of justice by misleading a witness into changing her statement.

Wallace was 6 feet 2 inches tall. Mrs Johnston said he had walked from the window side of the body and was leaving the room when he noticed the mackintosh. To avoid Julia's head and the pools of blood, he would have had to have been standing approximately 3½ to 4 feet away from the mackintosh, close to the doorway. In a room lit by only one gaslight, on the right-hand side of the room, which would cast the shadow of Julia's body (in its original position) to the left, over the mackintosh, how could it have been possible for Wallace not only to identify the crumpled, misshapen piece of material as a mackintosh, but then to assume it to be his wife's – then his own? This would have been highly improbable – unless Wallace had indeed expected it to be Julia's mackintosh. If Wallace had planned Julia's murder, could part of that plan have required Julia to be wearing her mackintosh that night?

6

The Police Arrive

At around 9.10 p.m., a knock came at the front door. Hoping it was finally the police, Mrs Johnston rushed down the hallway to answer it, Wallace in pursuit. Despite twisting and pulling at the unfamiliar lock, the door would not open. 'Oh, you had better do it,' she said to Wallace as she stepped aside. Wallace fared no better; the door would not budge. According to him, the door had been bolted. Taking off the bolt, Wallace greeted Constable 191G Frederick Robert Williams with 'Come inside officer; something terrible has happened.' Upon being asked at the Assize trial if he had heard the sound of the bolt being undone, Williams was to say that he had heard nothing. Wallace was adamant that the bolt had been on, hence the reason Mrs Johnston could not open the door. Mrs Johnston, however, could throw no light on the subject:

> When the first policeman came, Mr Wallace and I went running to the front door, and Mr Wallace opened it. I was very, very upset and cannot say how he opened the door, or whether or not he had to unbolt it. I could not contradict him if he said he had to unbolt it.

This has led to much speculation that Wallace was lying and the bolt was not on. However, we should examine part of Wallace's second statement, given to Inspector Gold on 22 January, where he states, 'I answered it and it was thus I found the front door was bolted. The safety catch was not on the latch-lock. I opened the door and admitted the constable.' Here, Wallace indicates that what he was terming 'bolted', did not mean that a large bolt had been drawn to lock the door, but that a latch (a 'snib') had been pressed on the lock in order to prevent the lock from turning even with the use of a key. Due to the size and positioning of the latch (on the lock itself), it would be highly unlikely that Mrs Johnston would have seen him unlatch the lock, nor PC Williams hear him.

Upon entering 29 Wolverton Street, Williams headed straight for the crime scene. In the parlour, Williams eyed the devastation, noting that Julia 'was lying on her stomach in a twisted position on the mat in front of the fireplace, her head towards the door and her feet towards the fireplace'. Near to her head, he also noted a crumpled piece of material, covered in blood. He took hold of her right wrist, and though it was still slightly warm, there was no pulse. 'How did this happen?' he asked. 'I don't know,' Wallace said and told him the tale of his fruitless journey to Mossley Hill in search of business from Mr Qualtrough. At the end of the statement, there was another knock at the front door; Williams moved Wallace into the hallway and closed the parlour door. As Williams spoke to two ambulance policemen, Mrs Johnston joined Wallace in time to catch the Wallaces' black cat edging its way through the forest of legs. 'Don't let him go into the front room!' she yelled needlessly as the cat continued on into the kitchen. Once it was explained that Mrs Wallace was deceased and the parlour was a crime scene, the ambulance police went on their way. Deciding to begin his investigation of the house, Williams trooped Wallace up the stairs.

From Williams's evidence, it would appear that sometime between Wallace and Mrs Johnston's last visit to the parlour (when Wallace identified the mackintosh to Mrs Johnston) someone had moved Julia's body into the position shown in the police photographs. This position of Julia's body was also noted by Medical Examiner Professor MacFall upon his arrival at the crime scene: 'In the front parlour, I saw the dead body of a woman lying on the hearthrug face downwards face turned to the left. The left arm was extended and the right arm by the side of the body.' As we now know from statements given by Mr and Mrs Johnston and the drawing contained in Hector Munro's files, Julia's body was resting on its right side; the right arm was hidden underneath her body and the left arm was resting on the left side of her body, bent at the elbow, the lower arm extending outward, the fingers almost touching the floor. Constable Williams states that upon examining Julia:

> She was lying on her stomach in a twisted position on the mat in front of the fireplace, her head towards the door and her feet towards the fireplace … I felt the right wrist of deceased but could feel no movement of the pulse. The flesh was slightly warm.

At the trial, Hemmerde referred Williams to the parlour photographs and asked him:

> *Just look at photograph No. 6* [the photograph taken from the doorway; same handed to witness]. *Does that represent the position in which you found her?* That would be the position of the body.

This was *not* the original position of the body. If the only two people in the house were Wallace and Mrs Johnston, and neither of them reported any repositioning of the body, who had moved Julia's body? In taking Julia's pulse at her right hand, had Williams pulled it from underneath her, forcing the body to slump forward? If this was the case, he must also have deliberately repositioned Julia's left arm and feet. Constable Williams was as good as chastised by Roland Oliver when being questioned about his notes taken after his arrival at the crime scene. According to Williams, he did not take any notes at all whilst he was there alone; he only took them when Superintendent Moore had arrived at around 10.30 p.m. – one hour and twenty minutes after he had arrived. This meant that his notes were taken in retrospect whilst other officers and Professor MacFall were investigating the crime scene themselves. Could this be why his evidence is wrong? Did Williams note the position of Julia's body when he first entered the room or, more likely, did he note it when he was making up his notes at 10.30 p.m? Could there have been an 'agreed' version of the investigation of the crime scene in the light of the official photographs? Surely, the priority even then would have been to document the crime scene first – then start investigating it.

After finding Wallace's laboratory in order, Wallace and PC Williams entered the bathroom. Williams queried Wallace about the burning light and was told, 'We usually have a light here.' In the middle bedroom, he also noted the gas jet was burning. He asked Wallace if the light was burning when he came into the house. Wallace replied, 'I changed myself in this room before leaving and probably left it on myself.' Wallace picked up the jar on the mantelpiece, took hold of the notes inside and, as he was extracting them, explained, 'Here is some money which has not been touched.' Williams told him put the notes back where he found them. Noticing a curtained alcove to the right of the fireplace, Williams approached it as Wallace informed him that that was where Julia's clothes were and had not been touched. Williams checked nonetheless and found all, apparently, in order. As they left the room, Wallace muttered, 'There appears to have been no one here.' Upon entering the front bedroom, Williams found it was still in darkness, as Wallace had found it earlier:

> The room was in a state of disorder: the bed clothes were half on the bed and half on the floor; there were a couple of pillows lying near the fireplace; there was a dressing table in the room containing drawers and a mirror, and also a wardrobe: the drawers of the dressing table were shut and the door of the wardrobe was shut.

Back downstairs, Williams lead Wallace into the kitchen and noticed the broken piece of the door of the photographic cabinet lying on the floor by the cupboard, near to the towering bookshelves. Pointing to the top shelf, Wallace explained about the £4 he had found to be missing from his cash box. Taking Julia's handbag from the chair under the table, he pulled out the cash from inside, muttering something about Julia's money – but Williams did not catch it.

Ushering Wallace back into the parlour for another look at the crime scene, Williams stood just inside the room, Wallace close behind him. As Williams was scanning the room for more details, Wallace eased himself between Julia's body and the sideboard and lit the left-hand gas mantle. Once again, the pair left the room, returning to the kitchen as Williams closed the parlour door behind him.

Once in the kitchen, Williams asked, 'Were there any lights burning when you entered?'

'Excepting for the two lights upstairs, the house was in darkness,' Wallace responded.

Wondering if light from the kitchen would have somehow escaped from between the heavy curtains, Williams parted them, asking, 'When you first came up the yard did you notice any light shining through the curtains?'

'The curtains would prevent the light from escaping,' Wallace answered.

Unsure, Williams wanted to test his supposition, but Wallace pointed out that would be fruitless now because he had moved the curtains.

Constable Williams stated that, upon his arrival at 29 Wolverton Street, after his initial examination of the parlour, he had closed the door in order to undertake an examination of the house with Wallace. Again, after visiting the room for the second time with Wallace (when Wallace lit the left-hand gas mantle), he claimed that upon leaving the room he had closed the door. This, however, according to his own testimony, would have been impossible. Upon being questioned by Edward Hemmerde at Wallace's trial, he was shown the

photograph taken from the doorway and asked to give his opinion as to the positioning of
the chair resting in front of the sideboard as he remembered it: 'The one near the sideboard
here appears to me to have been moved … I think it was this side of the sideboard near the
door.' Upon being shown the photograph taken from behind the settee, where the chair is at
the side of the sideboard, close to the door, he stated, 'That is the correct position.' Assuming
Williams to be correct, this would have meant, upon leaving the room, he could not have
closed the door; likewise, Wallace, upon entering the room for the first time that night,
would not have been able to open it – and the murderer, unable to escape, would have still
been in the room. An interesting observation of the photographs of the parlour in respect of
this seemingly superfluous and obstructive chair is the fact that the parlour contains a piano
– but no piano stool. Could this chair have been Julia's piano stool? If so, why had it been
placed against the sideboard in a very awkward position, rather than under the piano? Could
the chair have been moved away from the piano by Julia's killer in order to give him more
room for his attack?

At around 9.30 p.m., Mr Johnston was still waiting at Anfield police station when an
ambulance arrived and reported to Constable Saunders. Having been at 29 Wolverton Street,
they had found the woman to be deceased. Upon hearing the news, Mr Johnston decided
to make his way back to Wolverton Street as Constable Saunders reached for a phone and
tried to contact the Divisional CID. Unable to do so, he telephoned Superintendent Hubert
Moore (whose daughter, Imelda, was Richard Gordon Parry's father's secretary at the City
Treasury) at his home at 25 Belmont Drive, Newsham Park – a mere mile from Wolverton
Street. Upon receiving the call, Moore immediately phoned the CID office in Dale Street
and instructed a Constable Harrison to call all CID inspectors in the city and inform them
of the message he had received from Saunders, telling them to get themselves and their men
on standby for instructions.

By 9.45 p.m., Mr Johnston was back at the house. Williams and his immediate superior,
Police Sergeant 5G Joe Breslin, were in the parlour whilst Wallace hovered around the
doorway. Joseph Michael Breslin, father of six children, was 48 years old at the time and
living with his family at the house attached to Anfield police station. Born in Northern
Ireland in 1882, he had joined the Liverpool Police Force in 1904; he was to retire in May
1937, and died on 11 January 1948. As Breslin got the measure of the crime scene, Williams,
thanks to the additional lighting, suddenly realised that the material he had noticed close to
Julia's head was a mackintosh. Pointing to it, he exclaimed, 'That looks like a mackintosh!'
Immediately Wallace turned toward the coat rack in the hallway and informed the two
officers, 'It's an old one of mine. It usually hangs here.' At about this time there was another
knock at the front door and Professor John Edward Whitley MacFall lurched into the
hallway. At 6 feet 3 inches tall, his presence was as imposing as Wallace's. Liverpool Bridewell
Surgeon, Honorary Advisor to the Liverpool and Birkenhead Criminal Investigation
Departments, Chair of Forensic Medicine at the University of Liverpool and Examiner in
Medical Jurisprudence at four others, MacFall had impeccable credentials. His colleagues
at the Medical Faculty in the University of Liverpool were, however, less than impressed.
Besides considering him a careless diagnostician, they also felt he was abusing his position by
using it as a springboard to greater acclaim.

Heading straight into the parlour, MacFall cleared the room of unwanted and unneeded spectators and spent some time with Wallace alone. After that, he set about his examination of the victim and the crime scene. Except for several sketches, he would make no written notes of any of his examinations. Beginning with the most obvious point of reference, Julia's head, MacFall observed a large void, 2 inches wide by 3 inches long, through which bone and brain tissue were protruding. Attempting to examine the back of Julia's head through her blood- and brain-matted hair, he noticed that there was a great depression at the back of the skull, on Julia's left-hand side. The skull had been fractured by a number of blows (though at that point he could not determine how many) which had forced the back of the skull out of shape, forcing it up toward the crown. Close by Julia's head lay a pad, used by Julia for pinning under her hair at the back of her head to form a bun; matted with blood and brains and still attached to her head by strands of hair, it looked as though it had been ripped off her head. He observed that Julia's hands were blood-stained, though nothing was in them and there was nothing under her fingernails.

His next step was to attempt to determine time of death: a crucial calculation in any murder investigation and a hotly debated one in this particular case. In determining the time of death, MacFall opted for the greater of two evils – progression of rigor mortis. During the course of the night, he would examine Julia approximately every 15 to 20 minutes to check its progress. In determining the time of death, there were two methods one could apply (usually used in combination): monitoring body temperature or the progression of rigor mortis – the amount of time it takes for the body to become rigid. Both of these methods are notoriously inaccurate, though the latter is more inaccurate than the former. In basing his estimation of the time of death solely on the progression of rigor mortis, McFall initially gave the time of death as two hours before his arrival – approximately 8 p.m. Later on, he amended this to four hours prior to his arrival – 6 p.m. During Roger Wilkes's radio programme, the then Home Office pathologist Dr Charles St Hill gave his opinion of MacFall's method of determining time since death:

MacFall's responsibility when he came to the scene of the crime was to determine, first of all, how death occurred, when death occurred and to make observations which might help determine who was responsible. The important point in this particular case was when death occurred. For some reason, MacFall only concentrated on the progress of rigor mortis and did not take any body temperatures. It may be he'd lost or broken his thermometer and of course, in those days they weren't too easy to replace. It may be he didn't want to disturb the body. But, by not taking the temperature, he didn't carry out the least inaccurate method of determining time since death.

Rigor mortis can start between 2 and 6 hours after death. MacFall observed, when he first came to see the body, that rigor mortis was just commencing. At first, he said that this indicated that death had occurred some two hours prior to the arrival and this, in fact would, of course, put the time of death some 50 minutes after, or even an hour after, Wallace was known to have left the house. Later on, he increased this time of death to some 4 hours prior to his arrival, which would have put the time of death when Wallace was still there. In other words, he changed his mind, and then gave an accuracy of time since death based entirely on the observation of rigor mortis very accurately – far more accurately than I think is justifiable.

Given that MacFall gave the time of death at around 6 p.m., and that Wallace stated he did not leave the house until 6.45 p.m., not only did this place Wallace in the right place at the right time, but just as significantly it would go a long way in absolving other potential suspects – Parry and Marsden – if the murder had taken place at any time later that night. Parry had witnesses to prove he was 43 Knoclaid Road until 8.30 p.m., while Marsden, if he was working that day, would have been ensconced in his office at Bernard Murphy & Son in Birkenhead.

What has to be remembered is that, when determining time of death through progression of rigor mortis, a number of factors have to be taken into consideration: age, frame size, musculature, environmental temperature and conditions, and so on. MacFall determined Julia to be a small, frail woman of about 52 years of age and thus his determination of the progression of rigor mortis was based upon this. What he didn't realise (as, it would also appear, not even Wallace himself did) was that Julia was not 52 years of age; she was, in fact, almost 70 years of age. In determining the progression of rigor mortis, this is a very important factor. In his cross-examination by Roland Oliver as to the validity of using rigor mortis as an accurate determination of the time of death, MacFall underlined this point himself:

That seems a flimsy test on which to rely? I took the age of the woman into account. Extremes of age bring it on quicker. In middle age, it will come on from 4 to 6 to 8 hours after death and in a not too warm or cold room the extremities, the legs and arms were cold when I arrived. That meant that death with the cooling and the rigor would make it about 6 o'clock.

In effect, the onset and progression of rigor mortis in Julia's body would have advanced much faster than he had calculated, increasing the amount of time (based upon MacFall's belief that Julia was 52) she would have been considered to have been dead. According to Julia's autopsy report, her stomach contained 'about four ounces of semi-fluid food consisting of currants, raisins and unmasticated lumps of carbohydrate'. According to Wallace's statement, this was the remains of the meal (tea and scones) he and Julia had had at 6 p.m. If this is so, this could indicate that Julia may have been murdered sometime between 7.30 and 8.30 p.m. (an hour and a half to two and a half hours after her meal), not between 6.30 and 6.45 p.m. If Julia had been murdered between the latter times, the food in her stomach would not have been as broken down by digestive fluids, as the process would have been halted by her death. We should add to this the testimony of Mrs Johnston; upon entering the house with Wallace and her husband at 8.45 p.m., she noticed that:

The kitchen fire was nearly out and Mr Wallace and I put some wood on and he helped me to get it going by stirring the few live embers at the bottom. Mr Wallace put the coal on after the chips had caught. From the appearance of the fireplace when I went in, it looked as if there had been a good fire and that it had burned out.

The fire in the kitchen range, despite the possibility of it having been a 'good fire', can clearly be seen in the photograph of the kitchen to have been only a small fire. If Julia had truly been murdered between 6.00 and 6.45 p.m., before Wallace left to go to Mossley Hill, would not the fire in the kitchen have completely been burned out and the ashes gone cold by 8.45 p.m. – over two hours later?

Could it then be that Julia Wallace was actually murdered at sometime between 7.30 and 8.30 p.m. as Professor MacFall had originally proposed? If this is the case, then neither Wallace nor Parry could have been her killer. Both have a cast-iron alibi.

In examining the parlour, MacFall found a large grouping of blood splashes that ran in a line from the edge of the sideboard, around the corner over the two-seater chair holding Wallace's violin case, across the violin case and above the marble shelf of the fire grate. Several of these splashes reached a height of 7 feet, though the majority were around 4 feet from the ground. There were also a small number of tiny blood splashes on the wall between the parlour door and the piano. In his initial report, MacFall concluded that Julia must have been sitting on the two-seater settee, her head lowered and inclined to the right as if in conversation with somebody. In this position, he surmised, the perpetrator administered the first of ten blows to the back of her skull. Due to brain matter and bone being present only in the clots of blood surrounding Julia's head (and not under it) whilst lying on the floor, he concluded that it was whilst lying across the rug that Julia received the deathblow which caused the large hole through her skull. Ruling out the possibility of the staining in the corner of the room as having been caused by the whirling around of a blood-stained weapon, he concluded that these initial blows would have caused a bursting of the head that would have produced the pattern he had found: 'Like hitting and bursting a bag with a wet sponge in it.' Indeed, he thought the impact of that first blow to the back of the head may have produced a reaction sufficient to have produced the small spots of blood present between the door and the piano. In all, MacFall estimated that Julia was struck eleven or twelve times. He could not accurately account for how many times she might have been struck in order to produce the gaping hole in her skull, either once or twice, so he put his final estimation at eleven blows. If, however, we look closely at the photographs showing the wounding on the back of Julia's head, it can be clearly seen that two pairs of these 'incised' wounds lie almost perfectly parallel to each other and between each pair of wounds is a flat indentation. Could these pairs of incised wounds have been produced by the edges of the weapon that was used to inflict them – a weapon with a square or rectangular cross-section? If this is the case, and the remaining six wounds were also found to be in parallel pairs, Julia may have been struck by her assailant (including the single wound estimated by MacFall to have produced the hole through her skull) as little as six times.

It was whilst giving evidence at the committal proceedings on 3 February that MacFall changed his diagnosis:

> The brain substance was found only around the head and not beneath it, which I took to be evidence that the last smashing blows were made while the head was on the ground. The front of the head had been smashed in first, in my opinion.

Expanding upon this whilst giving evidence at the Assize trial, MacFall went on to explain that, in finding only bone and brain matter in the blood clots surrounding the head, this was a strong indication that the blows to the back of the head were administered after an initial blow (whilst Julia sat on the two-seater couch) had opened the skull and whilst Julia was lying across the rug. In striking the back of the head, pressure had built up inside the skull, squeezing the brain matter and bone out to pool around her head.

In the parlour, MacFall had not long sat down on the arm of the two-seater couch to make a quick sketch of the crime scene when, at around 10.05 p.m., Williams opened the front door to Superintendent Hubert Moore and Sergeant Adolphus Fothergill, on a flying visit to assess the situation. Entering the parlour, Moore took a quick glance at the crime scene and then moved into the hallway and took a statement from Williams before entering the kitchen to question Wallace and the Johnstons. Wallace not having a telephone, Moore and Fothergill left Wolverton Street for Anfield police station to telephone Assistant Chief Constable W. E. Glover (who some time later would arrive at the house and, after a consultation with MacFall, would summon Chief Medical Officer Hugh Pierce to the scene) and an Inspector Wallace at CID Special Branch to tell him to phone all divisions and have them do a search of lodging houses, railway stations, night cafés and anywhere else they though a heavily blood-stained man might be hiding out.

Hubert 'Rory' Moore was born in Country Leitrim, Ireland, in 1879. A one-time miner, he had joined the Liverpool Police Force in 1900. After walking a beat for three years, in 1903 he married Ann Connor, daughter of marine engineer James Connor and his wife Elizabeth, who were both from Ireland and the owners of the house he was boarding at as a 22-year-old Police Constable in 1901: 31 Salisbury Street, Everton. After serving as a court official in the Warrant Department, he began his detective career in 1912. That same year, Moore and his wife moved into 1 Auburn Road, Tuebrook, with their three daughters: Imelda, Edith Veronica and Elsie. Rising through the ranks of Constable, Sergeant and Detective Sergeant – having been one of the officers responsible for the capture of William Henry Kennedy at a house in Copperas Hill, Liverpool, on 25 January 1928 (who, along with Frederick Guy Browne, was hanged for the murder of Police Constable George William Gutteridge of the Essex Constabulary) – Hubert Moore became a Detective Inspector. During 1929 came another promotion to Chief Police Inspector. In February 1930, he was promoted yet again, and became Police Superintendent of the Liverpool CID. It was at this time, after thirteen years living at 1 Auburn Road, the family moved to 25 Belmont Drive, Newsham Park; it was apparently here, at home, he had been informed of Julia's murder. Jonathan Goodman offered the following description:

> [R]etaining a strong brogue in his speech, Moore was a devout Roman Catholic … he looked less like a policeman than a prosperous butcher. A heavily-built man, with dark red hair brushed away from a centre parting, he sported a large moustache – which, according to one of his compatriots, 'was waxed almost lyrical'. Lacking in imagination and humour (it was said that if you wanted to make a joke with him you had to arrange an appointment first), Moore was an able and hard-working policeman, but by no means a brilliant detective.

Over the past ten years the effects of two very different forms of rebellion had assisted him in his rise to the high rank of superintendent.

The Police strike of 1919 had resulted in the dismissal of many, if not most, of Moore's competitors for promotion. It had provided him with a golden opportunity for advancement – all that he needed was an equally golden chance to impress the men at the top. He did not have to wait long. Soon after the strike he was appointed as an inspector in the Special Branch, a position which, at that time, fitted his talents like a glove. He was in the right job at the right time.

During the 1920s Liverpool was the main centre of Sinn Fein disturbance in this country. Fighting for full Irish independence, the Sinn Feigners used arson, sabotage, and armed violence as the means of publicizing their cause and forcing the British Government to accede to their demands. It was the duty of the Special Branch to combat the terrorists, and Moore was ideally suited to the task. Himself an Irish Catholic, he understood and agreed with the motives of the Sinn Feigners, but hated them for the methods they used. These methods, he felt, could only defer the freedom they demanded. He fought them with the passion and ruthlessness of an extreme patriot – an Irish patriot – and, before long, he was as much admired by the people of Liverpool as he was hated by the Sinn Feigners.

At the beginning of 1930 he was promoted to the rank of Superintendent; at the end of that year he was placed in charge of the CID. He had reached the top. Now the only direction in which he could travel was down. If he fell he would fall a very long way, and nobody would bother to help him up again.

Occurring so soon after his appointment as Head of CID, the murder of Julia Wallace provided a personal test for Moore – probably the greatest challenge of his career. The thud-and-blunder methods he had used so successfully in the fight against Sinn Fein were of no use in dealing with a murder case, and his detractors said that these were the only methods he knew. He had to prove his detractors wrong. If he did not, then his position would be very insecure indeed. It was not just his reputation, but possibly his whole future, that was now at stake.

At around 10.30 p.m., Moore arrived back at the house to find that Detective Inspector Herbert Gold, Inspector Langford and Sergeant Harry Bailey had arrived. Inspector Gold, like PC James Edward Rothwell, had also been a customer of Wallace's. During 1922, Gold and his family had moved from 22 Chrysostom Street, Everton, to 10 Grenfell Street, Clubmoor; it was whilst living here that Wallace made his collections from Gold. After eight years at Grenfell Street, Herbert Gold and his family moved, in 1930, to 95 Queen's Drive, Stoneycroft. Gold may have known Wallace for all of these eight years.

In the kitchen, Wallace was being comforted by his sister-in-law Amy and his nephew Edwin, who had not long arrived. Mrs Johnston having sent her daughter Norah along with her boyfriend, Francis George McElroy, to their first-floor flat at 83 Ullet Road, Sefton, at around 10 p.m. to inform them of the tragedy, Amy and Edwin had rushed to Wolverton Street by taxi. Upon their arrival, they had been ushered into the house via the back door, where they came upon Wallace slumped in a chair by the kitchen fire. Turning to Mrs Johnston, Wallace had said despairingly, 'Tell them, please; I can't.' Edwin Wallace recalled:

> He was awfully upset, and had his handkerchief to his eyes, as he was crying profusely. Someone told me that my aunt had been murdered. I understand that my uncle had been given brandy. My uncle was able to speak to me, and said that my aunt had been hit about the back of the head and that his locker had been smashed (I saw this for myself in the back room, and half the door of the locker was lying on the floor). I told my uncle I was terribly sorry, and he said 'yes, I realise that, and nothing said at this time can help'.

In the meantime, Moore had begun his own examination of the property. With the thought of a recent spate of local burglaries perpetrated by the so-called 'Anfield Burglar' in mind, he paid close attention to the windows, doors and locks of the house and checked for any signs of a break in. Returning to the kitchen, he questioned Wallace about his whereabouts that night. Wallace, once again, repeated his statement of the night's events and showed Moore the broken photographic box. Whilst observing the broken door of the box on the floor, Moore noticed the half-crown and two separate shillings on the floor by the bookcase. Wallace pointed out the cash box on top of the bookcase and told him £4 had been stolen. Moore asked him where the box was upon his return. 'Where it is now,' Wallace told him. Lifting the box from the bookcase, Moore examined it, noting that, besides being empty except for a dollar bill and some stamps, the box had a broken hinge. Closing the lid, he said to Wallace, 'I cannot understand why a thief would go to all that trouble, putting the lid on the box and placing it back where he had found it.' He asked Wallace to accompany him upstairs.

In Wallace's laboratory, Moore noticed there were tools there that could have been potential weapons. In asking Wallace to check them carefully to see if any were missing, Wallace assured him all was correct. In the middle bedroom, he examined the jar on the mantelpiece where he observed that 'Four £1 Treasury notes were in a small jar on the mantelpiece and there was what appeared to be a bloodstain on one of these notes' (the jar also contained a postal order and a half-crown). Entering the front bedroom, Moore noted the disturbance:

> There was no light in the front room and the blinds were not drawn. The bedding was disturbed on the left inside the door, it appeared to me as though a person had just come in and taken the two pillows and flung them across the bed to the window side of the fireplace, one was practically on top of the other, and the bed clothing was pushed over the fireplace … exposing a portion of the mattress. On that mattress, there were two lady's handbags and two lady's hats, old hats, and on the bed clothing close to those hats, there was another hat, three lady's hats and two handbags … There were some articles on the dressing table in the position in which they should be. Nothing was disturbed on the dressing table; the wardrobe door was closed; I opened it and looked in, and there was some lady's clothing and everything appeared to be intact … It did not give the impression of a thief looking for valuables.

Moore asked Wallace if the bedroom was like that earlier in the day. Wallace said he had no idea; he had not been in that room for a fortnight. As mentioned previously, in the photograph of the kitchen, a brush is clearly seen on the corner of the table near to Wallace's chair – the bed sheet having been pushed back in order to accommodate it. The bed sheet had to have been draped across the tablecloth that evening at the time of their evening meal and when Wallace was just about to leave for his appointment with Qualtrough. Surely, if he did not already know, he had to have wondered and enquired of Julia why a bed sheet was cluttering up the table. Upon seeing the condition the front bedroom was in, could not this well-educated, intellectual, scientifically minded man not have put two and two together and told Superintendent Moore that Julia had probably left it like that when she had fetched the bottom bed sheet that was to be seen covering the kitchen table? On the other hand, had he decided not to in order to add to the growing speculation that a burglar had entered the house?

In the meantime, MacFall, having finished his examination of Julia and the parlour at around 10.30 p.m., had been doing his own examination of the house, searching for traces of blood. Having found none anywhere else in the house, at about 10.45 p.m., whilst investigating the bathroom with a torch, he noticed a nailbrush resting on the side of the bath; its bristles were still moist and the wooden handle had the appearance of drying after having had been used some time before. However, once again, he could see no signs of blood. Then, on the right-hand side of the pan of the toilet, near to the front, he claimed that his torch beam fell upon a single clot of blood. He explained that, hidden in the shadow caused by the overhanging washbasin, it had remained, seemingly, unnoticed. Sized three sixteenths of an inch in diameter and an eighth of an inch in height, the blood clot was circular and had a somewhat unusual appearance. It was a little cone – not unlike a drip frozen in time, its tail still prominent. Thought to have been left by the blood-drenched killer as he washed himself down in the bathroom, this little spot of blood was at the centre of a mystery that grew way beyond its minute proportions as time went on. Later that night, at around 1 a.m., after the police had photographed it in situ, MacFall removed the clot for further analysis. Tests were done to ascertain if it could have been menstrual blood from Julia, but no epithelial cells (cells from the lining of the womb, excreted during menstruation) could be found, thus ruling out this possibility.

MacFall judged the consistency of the clot to be the same as the blood clots found around Julia's body. Could it have been dropped onto the toilet pan at about the same time Julia's blood was spilled, hence the closeness in age and consistency? This, too, was ruled out; if dropped as fresh blood it would have splashed and flattened. How would it have formed itself into a cone shape? A problem also arose inasmuch as, if the clot had fallen from the murderer and was of such age as to be able to retain its conical shape, this would have meant that the killer must have murdered Julia and then remained in the house soaked in her blood for quite some time, possibly as much as an hour, before he had cleansed himself in the bathroom – highly unlikely.

In an attempt to ascertain how old the blood would have to have been in order for it to have retained the shape of a fallen drip, in addition to MacFall, three other eminent scientists were asked to carry out tests: Professor William Henry Roberts, City Analyst; Professor James

Henry Dible, MB, FRCP, Professor of Pathology, University of Liverpool, formerly Professor of Pathology, University of London; and Dr Robert Coope, MD, BSc and Member of the Royal College of Physicians. Between these four scientists, innumerable experiments were undertaken in an attempt to find how old the blood would have to have been, from what height it would have to have fallen and how long it would have to have been sitting upon the toilet pan for it to have attained the consistency and cone shape in which it was found.

Unfortunately, a satisfactory solution was never reached. The only alternative theory put forward as to how this spot of blood reached its final destination was that one of the investigative team (or one of the many official waifs and strays who had straggled in from other divisions and who neither gave a statement nor evidence) had unknowingly carried it there. I, for one, am an advocate of this theory. By using the official police photograph (taken by Harry Hewitt Cooke at around 1 a.m. on 21 January 1931) with some simple digital manipulation, it can easily be seen that, with the toilet seat closed, the right-hand foot of the seat rests exactly upon the blood clot. The simple answer is that somebody who had been examining Julia and had blood on one of his hands (possibly the same person who had touched the notes in the jar in the middle bedroom, producing a smear on one of them) had closed the lid (possibly to stand on it to examine around the toilet cistern looking for hidden weapons), and in doing so had inadvertently wiped the clot of blood onto the foot of the lid. With the lid closed, the clot had transferred to the toilet pan. In opening the lid, the clot had stretched slightly, and then snapped back to the rim of the pan, causing the conical 'drip' shape. Until the lid had been closed, the toilet pan would have been observed to have been clean as far as any signs of blood were concerned. Only in lifting up the lid once the clot had been transferred would it have been noticed. It was later proven that nobody contaminated with blood had washed themselves anywhere in the house when thorough tests of the bathroom, back kitchen and drains were carried out using the 'benzidine test'. It was found that no blood had been washed through the system, via the bath, the sinks or the toilet. Benzidine (first used as a test for blood in 1904), a colourless crystal, is dissolved in a small quantity of glacial acetic acid and hydrogen peroxide. When administered to any surface thought to have been in contact with blood, it gives an immediate blue colour, turning purple if blood (or anything that superficially resembles blood, such as certain fruit juices) is present, and is accurate in a dilution of blood to water in the ratio of 1:20,000 to 1:200,000.

In the light of Wallace's statement that he had not been able to open the front door with his key when he had first arrived at the house because it was faulty, upon arriving back downstairs, Moore and Gold examined the lock. Moore asked Wallace for his key. Pushing it into the lock, he gave it a few twists and found that it was, indeed, faulty. However, once one became aware of the problem, the lock could be made to work normally. To test this, Moore went out of the house, closed the door and opened it almost immediately. The lock was eventually given to James Sarginson, a locksmith, for examination; he found it to be a 'two lever night latch' and noted that the springs from the wards of the lock were missing – the wards being raised in a 'neutral' position. The wards add security to the lock. In their normal position, with the springs present, the wards are permanently down. You cannot open the lock until the correct key is inserted and turned, raising the wards above a certain height.

In the lock's present condition (which, in Sarginson's opinion, it had been in for some considerable time) the key would simply spin in the lock, which, after a certain point, would lead to the lock remaining closed. It would require experience of the lock to know when to stop turning the key in order to open the door. Upon entering the house, Moore exclaimed, 'I could open the door all right but the lock is defective.' Wallace replied, 'It was not like that this morning.' This statement is dubious on two counts. Wallace always maintained that during the daytime, he always used the back door, only using the front door of a night, so he should not have used the back door that morning. As well as this, Sarginson had stated that the lock had been in that condition for quite some time. Wallace had to have been aware of the fault and was therefore lying.

As the house search progressed, Wallace returned to the kitchen to be comforted by Amy Wallace and her son. Moore re-entered the parlour and, taking out his torch, he crouched down and examined the material close to Julia's head. In his opinion, it had been placed close to Julia's right shoulder and tucked in by the right side 'as though the body was a living person and you were trying to make it comfortable. No portion was resting under the body.' Realising it was a mackintosh, he called Wallace in from the kitchen. Wallace hovered in the doorway next to Moore. 'Is this your mackintosh?' Moore asked. Wallace stooped slightly and, rubbing his chin, remained silent. Moore probed further: 'Had Mrs Wallace a mackintosh like this?' Once again, Wallace remained silent (despite having already admitted it was his mackintosh to Mrs Johnston, Constable Williams, Sergeant Breslin and an unidentified, tall policeman who had entered the kitchen earlier and asked Wallace, 'What about this mackintosh, Mr Wallace?'). 'Take it up!' Moore ordered Bailey, who quickly unfolded the mackintosh and held it out. Moore took hold of the right sleeve and stretched it out. 'This is a gent's!' he observed. Wallace began to finger the garment, scrutinising it.

The City Analyst William Henry Roberts described the condition of the mackintosh:

> The Mackintosh was extensively and heavily stained with human blood on the right side, both inside and outside, and on the upper inner side of the right sleeve. The outside of the left cuff and a large area near the left pocket were similarly stained. A considerable portion of the bottom right side of the Mackintosh had been recently burnt away. I had visited the house on January 21st, and then formed the conclusion that the Mackintosh had been burnt in the Parlour on the night of the murder.

Wallace, still not committing himself, said:

> If there's two patches on the inside it's mine … it's mine. I wore it this morning, but the day turned out fine; I wore my fawn coat this evening. Of course it was not burned like that when I wore it.

Moore asked him where he had left it: 'Hanging in the hall at half-past one.' On 8 October 1928, Wallace had sent a letter to the Liverpool City Engineer's Office, complaining that after having called to the office seeking compensation for having had his mackintosh 'torn on a projecting nut on the barricades erected in connection with the sewer construction' in Knoclaid Road the previous Monday (1 October), he had had no word on the matter. On 18 October, Mr Thomas Peirson Frank (who was knighted in 1949 in recognition of his work as Coordinating Officer for Road Repairs and Public Utility Services for the London area during the Second World War – in spite of the severest air raids, Peirson Frank directed the road repairs that allowed London to carry on) told Wallace:

> I cannot trace having received a previous communication from you in respect of your claim for damaged macintosh [sic], but I have made enquiries into your complaint and regret I cannot recommend my committee to accept any responsibility in the matter.

Could the two patches on the mackintosh that Wallace was referring to have been caused by this event?

At 11.15 p.m., about a mile away from Wolverton Street, 24-year-old garage hand John Parkes was wending his way through the chilled back entries from his home at 1a Tynwald Hill, Stoneycroft (only one street away from the home of Richard Gordon Parry) to start his night shift at Atkinson's all-night garage at 1a Moscow Drive. Parkes worked as a cleaner and general dogsbody from 11.30 p.m. to around 9 or 10 a.m. the following morning. Well liked by the Atkinson family, he was called 'Pukka' by them. Owned by William Atkinson, who ran it with his three sons, Wilfred, Herbert and Arthur, the garage not only found business through private customers, but also ran a fleet of taxis. With a small flat above the garage, it was sometimes used as a late night/early morning drop-off centre for some of the customers, who would call in for a chat and a drink. One of these customers was Richard Gordon Parry. Parkes had known Parry since his childhood; the pair had gone to Lister Drive School together. Despite the longevity of their acquaintance, there was little love lost between the two youths. Parkes thought Parry arrogant, suave, a bit of a ladies' man – and, besides which, he was afraid of him. Parry had asked Parkes at one time, 'Do you like me?' Parkes had told him, 'I don't trust you.' For some time, Parry was a regular at the upstairs flat in the garage, often staying until 3 or 4 a.m. One night, he was caught rummaging through a wardrobe where one of the Atkinsons stored money. After the incident, William Atkinson told his sons and Parkes, 'Close the door of a night and don't let him in; things aren't safe.'

At about 11.40 p.m., Moore asked Wallace to accompany Gold and Bailey to Anfield police station in order to take a formal statement. At the same time, he ordered other officers off to the Central Fire Station to borrow any powerful lamps they might have. These would be set up in the street, outside No. 29, and set to glare through the windows. Once the lights were in place, starting outside the parlour door, Moore scoured the floor, continuing on into the kitchen. Examining the carpet up the stairs and the staircase walls, he proceeded onto the landing outside the bedrooms. Moving into the street, he also examined the front and back doors, and the window casings of the parlour and the kitchen – no bloodstains or evidence of forced entry could be found. At around 11.50 p.m., Dr Hugh Pierce, official Police Surgeon, arrived to assist MacFall. After examining Julia, he concluded that she had died at about 6 p.m., with a two-hour limit either side: effectively, sometime between 4 and 8 p.m. Joining MacFall in the vigil to determine the progression of rigor mortis, he, too, used no other method of obtaining a more accurate time of death, nor did he take any notes whatsoever. At 12.20 a.m., in the glare of the huge spotlights, MacFall took Pierce to the bathroom to ascertain his opinion of the blood clot on the toilet pan.

By this time, at Anfield police station, Wallace had given his initial statement. His clothing had being scrutinised for any signs of blood and none had been found. He was now being interrogated by Inspector Gold. Wallace told him that, upon leaving the house, he had seen no one suspicious lurking around and, upon his return journey, had spoken to no one before he saw the Johnstons. Upon arriving at the house, though he could hear nothing, he had thought there was someone in the house because he was locked out. As far as he knew, Julia had no friends he did not know about and the only person he would have expected to call was the paperboy – though he may have called before he left. If anyone was likely to call, they would be shown into the house only if Julia knew them personally – and then, only into the parlour. In a letter sent to Hector Munro on 18 March 1931, and simply signed 'Woman lover of justice', the writer states:

> I do not know them [the Wallaces], but from friends of theirs I understand that Mrs W was always nervous about having money in the house and seldom opened the door for anyone without first going into the sitting-room and looking through the window.

On the topic of Qualtrough, Wallace knew no one of that name, nor anyone who would have left him the message at the Chess Club. As far as he knew, there was no one who knew he would be going out that night; he had told nobody. Though Julia did have some money about the house, he had no idea where she kept it and, as far as he knew, the only thing stolen was the contents of the cash box which, in his estimation, amounted to a £1 note, three 10s notes, thirty to forty shillings in silver, a postal order for 4s 6d from a 'W. L. Springer, 41 New Road', a cheque drawn on the Midland Bank, Dale Street, for £5 17s payable to himself and crossed. There were also four 1d stamps, but they were not stolen.

By 1 a.m., just as MacFall and Pierce were about to leave Wolverton Street, MacFall observed that rigor mortis had progressed to Julia's right arm and right leg. By this time, Harry Hewitt Cooke, the official police photographer, had arrived and preparations were under way to take the parlour door off its hinges in order to take a clear shot of the room from that perspective. At 1.15 a.m., Detective Sergeant Harry Bailey arrived back at Wolverton Street and escorted Julia's body to the Princes Dock Mortuary. As the assistants prepared Julia for examination, Bailey noted down articles of jewellery being taken from the body – a brooch and her wedding ring. Whilst her clothing was being removed, Bailey noticed that her skirt was burnt at the front, in her groin area. As Bailey put it:

> I noticed as I turned over the body the skirt was burnt in the front … Directly opposite her private parts … as worn, where you fasten it up … The flap was here in the front and I should say that the flap should be at the side from what I know of female wear.

In its usual position, this 'flap', or placquet (usually hiding either buttons or a zip), would have been on Julia's left hip. There were, however, no signs of burning on her underskirt. The City Analyst, reporting upon the condition of Julia's skirt, said:

At the bottom of the Placquet there were 3 recent horizontal burns, which could have been caused by contact with the hot fireclay of a gas fire such as was in the Parlour at 29 Wolverton Street. The front of the skirt was heavily stained with Human Blood.

Given the City Analyst's report concerning both the burns on the mackintosh and the burns on Julia's skirt, it should have been plain to see that there having been an intruder in the house was not consistent with the evidence, and the 'robbery gone wrong' theory should have been immediately dismissed. Julia would have had to have known her attacker; she had allowed him into the house and invited him into the parlour in order to make him comfortable, lighting the gaslight and the gas fire for his comfort. If her attacker had been disturbed by Julia in the process of stealing the money from Wallace's cash box, why was she in the process of making him comfortable in the parlour? Surely, upon being discovered, he would have beaten Julia to death where she stood. If, for argument's sake, we say that the guest had managed to get away with the money unbeknownst to Julia, when Wallace returned and eventually opened the cash box and found it empty, he would, of course, have asked Julia about it. Julia would then have had to remind him that the only person who had been in the house over the past couple of days was the visitor on the Tuesday night, who would still have been caught. It would have been a no-win situation.

According to Goodman in *The Killing of Julia Wallace*, as the rest of Julia's clothes were removed, Bailey was struck by her peculiar underwear:

> The underskirt, which was obviously home-made, was fashioned from a length of woollen material only slightly lighter in weight than the skirt itself … The corsets were frayed and loose fitting, and it seemed to Bailey that they had been worn, not for support, but simply as a means of suspending the stockings. What at first sight appeared to be a small patch on the side of the corsets turned out to be a pocket containing a one-pound note and a ten-shilling note. The oddest of all Mrs Wallace's odd undergarments was the last to be taken from the body – an unhemmed square of white flannel, folded into a triangle and pinned in the position of a diaper.

What could possibly have been the function of such an item of clothing as a corset sporting a pocket? If Julia was to either put money into or take money from the pocket, this would have required her to raise her skirts. The only place this could be accomplished with any amount of decorum would have been in the house, surely defeating its purpose. As for the 'diaper', Julia was not known to have been incontinent and the Wallaces were not so short of money that Julia could not afford knickers (Julia had £1 10s in the pocket of her corset – the modern-day equivalent of over £70).

At around this same time, a Swift motor car tore up Moscow Drive and into Atkinson's Garage. John Parkes was busy cleaning cars with a high-pressure hose dangling from the rafters. Parry was almost out of the driver's door before the Swift screeched to a halt. He raced over to Parkes, saying, 'I've brought the car in. I want you to wash my car down!' Parkes stemmed the flow of the hose and dragged it over to the Swift; as far as he could see, the car was clean. He turned the hose on as Parry, shifting nervously, watched the hose play around the skin of the car:

His car was clean, as far as I could remember, but I got the high-pressure hose and went all over the car: underneath, on top, inside, all the back – everywhere … Every particle of the car was washed; where, in other places, they don't wash cars inside like I did. And he stood over me while I did it, and was telling me where to do, what to do and all this. I went all over it. I went completely all over it.

Whilst inside the car, Parkes noticed something in the glove compartment:

I seen the glove there and I pulled it out. I pulled it out cos that would get wringing wet and he snatched it off me as it was covered with blood, and he said to me: 'If the police got that … that would hang me!'

Parkes was shocked:

I realised then he wanted me to swill the box out and the glove an' all. But I didn't. I got the glove out before I started that. It was a thumb and all fingers; this part was all fingers and just the thumb … After that, he started rabbiting again. He said about the bar, said he's hid the bar in a doctor's house. He said he's dropped the bar down the grid outside of a doctor's house in Priory Road. He was in an agitated state, I can remember that. I could tell by what he said. And when I was washing the car down, I knew why I was washing it down and I daren't say anything.

Once Parkes was done, Parry paid him 5 shillings and left the garage.

At 4 a.m. that morning, Superintendent Moore was on his way from Wolverton Street back to Anfield police station. Upon his arrival, he sauntered into the smoky interview room where Wallace was still waiting, drained and exhausted. After quietly conferring with Gold, Moore faced Wallace and threw his statement down onto the table between them. He, too, was exhausted.

'Is there nothing more you'd like to tell us, Mr Wallace?'

'What about?'

Moore stared blankly at him for a few seconds, picked up Wallace's statement and left him at the table to rejoin Gold for another hushed conference. Soon after, at around 5 a.m., Wallace was driven, with Inspector Gold, to his sister-in-law's house at 83 Ullet Road, where a makeshift bed had been set up for him on the settee. Accompanying Wallace into the first-floor flat, Gold took statements from Amy Wallace and her son Edwin (these statements are no longer to be found in the police archives), then left. According to Amy Wallace, when Wallace arrived at her house, 'Mr Wallace was very deeply upset. He did not take his clothes off at all that night. I made a couch up for him in the lounge.'

Throughout that long night, police had been less than impressed by – in fact, suspicious of – Wallace's calm, almost indifferent demeanour toward the whole event. Not only had his wife been so brutally murdered, but he had been the one to find her battered body in a room covered with her blood – and yet there was little outward indication of either shock or grief. Under examination by Edward Hemmerde at the Assize trial, MacFall was questioned about this:

Can you tell my Lord and the jury what was the demeanour of the accused when he was there? I was very much struck with it: it was abnormal.

In what way? He was too quiet, too collected, for a person whose wife had been killed in that way that he described. He was not nearly so affected as I was myself.

Do you happen to remember anything particular that led you to that conclusion? I think he was smoking cigarettes most of the time. Whilst I was in the room examining the body and the blood he came in smoking a cigarette, and he leant over in front of the sideboard and flicked the ash into a bowl upon the sideboard. It struck me at the time as being unnatural.

To do that would he have to lean across anything? He did not come forward. I can recall his position at the moment: he leant forward so as not to step on the clot.

Detective Sergeant Harry Bailey was asked a similar question by junior prosecuting counsel Leslie Walsh:

What conclusion did you come to about his demeanour; what was he like? He impressed me as a very cool collected man – cool under the circumstances.

Inspector Herbert Gold was likewise quizzed:

What do you say about his demeanour? He was cool and calm. He did not seem to be in the least upset. I did not see any sign of emotion in him at all at the death of his wife.

Was there anything particular which drew your attention to that? When I first went into the house on the night of the murder, he was sitting in the kitchen. In fact, he had the cat on his knee and was stroking the cat, and he did not look to me like a man who had just battered his wife to death.

In defence of his behaviour, Wallace responded to Roland Oliver's questioning:

Do you know what your demeanour was the rest of that evening? It was said you were extremely quiet or cool and collected. One witness said you occasionally broke down, other witnesses say you smoked cigarettes. Do you really remember what your demeanour was? Well, I remember that I was extremely agitated and that I was trying to keep as calm and cool as possible. Probably I was smoking cigarettes for something to do, I mean to say, the inaction was more than I could stand. I had to do something to avoid breaking down. I did sit down in a chair on one or two occasions and I do remember I did break down absolutely; I could not help it or avoid it. I tried to be as calm and as cool as possible.

As a disciple of the Stoic philosophy, it could be argued (and often has been) that in this highly emotional situation, Wallace was simply showing how entrenched in this way of life he truly was. However, as Wallace had pointed out, there were moments during that night when the stoical walls he had built over the years crumbled, allowing his emotions to pour through. Had these walls been breached at least once before? Had these breached walls then allowed, not grief, but a torrent of bitterness and resentment to pour through the open chasm, leading Wallace to conceive a plan to bring about Julia's demise?

At the time of the murder, many rumours began circulating concerning Wallace's relationship with his sister-in-law – especially in light of the fact that he was then staying at her flat. These rumours began in suggesting that Wallace and Amy had been lovers for many years under the nose of the unwitting Julia. These were then expanded into Amy taking part in the actual murder itself. However, if we look at the facts, I feel these speak for themselves.

As previously stated, when Wallace went to work in India in 1902, his brother, Joseph Edwin, was already working as a printer for the British government in Singapore. Joseph returned to England on Monday 22 June 1909, arriving in London on the British Indian Steam Navigation Company ship SS *Jelunga* after sailing from Calcutta on 13 May. During the autumn of that same year, he married his childhood sweetheart, Amy Margaret Blackwell, in Dalton-in-Furness, Cumbria. After their marriage, the couple had moved to London, where their only child, Edwin Herbert Wallace, was born on 6 June 1911. Soon after, Joseph took his family back to the Malay States.

On 23 February 1929, whilst living in Kuala Lumpur, both Joseph and Amy were issued visas at Singapore. On 10 April that year, they sailed from Hong Kong on the Canadian Ocean Services ship *Empress of France*, arriving in Victoria, British Columbia, Canada, on 27 April 1929. Their ultimate destination was (as it ostensibly was on the rare occasions the couple visited England) The Schoolhouse, Watton Road, Ashill, Norfolk, England – the home of Amy's older sister, Mary Ann.[5] However, whilst in Canada, Joseph and Amy took a trip to Shelton, Mason County, Washington, USA, where they spent three weeks with another of Amy's sisters, Ellen Maud and her husband Horace Willows Skelsey.[6] At the time of Joseph and Amy's visit in 1929, the family were living at 12 Wynadotte Avenue, Shelton, Mason County, where Horace was a machinist for the railroad. On 17 May 1929, the couple left Montreal on the Anchor-Donaldson Line ship *Letitia*, arriving in Liverpool on 26 May 1929. It would appear from the records that both Joseph and Amy had every intention of returning to the Malay States after their visit to England. At the time of the murder, Edwin was 19 years old and was a medical student at Liverpool University. At the time of his parents' visit in 1929, he was almost 18. Given that it was only May when they arrived, it might be safe to assume Edwin's parents had remained in Liverpool to celebrate his 18th birthday on 11 June and spend some time with him before he began his studies in September. For some reason, possibly during the journey, or after their arrival, Amy decided not to return to the Malay States with Joseph. During the June of 1929, instead of making her way to Norfolk, she stayed at the Wallaces' for two weeks, sleeping in their front bedroom. After this, she moved in with relatives in the city until September 1929, when she moved into 83 Ullet Road with Edwin. This is given credence by the first entry in Wallace's diary to mention a 'Visit to Ullet Road' being on 3 November 1929. During the time of her arrival and moving into Ullet Road, Amy went on holiday with the Wallaces to Caemas Bay, Anglesey, Wales. These trips were usually taken at 'Rose Villa' during July. At the time of the murder, after Joseph had arrived in Liverpool, he rented a house at 31 Bentley Road, Princes Park, Liverpool. Amy and Edwin moved in with him.

In relation to the rumours concerning Wallace and Amy, the above details show that that the couple could not have had a long-term illicit relationship. They were not even in the same country for many years – let alone the same city. After Wallace's successful appeal, Wallace, Joseph and Amy all took a holiday to Broughton-in-Furness, staying at Lathom House. Upon Wallace's return to Wolverton Street, Joseph and Amy returned to Malay together, whilst Edwin – possibly due to the pressure, stress and unwanted attention he might have been receiving because of the case – changed university and went off to Glasgow, graduating in 1935. It would appear that Joseph and Amy remained in Malay until after Wallace's death on 26 February 1933. On 28 April 1933, Amy arrived in London after sailing from Yokohama, Singapore, on the P&O Line *Comorin*. Giving her last permanent address as Malay, she recorded her future permanent residence as 22 Union Street, Dalton-in-Furness – not only in her hometown, but also yards from her birthplace, 88 Chapel Street. Joseph Edwin Wallace died on 5 June 1950 whilst the couple were living at Mylnebeck House, Lake Road, Windermere, Westmoreland, England. Joseph left his whole estate – £10,134 12s and 7d (a modern-day equivalent of about £263,000) – to his wife, Amy Margaret Wallace. Joseph Edwin Wallace was a very intelligent and astute man; if there had been anything going on between his brother and his wife, why did he not only remain with her, but also leave her the whole of his fortune? This could quite easily have gone to their son Edwin. Amy died during the autumn of 1960, having returned to Dalton-in-Furness.

Add to this the strong possibility (as I will discuss later) that William Herbert Wallace may have been impotent, and an illicit relationship with anybody, let alone Amy Wallace, is extremely unlikely.

7

The Aftermath

The following morning, after a sleepless few hours, as Wallace made his way to a ten o'clock appointment at the Detective Office in Dale Street, the CID were already on their way to Anfield to begin door-to-door enquiries and scour the area around Wolverton Street in the hope of finding a murder weapon or blood-stained clothing. More detectives had been dispatched to track down all of the potential witnesses named in Wallace's statement, with Detective Sergeant Harry Bailey being given the thankless task of tracking down everyone in Liverpool with the name Qualtrough. As Wallace arrived at the Detective Office, at Atkinson's Garage, John Parkes was relating the night's disturbing events to his boss, William Atkinson:

> I don't think I told anyone that night. I told the sons and the father in the morning what I'd done … and how much Parry had given me – the five shillings. He'd given *me* the five shillings, but it really wasn't mine … it was the firm's money. He'd paid me, where he should have paid the boss. So, the boss said: 'Keep the five shillings.' He was a bit disturbed, but he says 'don't have anything to do with it.' When I told the sons, they didn't want anything to do with it, because they were being advised by their father. I told Mr Atkinson. I said: 'If Wallace is convicted, we'll have to come forward.' So he says, 'Aye, okay.'

Still exhausted after the events of the previous night and his prolonged detention at Anfield police station, Wallace entered the Detective Office resignedly and sat down, unaware that he wouldn't be leaving until twelve hours later. He began this interrogation by retracing his steps to Mossley Hill in search of R. M. Qualtrough and 25 Menlove Gardens East, trying his best to account for every person he had encountered on that journey. Besides the eventual length of his visit, what he also didn't know was that Superintendent Moore thought he had an ace up his sleeve. Earlier that morning, amongst the barrage of telephone calls received at the Detective Office concerning Julia's murder – in between the cranks, the busybodies and the pranksters – an anonymous male voice had proclaimed that the Wallaces had a maid with whom Wallace was having an affair. He implied that it didn't take a genius to figure out why Mrs Wallace had been murdered. Wallace denied the couple had ever had a maid. They had a charwoman who came on Wednesday mornings to help Mrs Wallace about the house; he didn't know her name, but knew that she lived somewhere in West Derby. Moore duly passed the task of locating the charwoman onto Inspector Gold and, at about 11 a.m., Moore and Gold left the Detective Office and headed toward Wolverton Street. As their car pulled up outside the front door of No. 29, Gold was surprised (and relieved, no doubt) to discover that the identity and location of the 'mystery woman' had already been solved. With it being a Wednesday morning, the charwoman had turned up for work and, upon being turned away by one of the uniformed officers in the house, had left her details: Sarah Jane Draper,[7] 38 Tollerton Road, West Derby. Gold was immediately dispatched to interview her. Mrs Draper had been estranged from her husband, James, for at least three years, when, upon the recommendation of a friend of the Wallaces – Alice Ann Jenkinson of 112 Moscow Drive, Stoneycroft – during May 1930, she had been employed by Julia as a charwoman. Wallace and the Jenkinsons had been friends since the Wallace family had move to Dalton-in-Furness in 1890 after Mr Wallace's life-threatening encounter with typhoid fever.[8]

Entering the Wallace home, Moore was greeted by Chief Constable Lionel Everett and Assistant Chief Constable Herbert Winstanley, who had both arrived earlier. Whilst outside the Wallace home, in the surrounding area, the police were busy searching for clues, inside No. 29 police activity was just as intense. Superintendent Moore and Chief Constable Everett went over the house with a fingerprint expert, but to no avail. They searched inside and outside the house, including the water tanks and the lavatory, and found nothing. Sometime between 11 a.m. and noon, William Henry Roberts, the City Analyst, and Professor MacFall arrived and went through the house looking for bloodstains. Roberts later estimated that Mrs Wallace had lost between ¾ of a pint and 1¼ pints of blood.

At some time between 1 and 2 p.m., MacFall had returned to the Princes Dock Mortuary and – Amy Wallace having already identified Julia's remains that morning – along with Police Surgeon Hugh Pierce, he set about performing a post-mortem examination on the body. In his autopsy report, MacFall concluded that Julia was a 'woman about 55 years', 5 feet ¾ inches tall and slightly built. Though there were no signs of rape, and no signs of violence on her trunk and limbs, there was a small, recent bruise on the inside of her left upper arm. Julia's hair, being 'matted with blood and brain tissue', was shaved off, whereupon he noted that 2 inches above her left cheekbone was 'a large lacerated wound 2" x 3" from which brain and bone were protruding'. At the left side of the back of Julia's head were ten diagonal wounds that he considered to have been incised. Removing Julia's scalp, he noted her skull at the front, left-hand side, beneath the open wound, had been 'driven into the front of the brain'. The ten diagonal wounds at the back of her head had caused the skull to have been 'driven in and broken to pieces'. These wounds were so violent as to have smashed the left side and left base of Julia's skull and practically destroyed the cerebellum at the base of Julia's brain:

> The appearance was as if a terrific force with a large surface had driven in the scalp, bursting it in parallel lines, with the appearance of several incised wounds, but the edges of these wounds were not sharp.

Concerning the stomach contents, he noted:

The stomach contained about four ounces of semi fluid food consisting of currants, raisins and unmasticated lumps of carbohydrate.

MacFall also noted that Julia was

> lightly built, prominent abdomen … The lungs, heart, kidney and spleen were normal … The small bowel was normal, the caecum ascending and transverse colon were enormously and chronically distended (typical constipation bowel) … The right ovary normal, left ovary 3½ by 2½ fibroid.

What MacFall diagnosed as 'typical constipation bowel' may well have been what we now term Ogilvie's Syndrome. This is a clinical disorder usually found in elderly people over sixty years old, giving the signs, symptoms and appearance of an acute large bowel obstruction. If the expanded colon is not deflated, the patient risks perforation, peritonitis and death. The symptoms of Ogilvie's Syndrome are abdominal pain, nausea, vomiting and fever; physical phenomena are abdominal distension, abdominal tenderness and bowel sounds. Could this explain Julia's bouts of illness? Perhaps her bouts of flu and gastritis (inflammation of the stomach) had been misdiagnosed.

During that afternoon, after interviewing her at her home, Inspector Gold brought Sarah Jane Draper back to 29 Wolverton Street to see if she could identify anything missing, out of place or additional in the house. Though she had not been to the house for a fortnight because of the death of her estranged husband, in touring the house with Gold, Mrs Draper made the following observations:

> There used to be two small steel pokers in the kitchen fireplace, one was about 1 foot long, that is here now, the other was about 9 inches, this one is missing, it had a small knob on it. There was a straight piece of iron kept in the parlour fireplace, it was about 1 foot long and about as thick as an ordinary candle, that is missing; last seen on January 7th. I used to clean the front bedroom and the bed was always kept made with blankets, sheets and pillows. Mrs Wallace use to have her hats spread out on it, I have never seen the bed in the state it is now. As far as I know, there was nothing the matter with the lock on the front door of 29 Wolverton Street. The catch on the back kitchen door was defective. When the knob was turned either from the inside or the outside, it would not bring the bolt back from the lock socket. This happened pretty regularly and on many occasions, I have had to ask Mrs Wallace to open the door for me and she used to do it by gripping the spindle close to the door. There did not seem to be any spring in the lock.

Before leaving Wolverton Street that night, Herbert Gold went through the house and gathered together numerous items of evidence to be examined by the City Analyst. At Wallace's trial, Edward Hemmerde asked Mrs Draper about the purpose of the iron bar:

> *Do you know what it was used for?* For cleaning under the gas fire.
> *I suppose cigarette ends and things get in?* Yes, and spent matches.

Mrs Draper told the court that the iron bar had been in that position ever since she had begun cleaning for the Wallaces, nine months previously. If the 12-inch iron bar had been by the side of the fireplace in the parlour for at least nine months, how did Wallace never notice it? By Mrs Draper's own evidence, she had used it to clear away cigarette ends and matches – more than likely to have been thrown there by Wallace when he and Julia were in the parlour playing music. How would it be possible not to have noticed something so conspicuous and distinctly out of place? If Mrs Draper did not bring it into the house and Wallace denied knowing even of its existence, then Julia must have introduced it herself. Where would Julia have discovered such an item?

That afternoon, it would appear that Wallace went to Joseph Crewe's office at 2 Great Nelson Street, off Byrom Street, and paid in his collection money from the previous week. Edwin Wallace accompanied him:

> Later, he also said 'If you get as good a partner in life as I had, you will do well'. These last mentioned words were said to me when he and I were walking back from the office of his Superintendent, near Byrom Street, on Thursday of that week I think [it was, in fact, the Wednesday]. I went with him on that occasion so as to keep him company and help him as much as possible.

Not 24 hours previously, this man had, apparently, stumbled upon the shattered and bloody body of his wife in his blood-drenched parlour; had been questioned until at least 4 a.m. that morning; had apparently not slept even when he had the opportunity; had arrived at Police Headquarters at 10 a.m. for more questioning; and yet, he had had the peace of mind to write out a cheque for the amount owing to his company from, presumably, his own bank account, and take it down to his superintendent's office to pay it in.

In attempting to denounce the theory that Julia's murder was a robbery gone wrong, Hemmerde was questioning Wallace's superintendent at the Prudential, Joseph Crewe, about the amounts of money collected by Wallace on his rounds and when he paid them in. In answering these questions, Crewe revealed another mystery concerning the collection money that was 'stolen' from Wallace's cash box:

> MR JUSTICE WRIGHT: What about 19th January?
> MR CREWE: The 19th January only £10 11s 0d was paid in, for the simple reason either the police or someone else had taken the cash and the police have a portion of that cash yet.
> MR HEMMERDE: What makes you say that?
> MR CREWE: Well, I understand the police have at least £18 cash and I have asked for it.
> MR HEMMERDE: What makes you say that; where did you get it from?
> MR CREWE: Because they took, it and I have asked for it.
> MR JUSTICE WRIGHT: When was the £10 11s 0d paid in? Was it paid in, in cash?
> MR CREWE: No, the £10 11s 0d was paid in on the Thursday (sic), the 21st January.
> MR HEMMERDE: Paid in by whom?
> MR CREWE: By Mr Wallace.

Later on in the trial, upon being questioned by Roland Oliver as to the amount taken in by Wallace during the week including 20 January, Wallace gave the following response:

> *On this particular week in which January 20th came, by January 20th how much money had you collected? Can you tell without a book?* I can give you an approximate amount. I cannot say to a penny, but I think about £14.

To ascertain how there came to be only £4 in the cash box, Oliver asked:

> *What had you done with regard to paying out, if anything?* As near as I can remember, I must have paid out something like £10 10s in sickness benefit out of what I had collected up to that time.
>
> *That is what you said. Out of the £14 you collected, you had paid away £10 10s which would leave you some £4 in cash?* Yes.

If this is the case, upon paying in that week's collection money on 21 January, Wallace should have paid in only £4; yet, according to Crewe, it should have been about £28 11s 0d – of which Wallace paid £10 11s 0d in by cheque. The fact that he paid the money in on Wednesday 21 January and not Thursday the 22nd is borne out by the paying-in accounts of the Prudential Assurance Company requested from the Prudential by Hector Munro.

That evening, having gained permission to leave the Detective Office for a short time, at 6.30 p.m. Wallace was at Lime Street station with Amy and Edwin Wallace, awaiting the arrival from Yorkshire of Julia's sister, Amy Dennis. Amy Dennis was to stay at Ullet Road with Amy and Edwin. Upon her arrival, a discussion ensued as to what Wallace was to do that night with regard to sleeping arrangements, the option being left open to him. During this meeting, Edwin Wallace described his uncle as being 'very deeply upset and seemed distraught'. At some point, his uncle told him, 'What a good friend I've lost.'

With Wallace gaining permission to leave the Detective Office in order for him to meet Amy Dennis off the train at Lime Street station, and Amy Wallace and her son already waiting at the station when Wallace arrived, all had to have known that Julia's sister was on her way. If, as the records appear to show, the Wallaces had had no contact with Julia's siblings since the time of their marriage, how could she have known of Julia's death only a day after the tragedy? Give that it was less than 24 hours after Wallace had found Julia's body, this rules out Wallace having sent a letter. One can only assume that she had to have received a telegram or telephone call from either Wallace, after being taken to Anfield police station the night before at around 11.40 p.m. (though I feel, under those circumstances, this is most unlikely), by Wallace on his way to the Detective Office that morning or, most likely, by Amy Wallace early that morning (Wallace may have asked her before he went on his way to the Detective Office). As stated above, Edwin Wallace saw his uncle during that afternoon and accompanied him to Crewe's office in Great Nelson Street. This may have been when he told Wallace the arrangements his mother had made to meet with Amy Dennis at 6.30 p.m. at Lime Street station. In order to accomplish this, Wallace had to either have had an address or telephone number for Amy Dennis.

Amy Dennis was running a guesthouse at 4 Denmark Terrace, Brighton, at this time (possibly with her sister Rhoda, who was also resident in Brighton at that time), so one presumes she would have had a telephone. According to Roger Wilkes, Amy was arriving at Lime Street station on a train from Harrogate. This information probably came from a statement given to Hector Munro by Edwin Wallace in which he states, 'At about 6.30 I and my mother were at Lime Street Station, to meet a relative coming from Yorkshire, a Miss Amy Dennis, one of my aunt Julia's sisters.' Wilkes must have assumed she would be coming from Harrogate, it being Wallace and Julia's last residence whilst in Yorkshire. The only other surviving member of Julia's siblings living in Yorkshire was her brother, George Smith Dennis, who was living at 40 Alfred Street, Redcar, Cleveland, North Yorkshire. Once Amy Dennis was contacted with the horrific news, she may have informed her sister Rhoda of the tragedy. With Rhoda staying in Brighton to manage the guesthouse, Amy travelled to Cleveland to see her brother. From Cleveland, she took a train to Liverpool. It would, of course, have to be assumed that the telegram or call to Amy Dennis had to have been very early in the morning on the day after the murder. As Wallace and Amy Wallace did not have telephones of their own, Amy Dennis had to have either have sent a telegram or have asked Amy Wallace to telephone her back at some point that day to confirm the arrangements she had made. How else would they have known to meet her at Lime Street station at 6.30 p.m? At the age of 67, this had to have been a very trying day for Amy Dennis.

At around 6.45 p.m., as Wallace was making his way back to the Detective Office, 14-year-old Douglas Metcalf, the Wallaces' morning paperboy, was doing his evening paper round in Richmond Park with his friend and colleague at Yates's newsagents, Harold Jones (who had finished his paper round earlier), when he bumped into 13-year-old Elsie Wright at the corner of Richmond Park and Breck Road. Elsie delivered milk for Close's Dairy in nearby Sedley Street, owned by the father of Alan Croxton Close, the young man who had delivered milk to the Wallaces' house the previous night. The three immediately began discussing the terrible event at 29 Wolverton Street, and Wright told the boys that she had been talking to Alan Close earlier that evening in the dairy when he told her that he had seen Mrs Wallace at 6.45 p.m. when he had delivered her milk the previous night. Metcalf pointed out that the local papers were saying that the last person to see Julia was the bread boy, Neil Norbury, at 4.30 p.m., and Close should go and tell the police he had seen Julia at 6.45 p.m. At this point, Metcalf spotted Kenneth Campbell Caird (son of Wallace's grocer friend James Caird) en route to the local library and shouted to him. Caird crossed the road and joined the discussion. Metcalf asked him, 'Close saw Mrs Wallace at quarter to seven and he wouldn't tell the police, and wouldn't you go and tell them if it was you?' Caird said he would. Just then, Alan Close himself wandered down Richmond Park on his way to meet with Elsie Wright to take her through the entry into Sedley Street (it being dark by this time and there being no lamp in the entry). He joined the gathering. Metcalf immediately queried him.

'Hey, Alan. What time did you see Mrs Wallace last night?'

'Well, when I took the milk it was quarter to seven.'

'What did she say to you?'

'She told me I had a bad cough and I'd better hurry up home, and she said she had a bad cough.'

'Well, the police ought to hear that, because in the papers it said that Mr Wallace went out at quarter past six, and if you saw her at quarter to seven, people couldn't think Mr Wallace done it.'

Close, however, was reluctant to go – appearing to treat the whole thing with some levity. Kenneth Caird told him he was a fool for not going, Metcalf telling him, 'I'd go if I were you, because that would help the police out a lot.' Metcalf, Caird and Wright offered to accompany Close to 29 Wolverton Street. Close agreed and the four children, like the Baker Street Irregulars, trooped off down the passage to Wolverton Street with Close pushing his thumbs under the armholes of his waistcoat, proclaiming, 'I'm the missing link – I'm the missing link!' Arriving at the Wallaces' front door, two plainclothes police officers responded to their knock. Close and Elsie Wright had already been to the house earlier that night to see if any milk was needed (and had been told it wasn't), so when the door was opened, one of the officers exclaimed, 'What; you back again!' Close told the officer, 'I saw Mrs Wallace at quarter to seven last night', and was taken into the house (at this point, a makeshift incident room), whilst the others waited on the doorstep.

According to Jonathan Goodman, the news about Alan Close's statement was not well received when it was phoned through to police headquarters. At the time, Superintendent Moore was in conference with other officers discussing the case. Inspector Gold left the meeting and went to another office to ask Wallace if he remembered the milk boy calling at the house. 'I can't say that I can remember the milk boy calling,' Wallace answered. 'He may possibly have called while I was upstairs, getting ready to leave the house – if so, I might not have heard his knock.' Meanwhile, Hubert Moore was already on the phone talking to MacFall. MacFall was nonplussed: 'I don't believe it; I still say the death occurred no later than six o'clock!' Moore probably thought that, on only the second day of the investigation, having already got to grips with his most important case to date, this little titbit brought him right back to square one. If MacFall was right, Wallace was innocent; he had stated that he had not returned home until 6.05 p.m. If Alan Close was right, Wallace was innocent; he had stated that he had not left home until 6.45 p.m. Moore dismissed this vital evidence with a brusque 'The milk boy is mistaken!'

The children did not see Alan Close until later the following night, when, according to Harold Jones, Close had been told by the police not to discuss the case with his friends. Subsequently, it was not until they read about it in the local paper, or were at the actual trial, that they learnt that Close had changed the time he had told them he had seen Julia from 6.45 p.m. to 6.31 p.m. However, in an important part of Douglas Metcalf's statement regarding the night of the murder, he relates:

I was in the Parochial Hall in Richmond Park giving Mr Davies, the Caretaker, a paper and there was a Lantern Lecture going on. I asked one of the men the time, as I wanted to go to a football match and he said it was twenty-five to seven. I then had to go across to Campbell's Dance Hall in Richmond Park and when I came out of there, I talked to some boys for a very short time, and then walked down the passage into Wolverton Street. I had just crossed over to 23 Wolverton Street when I saw a boy named Allison Wildman walking down the entry towards Redbourn Street.

James Allison Wildman was 16 years old and working for a haulage firm at Liverpool's Canada dock. In his spare time he delivered newspapers for his uncle, who had a shop at 156 Lower Breck Road (William Wildman's shop was at the corner of Lower Breck Road and Breckside Park, on the next corner from Dr Dunlop's surgery on the corner of Lower Breck Road and Suburban Road). Following this up, Hector Munro arrived on the doorstep of Allison Wildman's house (5 Twickenham Street, Anfield) and took a statement from the boy:

> I start work about 6.20 in the evening and first deliver at No's 11, 19, 21 and 28 Suburban Road, 42 Winchester Road, 34 Clarendon Road, 52 and 48 Claude Road and then go back to the shop, unpack more newspapers, and start on my second round on which the route is as follows: Hanwell Street, Taplow Street, by two entries to Richmond Park, along Richmond Park, down the entry by Campbell's Dancing Rooms into Wolverton Street and then along Wolverton Street where I deliver papers at No's 28, 27, 22, 20 and 18. There is an entry into Wolverton Street which I go down into Redford Street. Then I follow an entry into Richmond Park, go down Richmond Park and right along Richmond Park into Lower Breck Road.
>
> I deliver four papers in Hanwell Street, one in Taplow Street and two Richmond Park. I always glance at the Holy Trinity Church Clock in passing. When I passed on the evening of 20th January, it was twenty-five minutes to seven. Having passed Holy Trinity, it takes me about two minutes to get into Wolverton Street. I remember the time quite clearly, because when I read of the murder at 29 Wolverton Street next morning I thought over what time I had passed Holy Trinity.
>
> When I delivered the paper at 27 Wolverton Street, it would be about twenty-two or twenty-three minutes to seven. The door of No. 29 Wolverton Street was wide open and a milk boy was standing on the top step with two or three cans in his hand. He had a Collegiate School Cap on his head.
>
> When I left No. 27 Wolverton Street, the milk boy was still standing there.

Quite effectively, these two statements combined confirm that what Alan Close had originally purported to be the time he had delivered milk to 29 Wolverton Street, about 6.45 p.m., was correct. James Allison Wildman, according to his description of the route he took on his newspaper round, would have emerged from Tapwell Street opposite Holy Trinity church, where he could easily see the illuminated clock face (checked by the police at the time, the clock proved to have been correct). When Douglas Metcalf left the Parish Hall at 6.35 p.m., he crossed Richmond Park and took the same route into Wolverton Street as did Wildman – through the entry next to Campbell's Dance Hall. This brought them to the bottom of Wolverton Street, five doors away from No. 29, which would be on the right. Wildman said he delivered five newspapers in Wolverton Street, his last one being delivered to No. 18, two doors away from the entry on the left of Wolverton Street where Metcalf spotted him as he made his way to Redford Street.

Fifty years later, being interviewed for Roger Wilkes's radio documentary *Who Killed Julia?*, James Allison Wildman recalled:

It was only the following evening when I went up to the church club and started talking to Dougie Metcalf, and the other people in the club about the murder, that I happened to mention to Metcalf that I had seen Alan Close on the steps of 29 and, although Alan Close had said the time was 6.30, I knew it was seven minutes later than that, because I had seen the clock at Holy Trinity Church. Alan Close, the following day, went down to the solicitors, Herbert J. Davis, Berthen and Munro, and told them what I had told him and they came up in great haste to interview me, and the three of them – the three solicitors – walked with me around my paper round and timed everything. When they had satisfied themselves that the time that I had stated was perfectly correct and they had timed the journey for themselves, they then informed the police of my evidence, and an Inspector Gold came from the police and interviewed me and I told him the same thing – that the time was 23 minutes to 7 when Alan Close was standing on the steps of 29.

Why then, would Alan Close change the time he had originally stated, to a time nine minutes earlier? James Allison Wildman died in Liverpool in November 2005.

Also interviewed for Roger Wilkes's radio documentary, Douglas Metcalf gave the following statement:

It was only later I discovered that Alan [Close] had been persuaded by the police to change the time from a quarter to seven to twenty-five to seven … Alan changed his mind about the time and this was because, according to Alan, that when he went into the house, police started questioning him about the correct time, and Alan said, 'It was about a quarter to seven.' … several comments were passed by the police, and they said, 'Well, if you're not sure that it was quarter to seven, it could have been twenty-five to seven', and Alan said that he changed his mind and made it twenty-five to seven. This is what Alan told me later on.'

Douglas Metcalf died in Liverpool in April 1993 aged 75.

Unfortunately, at the time of the Radio City interviews, Kenneth Campbell Caird was unavailable and Alan Croxton Close had died during the early hours of 18/19 June 1940, aged only 23. Close was a Sergeant Pilot in the RAF – a member of 23 Squadron. On the fateful night, he was piloting a Blenheim Mk I fighter-bomber on night patrol when he engaged in combat with a Dornier 17 bomber piloted by Major Dietrich von Massenbach, Kommandeur of Luftwaffe bomber unit II/KG4. Close's plane was shot down. Massenbach was later shot down over Norfolk by another member of Close's squadron, Flight Lieutenant Raymond Myles Beacham Duke-Woolley. Close had married Daphne E. Warren in March 1940 (just three months before his death). The couple had met whilst on a visit to Llandudno, North Wales. Daphne (whose father, William Warren, had served in the Royal Flying Corps in the First World War) went on to join the Women's Auxiliary Air Force as a Corporal Plotter at Fighter Command. She later remarried and had two children and two grandchildren. Kenneth Campbell Caird died in 1988 in Rhuddlan, North Wales.

It was not until 18 February that Hector Munro took a statement from James Allison Wildman – the day before Wallace's committal trial was to begin. For some reason, Wildman was never asked to appear in that court to refute Alan Close's amended assertion that he saw Mrs Wallace alive at 6.31 p.m.

Before Wallace left the CID office at 10 p.m. on Wednesday 21 January, he had obtained permission to spend the rest of the night at 29 Wolverton Street. With Amy Dennis staying at Amy Wallace's house in Ullet Road, there was most likely no room. There were only two bedrooms: Amy Wallace had her own room, as did her son. Whilst Wallace was staying there, he had been ensconced on the settee. The arrangements for Amy Dennis were most likely that she take Edwin's room, whilst he slept on the settee. According to both Amy and Edwin Wallace, Wallace's sleeping arrangements for that night were left up to Wallace himself. Amy Wallace stated:

> The day afterwards, I think he had to go to the police. He did not come back to us at all that day. We expected him back later that night, but he did not arrive (we are not on the telephone).

Edwin Wallace said that

> as we have only two bedrooms, there was a discussion as to how everybody would be put up that night. Ultimately, it was left to my uncle to decide whether he would come to us that night ... My uncle did not come back to us on the Wednesday of the week although we really expected him notwithstanding for it had been left indefinite.

According to Wallace, he was driven to Wolverton Street by Inspector Gold and Sergeant Bailey. After seeing them off, he was left in the house alone.

Thursday 22 January 1931

Being left in his house alone for that single night appears to have had a dramatic effect upon Wallace. Despite many items from the house having been taken by Gold earlier that day (including pictures, photographs, Wallace's violin, the cushion from the chair it was resting on, the hearthrug and the toilet pan), the parlour still held both the essence of Julia and the nightmare that had brought her life to an end so violently, both indecently intertwined. The remnants of blood clots stained the floor close to where Julia would sit to play her piano, which was also flecked with her blood.

At around 10.45 a.m. the following morning Wallace was back at the Detective Office, sitting in front of Inspector Gold: 'He said to me, "I think I have some important information for you." He then related to me a statement which I afterwards took down in writing.' Contrary to the end of his first police statement, where, approximately 36 hours earlier, he said 'I have no suspicion of anyone', Wallace made this statement:

Dale Street Detective Office 22/1/31.
William Herbert Wallace further states:

Mr Gordon R. Parry [*sic*], of Derwent Road, Stoneycroft, is a friend of my late wife and myself. He is now an agent for the Gresham Insurance Coy [*sic*]. But I'm not quite sure of the company.

He was employed by the Prudential up to about 12 or 15 months ago, and he then resigned to improve his position. Although nothing was known officially to the company detrimental to his financial affairs, it was known that he had collected premiums which he did not pay in and his Supt Mr Crewe, of Green Lane, Allerton, told me that he went to Parry's parents who paid about £30 to cover the deficiency. Mr Crewe's office is at 2, Great Nelson Street. Parry is a single man about 22 years of age. I have known him about three years and he was with my company about two years. I was ill with Bronchitis in December in 1928 and Parry did part of collecting for about two or three days a week for about three weeks. I discovered slight discrepancies and I spoke to him about it. He was short of small amounts when paying in and he had not entered all the amounts collected in the book. When I spoke to him he said it was an oversight and that he was sorry and he put the matter right. Previous to Parry doing my work he had called at my house once on business and left a letter for me which he wrote in my front room. I was not in at the time but my wife let him in. While he was doing my work in Dec 1928 he called very frequently to see me about business, and he was well acquainted with our domestic arrangements. He had been in the parlour and kitchen frequently and had been upstairs in the middle bedroom a number of times to see me while I was in bed. I do not think he called to see me after I resumed duty in Jan 1929, but if he had have called my wife would have had no hesitation in admitting him. I have often seen him since he has been working for his new company and have spoken to him. About last November I was in the City Café one evening, I think it was on a Thursday, playing chess, and I saw Parry there. He was not playing chess. He was by himself walking across the room. I said, 'Good evening' and he returned my greeting. I think that was the last time I saw him. He is a member of an Amateur Dramatic Society which holds its meetings at the City Café all Thursday evenings. I do not think he drinks. He is engaged to a Miss Lloyd, 7 Missouri Road, Clubmoor. He would be on a weekly salary from his company plus commission on business and his earnings would be about £4 per week.

There was another man named Marsden who also did part of the work for me while I was ill in Dec 1928. I do not know his address. He was an agent for the Prudential Coy for two or three years and had left before he did my work. I gave him the job because he was out of work. Parry recommended him. I have heard that Marsden left the Prudential on account of financial irregularities. While he was working for me he often came to my house to see me on business. He also knew the interior arrangements of my house. I have seen Marsden several times since he worked for me. I do not know if he is working now and I do not know anything about his private affairs. If he had called at my house my wife would have asked him in. Both Parry and Marsden knew the arrangements of my business with regard the system of paying in money collected to the Head Office, Dale Street. There is a definite order of the company's that money must be paid in on Wednesday's but this is not strictly enforced and I paid in on Thursday usually. I have had the cash-box from which the money was stolen for about 16 years. I always put the company's money in that box, and it is always kept on the top of the bookcase in the kitchen during the daytime. At night I always took it upstairs to my bedroom. Parry and Marsden know I kept the money in the box because while they worked for me I always put the money into it when they called to pay over to me their collections. They had both seen me take it down and put it back to the top of the bookcase in the kitchen often. Marsden is about 28 years of age, about 5 foot 6/7 inches, brown hair, and fairly well dressed. Parry is about 5 ft 10 ins, slimmish build, dark hair, rather foppish appearance, well dressed and wears spats, very plausible.

Supt Crewe, his assistant, Mr Wood, 26 Ellersley Road, Mr J. Bamber, Ass Supt, 43 Kingfield Road, Orrel Park, employees of the coy would be admitted by my wife without hesitation if they called. There are personal friends of ours who would also be admitted if they called. They are Mr F. W. Jenkinson, his son Frederick, 20 years? [sic], his daughter 16, and his wife, they live at 112 Moscow Drive. Mr James Caird, 3 Letchworth Street Anfield, his wife and family. He has two grown up sons. Mr Davis, music teacher of Queens Drive, Walton, who is teaching me the violin. Mr Hayes, my tailor of Breck Road.

I forgot to mention that I believe Mr Parry owns a motor car or has the use of one, because I was talking to him about Xmas time in Missouri Road and he had a car then which he was driving. He gave me one of his Company's calendars.

When I left the house at 6.45 p.m. on Tuesday night last my wife came down the backyard with me as far as the yard door, she closed the yard door. I do not remember hearing her bolt it. On Monday night, the 19th inst I left home about 7.15 p.m. to go to the chess club. I got there about 7.45 p.m. and started to play a game of chess with a man whose name I think is McCarthy, but I am not sure of him and I do not know his business. He is a member of the club. We had been playing for about ten minutes when Capt Beattie came to me and told me there had been a telephone message for me from a Mr Qualtrough asking me to go and see him at 25 Menlove Gardens East at 7.30 p.m. on Tuesday the 21st [sic] inst on a matter of business. Capt Beattie had the name Qualtrough and the address 25 Menlove Gardens East, and the time and date of the appointment written on an envelope and I copied it into my diary. Mr Caird was present and we all discussed the best way to get to Menlove Gardens. When I left home on Monday night to go to the chess club I think I walked along Richmond Park to Breck Road and then up Belmont Road, where I boarded a tramcar and got off at the corner of Lord Street and North John Street.

When I was at Allerton looking for the address 25 Menlove Gardens East in addition to the people I have already mentioned I enquired from a woman in Menlove Gardens North. She came out of a house near the end by Menlove Gardens West. She told me it might be further up in continuation of Menlove Gardens West. I went along as suggested by her and came to a crossroad, I think it was Dudley Road, and I met a young man about 25 years, tall and fair, and I enquired from him but he could not inform me. I walked back down the West Gardens to the South Gardens and found all even numbers. I did not knock and came out on to Menlove Avenue itself, when I saw a man waiting for a tram by a stop where there was a shelter. I went up to him and asked him if he could tell me where Menlove Gardens East was, and he said he was a stranger and did not know. I think these are all the people I spoke to that night at Allerton.

When I got back home and after getting into the house and making the discovery of my wife's death, Mr Johnston went for the Doctor and Police. Mrs Johnston and I stayed in and sometime after a knock came to the front door. I answered it and it was thus I found that the front door was bolted. The safety catch was not on the latch lock. I opened the door and admitted the Constable. That was the first time I went to the front door after getting into the house.

When I left my house at 6.45 p.m. my wife was sitting in the kitchen, that is, when I had got my hat and coat on ready to go, and as I have already said, she came down the yard with me. The tea things were still on the table. When I got back the table had been cleared of the tea things.

There is a Mr Thomas, a member of the chess club and a Mr Stan Young who used to be an employee of our Coy, who would be admitted by my wife if they called. I do not know their addresses. My wife had no friends unknown to me as far as I know. I have now found by the calendar that Mr Parry's employers are The Standard Life Assurance Coy, whose head office is at 3, George Street, Edinburgh.

If we examine this statement closely, it would appear to be in three separate parts. The first part, an in-depth account of his relationship with (and knowledge of) Richard Gordon Parry and a 'mystery man' named Marsden, can only be interpreted as Wallace voicing his opinion as to their possible culpability. The second part is a quick list of thirteen people – work colleagues and personal friends – who Julia would allow into the house in his absence (lacking the depth of detail given to Parry and Marsden), with an addendum that he now remembered that Parry had the use of a car. The third part is a clarification of his alibi on the night of the murder, this time with two addendums – the first naming two more of his colleagues whom Julia would allow into the house in his absence, the second a declaration that could only have been included if the statement had been put together over at least two separate days and not a single sitting at the Detective Office: 'I have now found by the calendar that Mr Parry's employers are The Standard Life Assurance Company, whose head office is at 3, George Street, Edinburgh.' In order to have found the calendar, he would have had to have returned to Wolverton Street and looked for it. According to the record, he did not do this until the following day, Friday 23 January.

This statement is over 1,600 words long, half of which relate to Parry and Marsden. The police not having found any signs of forced entry at 29 Wolverton Street, part of the line of questioning the day after the murder, besides gaining Wallace's opinions as to who might have called after his departure, would naturally have been to gain his opinions as to whom Julia would have allowed into the house in his absence. In staying overnight at Wolverton

Street, had this given Wallace the opportunity to contemplate his answer to this latter line of questioning? His saying to Gold the following morning, 'I have some important information for you', would appear to confirm this – especially with regard to Parry and Marsden. Whatever the reason, after that night he was very eager to point the police in the direction of these two men – a little overeager, it could be said. On the whole, the part of his statement dealing with Parry and Marsden is extremely informative regarding Parry, though very scant regarding Marsden. In fact, Wallace makes him out to be almost a stranger to him. Wallace apparently knew only Marsden's surname, his approximate age, his hair colour and his approximate height. Wallace maintains that he does not know where Marsden lives, nor has any information regarding his personal life. In saying that it was on Parry's recommendation that he gave Marsden work, he immediately shifts any blame – should it be found that Marsden was the culprit – over to Parry, by implying that in questioning Parry they will gain more information on Marsden. His information concerning Parry, though very thorough, still implies there is some distance between them. He does not now know where he lives nor works – he gives the wrong address in both cases. There is, however, enough information concerning Parry to save the police having to dig too deeply in order to find him. Not only that, in revealing Parry and Marsden's 'unreliability' Wallace has even supplied the police with a line of questioning for them to pursue. Was this part of his reasoning in giving this statement – to reveal his knowledge of Parry, whilst distancing himself almost entirely from Marsden?

At the Assize trial, Roland Oliver had referred Wallace to the making of his second statement:

> *Before you gave the statement, which is Exhibit 44, in which you mentioned the names of people who might have done this, had you been pressed by Inspector Gold to give the names of people who could possibly have done it by the questions he asked you on the night of the 21st?* Yes. The questions were put to me in such a way that I felt that I had to give the names of people. It was put to me something like this: 'As near as you can remember would your wife admit anybody to the house?' I agreed she might, and he said: 'Can you tell me the names of anybody she would admit?', and I gave him the names of quite a number of people that my wife would know and would admit at night.

Here, Oliver's question gives the impression that Wallace had given a statement to Inspector Gold on the night of Wednesday 21 January. Wallace, however, had given no written statement during that day, nor on that night. He had given a statement on the night of 20/21 January after being taken from Wolverton Street to Anfield police station. His second statement would not be until Thursday 22 January – effectively two days after his first. There is no evidence to show what Wallace was questioned about after his arrival at the Dale Street Detective Office on the morning of 21 January or for the rest of that day. Oliver had to have been referring to Wallace's first statement, taken on the night of the murder, within which Wallace simply says 'I have no suspicion of anyone'. Wallace's reply to Oliver's question gives the impression that, upon being asked by Gold, during the taking of this statement, for the names of people Julia would admit into the house, Wallace had simply given a 'shopping list' of names. As has been seen, this was not the case. Wallace had volunteered this information on the morning of 22 January (after spending the previous night at 29 Wolverton Street) with no coercion from anybody, announcing it with 'I think I have some important information for you'. Upon providing Gold with this information, why had he not given a simple list of people? As can be seen in Wallace's second statement, he went into an unwarranted amount of damning detail regarding Parry, then coupled him with a 'mysterious' man named Marsden.

If it was the case that Wallace masterminded the death of his wife and Marsden and Parry were coerced by him into assisting in his diabolical plan, a major question arises: why would he have pointed the police in their direction in this second statement, given only 36 hours after the murder? The list of all people who might call to his house in his absence and be allowed in by Julia had to have contained (as it did), as well as friends, Wallace's colleagues at the Prudential – one of whom was Richard Gordon Parry. As will be seen, according to Parry's own statement, he had been to the house on several occasions prior to December 1928 and (despite Wallace's statement to the contrary) on several occasions after, under orders from Prudential Superintendent Joseph Crewe. It was known by the Prudential that Parry was untrustworthy and, though Wallace had been told this, Parry had assisted him when he was ill. Crewe might have told police so himself had he been asked; Parry would have been on that list anyway. As police invariably do to this day, all people named on such a list would have been subject to scrutiny as to their character and background. Parry is the weakest link; had Wallace not told the police of Parry's visits to the house and of his knowledge of Parry's misdemeanours, this would have raised immediate suspicions and the police would have started digging – and may have dug too deeply. In laying his cards on the table concerning Parry, Wallace was, in fact, allaying suspicion and directing the police enquiry into this matter. Similar reasoning might also apply to his reference to Marsden. If his name had been brought up, possibly by someone at the Prudential, as also having been untrustworthy and having been in association with both Parry (there had to have been some degree of association as, according to Wallace, it was Parry who recommended Marsden to assist when he was ill) and Wallace, in not telling the police, this would indubitably have aroused suspicion. It has to be remembered that at the time Wallace gave the police his second statement they had been properly investigating the case for only a single day. Their evidence and suspicions were weak – possibly non-existent. Hopefully, after eliminating Parry and Marsden from their inquiries so early in the investigation, the police would direct all their efforts elsewhere and the two men would soon be forgotten.

Regarding the information given about Parry and Marsden, Wallace distances himself from Parry by giving the impression that, whilst he knows Parry well, he did not know him well enough to ever have known his address (Wallace states this as being Derwent Road, Stoneycroft, when Parry actually lived at 7 Woburn Hill, Stoneycroft) or what his present employment was. However, in stating 'He is engaged to a Miss Lloyd, 7 Missouri Road Clubmoor', Wallace seems to want to make absolutely certain the police speak to the right man. Wallace, on the other hand, essentially dissociates himself completely from Marsden – giving the impression he knows him only by sight. Yet, in closely associating this mystery man with Parry, Wallace is giving a clear indication to the police that there is a more involved relationship between them. Had things not gone to plan and the police arrested Parry and

Marsden, Wallace most likely knew that the 'foppish' and immature Parry would crack and bring Marsden down with him. It is likely he also knew that both Parry and Marsden would undoubtedly implicate him and reveal the whole sordid plot to the police. Had this been the case, Wallace had already catered for this eventuality. The crime scene had been made to appear to be a robbery gone wrong.

In his second statement, Wallace had seemingly hedged his bets by highlighting the fact that both Parry and Marsden were ex-Prudential agents. Each, after having worked on Wallace's round when he was ill, would have a working knowledge of his business practice and how much it accrued. Each had access to his home and knew where his collection money was kept. Each would be allowed into the house by Julia in his absence. Most importantly, Wallace had highlighted the fact that each had 'irregularities' in their collection monies whilst working at the Prudential, underlining them as possible criminal types. Had Parry and Marsden claimed that they had carried out this crime because Wallace had coerced them into it, the police would have had only the word of two suspects in a murder case who might soon be facing a death sentence and therefore were likely to say anything to assist their case. It would be their word against that of a highly educated man of impeccable reputation and character who, as was the case, would have any number of respectable witnesses to confirm this. And added to this is the fact that, for both 19 and 20 January, Wallace had (what he considered to be) an unshakeable alibi. He knew that Parry could not have had an alibi for the time of the telephone call to the City Café (as he was making the call) and Marsden could not have had an alibi for the time of the murder (as he was at Wolverton Street murdering Julia) so why should police even consider Wallace a suspect? He may even have been hoping to use the same argument in his defence: why would a man involved in a murder point the police in the direction of his accomplices?

Also on 21 January, police discovered the approximate time the call to the City Café was placed and, more importantly, the district from which it had originated. Upon amalgamating the statements taken from Gladys Harley and Samuel Beattie, they now knew the call had been placed at approximately 7 p.m. from the Anfield district (Gladys Harley had stated that when the call had eventually been put through to the City Café by Annie Robertson, supervisor at the Anfield Telephone Exchange, she had said to her, 'Anfield calling, hold the line.'). This information was immediately relayed to Chief Constable Lionel Everett, who dispatched a letter to the postmaster at the General Post Office in Victoria Street the same day, urging him to make urgent enquiries in order to ascertain the number of the telephone from which the call was sent. Superintendent Moore, however, was wasting no time. He telephoned the Post Office Intelligence Department himself and, informing them of the approximate time of the call and the district within which it had been placed, he asked them if they could immediately attempt to trace the telephone number from which it had been made. Early that same evening Moore's wait was over; to his delight, the Post Office Intelligence Department informed him that not only were they able to provide him with the number of the telephone from which the call was made, but they were able to say that it was made from a phone box close to Wallace's house at 7.20 p.m. Moore made arrangements for the two Anfield Telephone Exchange operators (Lilian Martha Kelly and Louisa Alfreds) who had handled the call to meet him at the General Post Office building the next day in order to take their statements.

During that afternoon Dr C. G. Mort, the City Coroner, had opened the inquest into the death of Julia Wallace. Wallace, detained at the Detective Office all that day, did not appear. In his place, Amy Wallace appeared to formally identify Julia. Due to Julia's death being the subject of an ongoing murder investigation, the inquest would have been a mere formality had it not been for Amy Wallace's protestations to Dr Mort about the invasion of her privacy the previous day by the press. Reporters, apparently posing as CID officers, had gained entry to her flat in Ullet Road. Upon realising who they were, Amy had asked them to leave; however, they were unwilling to go until they got a statement from her. Dr Mort told her that, as this was an inquest, he was not empowered to take notice of the complaint. After allowing Amy to vent her disdain, Dr Mort quickly closed the inquest, adjourning it until 5 February, 'by which time we might know what the position is'.

That evening, whilst being questioned by Inspector Gold at the Detective Office, a Superintendent Thomas (Head of Criminal Investigation, Aliens and Firearms Registry) had spoken with Wallace and told him that the call to the City Café had been traced to a telephone kiosk in the Anfield district. Later that night Wallace left the Detective Office and headed off to Lord Street to catch a tram back to Ullet Road. Shortly after 10 p.m., the Thursday meeting of the Chess Club had ended and Samuel Beattie, James Caird, a Mr Barusch and another friend were making their way up North John Street toward the same Lord Street tram stop when Caird spotted Wallace: 'Mr Beattie; see who's there?' When Beattie looked down the street, he saw Wallace 'standing on the edge of the curb, right in the corner, with his back towards Lord Street'. Caird, Beattie and Barusch were talking to Wallace when he turned to Beattie and asked, 'That telephone message, can you remember what time you actually received that message? It may be very important.'

'About 7 o'clock,' Beattie replied.

'I'd like to get nearer than that if you can remember.' Wallace insisted.

'I'm afraid I can't,' Beattie retorted.

Wallace then went on to tell the men that the police had found many strange aspects to the case and he had just left their office having been cleared.

'Oh, have they?' Beattie asked.

'Yes, they've cleared me.'

Wallace declared to Beattie that he hoped the police caught the man, as there were a few things he would like to ask him.

By this time, Beattie had had enough and advised him, 'You know the police have been in touch with me over this business and I would advise you not to discuss it with anyone other than the police because any simple thing you might say might be distorted.'

Changing the subject, Caird asked him when Julia's funeral would be. Wallace told him he was not sure, but he was trying for Saturday. Seeing Wallace at this meeting, James Caird's opinion was that he was 'a man under a great strain, very much upset and shaken. He was dressed in mourning. He looked ghastly.'

It was now 10.25 p.m., a No. 8 tram arrived and, boarding it, Wallace went on his way to Ullet Road. Upon arriving at Amy Wallace's flat, Wallace found that, before leaving that morning to return to her home in Brighton, Amy Dennis had left a statement for the police (unfortunately, this statement is no longer available) and a brief letter for him:

Dear Mr Wallace,

I would ask for nothing that belonged to my late sister apart from her fur coat as a keep-sake in memory or her. When this trouble is over I would be grateful if you could despatch the coat to me by registered Post.

Yours

AMY DENNIS

Amy Dennis having been in Amy Wallace's company since she arrived in Liverpool, the main topic of conversation had to have been Julia. During the course of these conversations the subject of Julia's fur coat may have arisen – hence Amy Dennis's request. The coat was duly sent on to her and was received before 25 February. However, the formality of this letter shows graphically the condition of the relationship that must have existed between the Wallaces and the Dennises. This was even more poignantly displayed the coming Saturday when, despite three of her siblings still being alive (Rhoda, Amy and George Smith Dennis), none was present at Julia's funeral. In fact, on 26 April 1931, just after Wallace's conviction, Julia's brother George sent a letter from his home in Redcar to Chief of Police Lionel Everett asking him to communicate with him with regard to him claiming Julia's belongings – especially the £90 Post Office savings book he had been reading about in the newspapers. This would strongly suggest that Julia's siblings knew of their sister's sixteen-year age reduction. In all newspaper reports, Julia's age was consistently reported as being 52: if any of her surviving siblings had a problem with this, surely one of them would have rectified this gross mistake. A salacious little titbit like this would surely have hit the headlines, considering she was almost 70 years old and her husband was only 52. However, this was never reported. These communications also show that the Dennises had no axe to grind against Wallace; had there been any bad feeling, any reservations against Wallace or any accusations pointed in his direction, this would have appeared in Amy Dennis's statement to police (which she would not have left at Ullet Road for Wallace to see) and there would be some indication of this in the police documents concerning the investigation. There is none whatsoever. Rhoda Dennis died in Hove, Sussex, in 1943; George Smith Dennis died in Redcar, Cleveland, Yorkshire, in 1946; Amy Dennis (after marrying William Coleman in Eastbourne, Sussex, in 1934) died in Hove, Sussex, in 1956.

The time Wallace left the Detective Office that night is usually stated as being sometime between 10 p.m. and 10.15 p.m. Wallace went directly to the tram stop in Lord Street in order to make his way to Amy Wallace's flat in Ullet Road and ultimately bumped into James Caird and Samuel Beattie. However, according to Inspector Gold, Wallace left much earlier than that. In answer to questions put to him by Roland Oliver at Wallace's trial, Gold said:

He was with me on the 22nd in the Detective Office all day on the 22nd, up to 20 to 10 when I was taking his statement [Wallace's second statement]. Then he looked at his watch and said 'I do not want to be late to get to Ullet Road because my sister-in-law will be going to bed. I am not going to Wolverton Street', and he said 'Can I go?' And I said 'Yes', and he went and met Mr Beattie.

Gold said Wallace left the Detective Office at 9.40 p.m. He did not meet Caird and Beattie until 10.20 p.m. Where had he been for those 40 minutes? Why had he not gone straight back to Ullet Road? Why had he lied to Gold? After leaving the City Café, when Caird pointed Wallace out to Beattie whilst on their way to the tram stop, Beattie said Wallace was 'standing on the edge of the curb, right in the corner, with his back towards Lord Street'. This must mean he was standing looking down North John Street toward the City Café (which was on the same side of the road) and *not* at the tram stop: he was waiting to see Beattie. Upon receiving the news that evening from Superintendent Thomas that Qualtrough's call had been traced and its location pinpointed, had it shaken him? If so, why? From the moment he was told, it had to have been on his mind. At some point, he had realised that it was a chess night at the City Café and, if he was in time, he could ambush Beattie and see exactly where he stood over his evidence concerning the time he received the Qualtrough phone call. Nevertheless, why had he left the Detective Office at 9.40 p.m? He knew that tournaments at the Chess Club never finished until around 10.10 p.m. – if Wallace had simply wanted to ask Beattie if he had had any more thoughts on the time he received the call from Qualtrough, why had not he simply gone to the City Café when he left police headquarters at 9.40 p.m? The Chess Club meeting would still have been in progress; he could have asked Beattie there. Why, upon 'bumping into' Beattie, as he left the Chess Club, did Wallace blatantly lie to him when he told him he had been cleared by the police? Was he trying to convey a false sense of security to Beattie in order that he would reveal more than Wallace thought he otherwise would?

Now knowing that the police had traced the Qualtrough telephone call to the very telephone box where it was placed, was Wallace concerned because the police were getting too close to the reality of the circumstances of his plot to murder Julia? Had this new information gained by the police been so damning to Wallace that, in cajoling Beattie into being more specific as to the time of the call to the City Café, Wallace was desperately attempting to vindicate himself in the light of possible future events? As will be revealed later, Wallace knew that the location of that telephone kiosk held more significance as to his own guilt than simply being in the vicinity of his own home. The last man on earth he would want the police talking to was the man who made that call, the man who also knew what this greater significance was – Richard Gordon Parry. In order to protect himself, Wallace would have to make certain that there could be no doubt in the minds of the police that Parry could not have made that call. He would need an airtight alibi for his whereabouts at the time of the call, and Parry would need someone to vouch that he was in their company. If there was any doubt in the minds of the police as to his alibi, they could pester Parry and Wallace knew that, under such pressure, Parry was likely to break and the game would be up. Having pointed police in Parry's direction in his statement that morning, Wallace knew it would not be long before the police would be calling on both Parry and Marsden and so time was of the essence. Had Wallace left the Detective Office early in order to attempt to contact Parry and warn him to get an alibi together as quickly as possible? As previously shown, Parry's statement concerning 19 January was not only an incompetent debacle – it was an obvious pack of lies. If, as it appears, Parry had made the telephone call to the City Café posing as Qualtrough and if that call was *meant* to be logged, why had Parry not made absolutely certain that he had a credible alibi? Instead, the alibi he gave appears to have been quickly and ineptly cobbled together from the facts of Lily Lloyd's lesson with her piano pupil on Monday 19 January. Was this as a result of a panicked call from Wallace after his early departure from the Detective Office on that night?

As shown in the statements given by Parry, Lily Lloyd and her mother, it was usual for Parry to call at Lily Lloyd's house each night at sometime between 9 and 9.30 p.m. and leave at sometime between 11 and 11.30 p.m. Had Wallace known this, he may have telephoned the Lloyds' house and spoken to Parry about the tracing of the phone call. If this was the case, Wallace would have to have phoned the Lloyds' house sometime between 9.40 p.m., when he left the Detective Office, and 10.20 p.m., when he saw Caird and Beattie at the tram stop in Lord Street – also when Wallace would have been sure that Parry would have been at the Lloyds'. As will also be shown, Parry appears to have made his statement at Tuebrook police station late the following night, on Friday 23 January, finishing it in the early hours of Saturday morning. Had he called in at the police station on his way home from Lily Lloyd's house sometime after 11.30 p.m. on the night of the 23rd? In her statement, Lily Lloyd's mother describes the clothes Parry was wearing on Friday the 24th: 'On Wednesday and Thursday or Thursday and Friday he was wearing a navy blue suit, I think it was Thursday and Friday because on Saturday he had his striped trousers on again.' This shows that Parry was at the Lloyds' house at some time on Friday the 23rd. Had Wallace telephoned the Lloyds' house to warn Parry, this would have given him only 24 hours to come up with a credible, cast-iron alibi for the night of the phone call to the City Café. Could Parry have spent most of those 24 hours attempting to persuade Lily Lloyd to help him forge that cast-iron alibi? Did he leave her at the last possible minute after she refused, leaving him armed only with the facts of her day from which to concoct his alibi before he arrived at Tuebrook police station to give his statement? Did he hope to persuade her over the weekend to assist him? As will be seen, on the whole Parry's statement is very plausible and verifiable – except for the night of 19 January. The question still to be answered is, with the police now knowing the actual location of the telephone kiosk from which the call to the City Café was made, what parameters had changed as far as Wallace's possible guilt was concerned?

Friday 23 January 1931

The following day, Friday 23 January, Inspector Gold, Detective Sergeant Bailey and Wallace headed out to Wolverton Street. Here, the trio made a thorough search of the house. In a drawer in the dressing table in the front bedroom, Wallace recovered Julia's Post Office savings book, which showed her account contained £90. In the middle bedroom, Wallace retrieved Julia's jewellery from another drawer. As far as he could see, nothing seemed to be missing, except for a small axe used to chop firewood, but he had not seen that for around twelve months. Gold had another rummage around and eventually found the axe under a pile of old clothes under the stairs. The police had, up to this point, apparently undertaken numerous thorough searches of the house and yet had never thought to look under the stairs, where they would have found this most incriminating piece of evidence for themselves. How thorough can these initial searches have been? Had Wallace placed the axe there himself, whilst staying there the night before, as a possible red herring? Informing

Wallace that Mrs Draper had stated that a small poker from the kitchen and an iron bar
from the parlour were also missing, Wallace denied any knowledge of them: 'Perhaps she
has thrown the poker away with the ashes. I don't know anything about a bar of iron in the
parlour.' Wallace then showed the officers an insurance policy taken out with the Prudential
Assurance for Julia for £20. Gold asked him if there were any more. 'No; this is the only
one,' Wallace replied. Before returning to the Detective Office, Gold gathered together some
more items of evidence: the suit of clothes Wallace was wearing on the night of the murder
and the towel from the bathroom. At some time during that afternoon Wallace appears to
have paid a visit to Anfield cemetery to pay £16 6s for Julia's burial the following day. Whilst
he was there, as well as giving them the Coroner's Order for Burial, he also handed them a
'Notice of Burial' (required under the 1880 Burial Laws Amendment Act), informing them
that Julia's burial was to be officiated by a clergyman from a dissenting church and not
within the rites of the Church of England.

Returning to the Detective Office at around 6.30 that evening, Moore and Gold
confronted Wallace over his meeting with Beattie at the tram stop.

'You saw Mr Beattie of the Chess Club last night?' Moore asked.

Wallace told him he was simply waiting for a tram.

'You asked him about the telephone message and what time he received it?'

Wallace agreed.

'You told him the time was important.'

Once again, Wallace agreed.

'In what way was it important?'

'I had some ideas of my own,' Wallace replied cryptically. 'We all have ideas. It was indiscreet
of me. I can't say why I asked him. I admit it was an indiscretion on my part. I cannot say
anything further.'

Later that evening, in the company of Sergeant Bailey, Gold took another statement
from Wallace, his third. This merely reiterated the journey he took from Belmont Road to
Menlove Avenue.

At his trial, Wallace was questioned about his meeting with Beattie by defence counsel
Roland Oliver:

Why did you think time was important then? Well, I had just come from the police station
[as stated above, he had left the police station 40 minutes before]. I had been there all
that time and sometime during the evening Superintendent Thomas had come into
the room, I think it was Superintendent Moore's room, I am not sure, and another
gentleman I do not know who he was, but Superintendent Thomas had a conversation
with me regarding this telephone message which had been received and he gave me
the information that they had been able to trace that call to a call box somewhere in
the Anfield district.

That would be near your home? It was suggested to me that it was near my home. If
that was so and the time was stated to be about 7 o'clock, I was in this position. I felt
that if I had left home at a quarter past 7 and the telephone call had been made at 7
o'clock, and if the Police up to that moment had believed all my statements to be true

and I had no reason to doubt otherwise, then that automatically cleared me of having sent that message. That is what I thought about.

If it was a genuine message, you realised you would be an innocent man? Yes, quite.

Was it with that in your mind that you asked Mr Beattie if he could possibly remember the time? It was, because Mr Beattie was uncertain and I thought if he could fix it, as he thought it was about 7, that it was 7 o'clock and I left at a quarter past 7, at all events I could not have sent that message.

That, at all events, was what was in your mind? Comment is made that when the officers asked you next day why you were interested in the time you did not say why you said it was indiscreet of you? Yes, I did.

Why was that? When Superintendent Moore put these questions to me – I think it was Superintendent Moore – I realised that if he could tell me of meeting Mr Beattie somewhere around about a quarter past 10 the previous night and knew something of the conversation I must have been followed [surely one's first thought would have been that Beattie had informed the police of the conversation], my movements must have been under observation. That was the conclusion I arrived at. If I had been under observation I was therefore, to my mind, a suspected person and the argument that went through my mind was it was indiscrete of me, if I was a suspected person, to be talking to a man who may be called as a witness in any charge made in this case. I realised that was an indiscretion and that was why I was unwilling to say anything further about it.

Had Mr Beattie said anything about the night before? I do not know whether you remember what he said? I cannot give the words, but he advised me to say as little about the case as possible to outsiders.

Because I think he said, what you said might be misconstrued? Yes.

Do you agree with that? I agree it was misconstrued.

As can be seen from the above testimony, according to Wallace this was the time when he first felt that he was suspected of Julia's murder. He felt that police could only have known of his rendezvous with Beattie if he had been followed after he left the Detective Office. If this was true, surely he would have been questioned as to why he had not gone directly back to Ullet Road when he left police headquarters at 9.40 p.m. Could the fact of the matter be that it was Beattie himself who informed the police about the encounter? Had he informed Superintendent Moore or another officer? There was an Inspector John Beattie (Warrant and Reformatory) stationed at Dale Street Detective Office. Could he have been related to Samuel Beattie and have been instrumental in passing the information on to Moore? Could the fact that Wallace had actually left the Detective Office 40 minutes earlier have either paled into insignificance, got lost under the weight of this new information or could the police have known more about the circumstances of the murder than they were telling, making them reluctant to pursue the matter?

At the trial, upon being asked by Hemmerde about Wallace's assertion that he was being followed, Inspector Gold denied any knowledge of this. When Wallace was eventually followed by police, Gold maintained that he was being 'escorted' for his own protection:

Mr Hemmerde: Why was he being followed?

Mr Gold: Because he was going round his block collecting the insurance money and we were told that the people there were hostile to him, and we sent a man with him in case of necessity.

Mr Justice Wright: It was nothing to do with any suspicion.

Mr Hemmerde: Nothing whatever.

This 'charitable' act on the part of the police was, apparently, never requested by Wallace, nor was he informed by the police that he was being 'protected' in this way. According to Jonathan Goodman, Wallace was being covertly shadowed. 'Wherever Wallace went, one of three plain-clothes men – Frederick Austin, Thomas Cleater and Thomas Hudson – was never far behind.' Wallace himself had this to say:

But it was only the day after the funeral [Sunday 25 January 1931] that I realised definitely that I was suspected. The whole of that day I felt I was being followed. But when I saw a man stationed outside my sister-in-law's house where I was staying *I knew I was under suspicion* … Day by day on my collecting rounds the shadow walked behind me … my shadow, my tracker, treated me with every consideration, not unduly embarrassing me with his presence at my interviews with clients, and occasionally even chatting with me in complete friendliness and camaraderie. I knew that he was performing a distasteful duty and whatever his superiors might suspect him himself was under no illusions as to my guilt.

Sometime late that same evening (only a day after having traced the Qualtrough phone call), Richard Gordon Parry was at Tuebrook police station being interrogated by police.

Tuebrook Bridewell
23/1/31.
Richard Gordon PARRY says:

I live at 7, Woburn Hill, and I am an Inspector employed by the Standard Life Assurance Co., 28, Exchange Street East. I have known Mr and Mrs Wallace of 29, Wolverton Street since September 1926, by being in the employ of the Prudential Assurance Co., of which Mr Wallace was an agent. In December 1928 Mr Wallace was off duty ill and I did his work for two weeks. On the Thursday of the first week, and on the Wednesday evening of the second week I called at his house to hand over the cash, and settle up the books. The first time I called Mrs Wallace gave me a cup of tea and some cake while I was waiting for Mr Wallace to come downstairs. It was about 10.0 a.m. and I waited in the kitchen. I had been to Mr Wallace's house on several occasions prior to December 1928 on business matters for my Superintendent, Mr Crewe, and had also called several times after that date on similar business. I always looked upon Mr and Mrs Wallace as a very devoted couple. The last time I called at Wallace's was about October or November 1929, and then I called on business for Mr Crewe. The last time I saw Mr Wallace was about three weeks ago on a bus from Victoria Street. I got off at Shaw Street. I know that Mr Wallace is very fond of music, he plays bowls, and I have seen him at the City Café in North John Street; he is a member of a Chess Club which has its headquarters there.

I am a member of the Mersey Amateur Dramatic Society and previous to the production of 'John Glaydes Honour' on November 17th 1930, at Crane Hall, we were rehearsing at the City Café every Tuesday and Thursday. It was during these rehearsals that I saw Mr Wallace at the City Café on about three occasions. I did not know previously that he was a member of the Chess Club there.

On Monday evening the 19th instant, I called for my young lady, Miss Lillian Lloyd, of 7, Missouri Road, at some address where she had been teaching, the address I cannot for the moment remember, and went home with her to 7, Missouri Road at about 5.30 p.m. and remained there until about 11.30 p.m. when I went home.

On Tuesday the 20th instant, I finished business about 5.30 p.m. and called upon Mrs Brine, 43, Knockliad [sic] Road. I remained there with Mrs Brine, her daughter Savona, 13 yrs; her nephew, Harold Dennison [sic], 29, Marlborough Road, until about 8.30 p.m. I then went out and bought some cigarettes – Players No. 3, and the Evening Express from Mr Hodgson, Post Office, Maiden Lane, on the way to my young lady's house. When I was turning the corner by the Post Office I remembered that I had promised to call for my accumulator at Hignetts in West Derby Road, Tuebrook. I went there and got my accumulator and then went down West Derby Road and along Lisburn Lane to Mrs Williamsons, 49, Lisburn Lane, and saw her. We had a chat about a 21st birthday party for about 10 minutes and then I went to 7, Missouri Road, and remained there till about 11 to 11.30 p.m. when I went home.

I have heard of the murder of Mrs Wallace and have studied the newspaper reports of the case and, naturally, being acquainted with Mr and Mrs Wallace, I have taken a great interest in it. I have no objection whatever to the police verifying my statement as to my movements on Monday the 19th and Tuesday the 20th instants.

[Signed] R. G. Parry.

24th January, 1931.

As can be seen, Parry's statement begins on 23 January and ends on 24 January. It would appear that Parry was at Tuebrook police station late in the evening of the 23rd, finally signing the statement in the early hours of Saturday 24 January. As mentioned previously, might Parry have called at Tuebrook police station upon leaving Lily Lloyd's house at about 11.30 p.m?

If we look carefully through the statement, it can be seen that several of Parry's declarations are at odds with Wallace's second police statement. Wallace said, 'I have known him about three years and he was with my company about two years.' He says he had known Parry since 1928, presumably implying that he had known Parry since the Christmas he had done work for him. But according to Parry, he had known both Mr and Mrs Wallace since the September of 1926, two years earlier. According to Wallace, 'Previous to Parry doing my work, he had called at my house once on business and left a letter for me which he wrote in my front room. I was not in at the time but my wife let him in.' After being so adamant that Julia would never allow anyone into the house she did not know personally, in the above statement Wallace is saying that she had, in fact, allowed a perfect stranger into the parlour. According to Parry, he had been to 29 Wolverton Street on several occasions before December 1928 on business for his Superintendent, Joseph Crewe. Again, Wallace states, 'I do not think he called to see me after I resumed work in January 1929 but if he had have called, my wife would have had no hesitation in admitting him.' Parry states that he had called at Wallace's on several occasions after December 1928 on similar business, the last time being in either October or November 1929. One of them was, most assuredly, lying.

Another curious omission can be seen in this statement. The police seem not to have questioned Parry about Marsden. Wallace had named Marsden in association with Parry only the day before in his second statement. As has been previously mentioned, it is usually given that Sergeant Harry Bailey had questioned the Qualtrough families in Liverpool on the day after the murder, 21 January; given that Bailey's line of questioning included asking them if they knew anyone named Marsden, it cannot have been until after Wallace gave his second statement on 22 January. In not asking Parry about his friend Marsden, had the police already tracked down and questioned Joseph Caleb Marsden and taken his statement on the 22nd? If so, where is it and why were the police not corroborating it with Parry's? If not, why were they not gaining more information about him from Parry?

At around this time, according to Mrs Ada Cook, Parry's parents had called at her parents' home, 19 Halsey Crescent, West Derby, to plead with her father, a Chief Steward, to assist them by surreptitiously spiriting their son out of the country. Mrs Cook – born Ada Pritchard on 13 March 1913 – was the only daughter of Sidney McCulloch Pritchard, born in West Ham, London, in 1883 and Mary Ada Green, born in Liverpool in 1883. Married in Everton, Liverpool, in 1907, the couple had three children – Harry (1909), Ada (1913) and Charles Arthur (1914). In a signed statement given to retired teacher Thomas Brady whilst he undertook his own investigation into the case, Mrs Cook explained:

> The Parrys were close family friends. We attended the Primitive Methodist Church in Hilberry Avenue, Tuebrook … My father and Mrs Parry sang duets together with my mother accompanying them on the piano.

In fact, not only did the two families attend Hilberry Avenue Primitive Methodist Church, both William John Parry and Sidney McCulloch Pritchard were trustees of the church, William John Parry later becoming its treasurer. The relationship between the two families was so close that the Parrys named one of their daughters, Amy Muriel, after Mrs Cook's mother. Despite this, Mrs Cook went on to say:

> Our mother was constantly warning all of us, her children, not to get involved with Gordon and to stay away from him … Gordon had been in trouble with the police many times in his youth but had never had any punishment because his father used his influence to get him off. It was well known that there was heaps of corruption in the police and in the Liverpool council.

Regarding the time of Julia's murder, Mrs Cook stated:

> At the time of the murder, we knew that Gordon had been taken into the police station for questioning. He usually lay down and made a terrible fuss so that the police had to carry him in … Mr and Mrs Parry were over at our house shortly after the murder, and us children were sent upstairs. My brother, Arthur and I decided to listen at the sitting room door. I was about 16/17 years old at the time. Mr and Mrs Parry were asking my father to smuggle Gordon out of Liverpool by any boat he could find to take him away to the other side of the world. I remember Mrs Parry saying to my father, 'I am begging you, Sidney, on my bended knees to help us'. That night, after the Parrys had left, my parents had a blazing row during which my mother raved at my father not to help Gordon escape the punishment he deserved. My father, who was soft hearted, wanted to help them; my mother was adamant that he was not to do it as he would be helping a murderer. She was scared that father would end up getting in trouble with the police himself and she still had all us children to support. In the end, mother won, and father did not help him, and they still, remarkably, stayed friends with the Parrys. My mother was convinced that they knew their son, Gordon, was a murderer. Knowing Gordon as we did, we were sure he had done it too … After the murder, feelings in Liverpool ran very high and Ada Parry, Gordon's sister … was forced to leave Liverpool University after receiving hate mail. She moved to Dublin … I heard, I don't know where from, that the murder implement was dropped down a grid near the Clubmoor Cinema where Lily worked.

Amy Muriel Parry's relocation from Liverpool University to Dublin because of the unwelcome attention the case was bringing was also an experience shared by Edwin Herbert Wallace, Wallace's nephew, who had to relocate from Liverpool University to Glasgow in order to finish his studies.

Ada Pritchard was married in 1936 to Harry Burton Cook, a schoolmaster from St Helens, Lancashire. Having moved to St Helens shortly after their marriage, Mrs Cook related an encounter with Parry which will be given more credence later in the text:

> One day, in the early 1940s, I saw him [Parry] in St Helens town centre and he followed me into the fish shop – he was trying to 'chat me up'. I was sure he hadn't recognized me, and so, I addressed him by name and said 'Gordon Parry, I'm Ada Pritchard, and I know everything about you, so leave me alone'. I left the shop and waved down the first bus and got on it – he did not follow.

It is plain to see in this very damning statement that on the night the Parrys went to see their long-time friends the Pritchards, they never actually stated that they *knew* their son had murdered Julia Wallace; however, there are obvious, strong implications of their own beliefs as to his complicity. If it were found that their son was an accessory before and after the fact, this would have resulted in a sentence of death. What other explanation than their belief in their son's culpability can be given to justify William John and Lilian Jane Parry going to such extraordinary lengths, not only to pervert the course of justice, but in attempting to coerce their close friends into aiding and abetting a suspect in a murder enquiry?

According to various sources, Parry appeared to have been thoroughly investigated by the police. Parry's next-door neighbour at the time, Les Hill, stated, 'As for the murder, I knew Parry was questioned but how this came about I don't know. He was interviewed for about three hours at Atkinson's garage'. Why had the police not interviewed Parry at his home or at a police station? Interviewing him at Atkinson's Garage could only have been after Wallace's arrest. The police knew of no connection to Atkinson's Garage and Julia's murder until John Parkes gave them his evidence concerning the washing down of Parry's car. This was given after Wallace had been arrested. According Goodman and Whittington Egan's interview with Parry:

> The police [Parry said] were in and out of his home in Liverpool by the minute for two days at the time of the investigation. But they finally seemed satisfied as to his innocence for the Wallace murder when he was able to produce some people with whom he had spent the evening of the murder 'arranging a birthday celebration'.

As mentioned previously, there was no love lost between the Williamsons and Parry. It appears that it was only through Mrs Williamson's friendship with Lily Lloyd that they endured his acquaintance. Lily Lloyd had stated that on the night of the murder Parry had told her he had been to Mrs Williamson's house. Parry was an unwelcome guest at 49 Lisburn Lane, so why would he have been asked to help with arrangements for Leslie Williamson's birthday party? In addition, who were the 'friends' he was with? Once again, when Leslie Williamson phoned Radio City during the *Who Killed Julia?* phone-in, had they known how important to the case Williamson was, this would have been a prime opportunity for Roger Wilkes and Jonathan Goodman to clear up whether it was actually this 21st birthday party Parry was referring to.

After Liverpool's Radio City had broadcast Roger Wilkes's *Who Killed Julia?* programmes, Parry's sister Joan (then Joan Smith) had taken umbrage at the Goodman/Wilkes claim that her deceased brother had been Julia Wallace's murderer. Subsequently, a few days after the broadcast, an article appeared in the *Liverpool Echo* which stated:

> Her brother [Parry], she said, was thoroughly investigated by the police ... His alibi was checked out and forensic experts even took the seams out of his clothes and gloves for tests. After an exhaustive investigation, Mr Parry ... was completely cleared of implication.

It has to be noted that Mrs Smith was only three years old at the time of the murder so this information had to have been related to her by somebody else a long time after the event – possibly Parry himself.

Saturday 24 January 1931

At 10.30 a.m. on Saturday 24 January, under a veil of secrecy, Julia was buried at Anfield cemetery. Only three mourners were present: Wallace, Amy Wallace and Edwin Wallace.

The only other people present were the minister, the Reverend James Edward Stevenson of the Congregational Church in nearby Queen's Drive, the undertakers, Jonathan Leary of 188 Breck Road and (according to Goodman) Wallace's police shadow. Edwin Wallace noted of his uncle that 'during the sermon in the church he was crying a little'. The original gravesite had neither monument nor upright gravestone; instead, Wallace had a stone border placed around its circumference, the inscriptions being etched upon this. When Goodman visited the grave during the 1960s, he noted that it was 'difficult to find. The grass is high around it, and the weeds. The inscription on the plain stone surround is not easily read'. This inscription, which by then included Wallace's own name (following his death in 1933), was as follows:

> In loving and affectionate remembrance of Julia
> Beloved wife of W H Wallace
> In loving memory of William Herbert Wallace
> R I P

During April 1973, possibly because the stonework had been damaged by lawnmowers (or vice versa), the border was sunk by Liverpool Council and an upright gravestone was put in its place. It has to be noted that the present gravestone gives a wrong impression of the orientation of the actual grave position. Originally, Julia's grave ran lengthways, parallel to the pathway beside it. The present gravestone has been placed in the centre of the grave, the inscription facing the pathway. When one visits the gravesite, both Julia's and Wallace's heads are to the right of the stone, their feet to the left. In addition to the replacing of the border with a headstone, the original inscription was not only replaced, but also augmented to include the occupants' ages and dates of death, gleaned from the burial registers.

That evening, 24 January 1931, a man was ushered into Moore's office. Introducing himself as Mr Hall, he gave Moore an envelope, telling him it was from his daughter who was ill in bed: he was going to post it but had decided to drop it in himself. The letter was a statement from a Miss Lillian Hall stating that she had seen Wallace on the night of 20 January at around 8.35 p.m. talking with another man in Richmond Park. Moore made arrangements with Joseph Hall to call to his home and take a statement from his daughter. The next morning he arrived at 9 Letchworth Street and took a statement from Lily Hall.

Sunday 25 January 1931

9 Letchworth Street, 25 January 1931.
LILY HALL says: I am a typist employed at Littlewoods Ltd, commission agents, Charles Street, off Whitechapel, and I live with my parents at 9 Letchworth Street.

I have known Mr Wallace for 3 or 4 years by sight and about a fortnight ago, I learned his name from Mr Johnston, junior, of 31 Wolverton Street. I was there visiting them.

On Tuesday night, the 20th instant, I left business at Charles Street soon after 8 p.m. and took a tram home at the corner of Lord Street and Whitechapel. I got off the tram at the tram stop in Breck Road at the corner of Walton Breck Road. I had arranged to go to the pictures that night if I got home in time and when I got off the tram, I looked at Holy Trinity Church clock, which is near the tram stop, and saw that it was then 8.35 p.m. by that clock.

I came straight home along Richmond Park and as I was passing the entry leading from Richmond Park to the middle of Wolverton Street, I saw the man I know as Mr Wallace talking to another man I do not know. Mr Wallace had his face to me and the other man his back. They were standing on the pavement in Richmond Park opposite to the entry leading up by the side of the Parish Hall. I crossed over Richmond Park and came up Letchworth Street and home. When I got into the house, our clock was just turned 8.40 p.m. but it is always kept 5 minutes fast. It takes me not more than 3 minutes to walk from the tram stop to our house. The next morning I heard Mrs Wallace had been murdered and when I got home that night, I told my parents that I had seen Mr Wallace the previous night. Mr Wallace was wearing a trilby hat and a darkish overcoat when I saw him talking to the man in Richmond Park on Tuesday night. The man he was talking to was about 5ft 8ins and was wearing a cap and dark overcoat; he was of a stocky build.
[Signed] Lily Hall.

Jonathan Goodman strongly contested this statement on four separate grounds:

i. Despite repeated police appeals, the man she claimed to have seen talking with Wallace never came forward. There was little doubt that if Wallace murdered his wife he committed the crime without the aid of an accomplice; even supposing that Wallace did employ an accomplice, it was hardly likely that he would have stopped to chat with him in full view of anyone who happened to be passing. It was virtually certain, then, that if the man existed he had no reason to fear police questioning – and, therefore, no reason (apart, perhaps, from extreme shyness) to ignore the appeals.

If this rendezvous was legitimate, this man, for whatever reason, might simply have not wanted to be interviewed by the police, especially considering the fact that the crime they were investigating was murder. Then as now, this is often the case. Many people, no matter how small the crime, simply do not want to get involved. Goodman dismisses the fact that Wallace might have been meeting an 'accomplice'. It could have been the case that the accomplice might well have been an unwilling accomplice and had no choice in the matter. Giving testimony at the committal trial, Lily Hall said:

I last saw him at 8.35 p.m. on the 20th January last at the bottom of the entry by the Parish Hall. It is the entry shown on the plan WHW14 running at right angles to Richmond Park and parallel with Letchworth Street.

In her statement given to Hubert Moore, she said, 'Mr Wallace had his face to me and the other man his back.' As Miss Hall was on the side of the road opposite the Parish Hall, this would suggest that Wallace was standing with his back to the entry at the side of the Parish Hall – the entry he had told Inspector Gold he had walked up when going in search of Menlove Gardens East and the entry he came down upon his return. Having his back to the entry would be correct if he had done this upon his return. The man Lily Hall saw Wallace talking to was standing with his back to the entry leading from Wolverton Street – the entry Wallace had used when he left his back door at the start of his journey to Mossley Hill that night – so the man Wallace was talking to was standing in the correct position if he had left the entry from Wolverton Street and crossed the road to meet Wallace.

ii. Why should Wallace have told such a deliberate and unnecessary lie? In so doing, he must have recognized the possibility that the man (and Lily Hall – since if she saw Wallace it was reasonable to suppose that he must have seen her) would come forward with an account of the meeting, and so expose him as a liar. No one was able to explain why Wallace should have lied so recklessly – or indeed, why he should have lied at all. He could have admitted the encounter and still stuck to his statement that he was in a hurry to get home – all he would have needed to say was that he was not in so great a hurry as to ignore anyone who approached him in the street.

The only answers Wallace could give in reply to Miss Hall's assertion that she witnessed him in conversation with another man were, yes, he was talking to someone, or no, he was not. In admitting he had been talking to someone, he would then have been asked by Moore who it was. Once again, there are two alternatives: a complete stranger who had asked him for the time, directions or some other sundry question, or somebody he knew. If it was a complete stranger, Moore would have asked for a description. Being in such close contact with the man, Moore would have expected the description to have been fairly precise. Wallace had no idea how well Miss Hall had described the man. If he lied, Moore would have found this highly suspicious and the case would have taken a whole new direction there and then. If he knew the man, Moore would have asked for his address. If it was a legitimate meeting, Moore would have been given that address. If it was a covert meeting with Julia's killer, Wallace could give neither description nor address. The path of least resistance was to deny any knowledge of the incident; Moore would only be left with Wallace's word against Lily Hall's.

iii. Lily Hall said that she was 'able to fix the time definitely as 8.35 p.m., because I was on my way to the pictures and I looked at Holy Trinity Clock'. But this statement was contradictory. If she was on her way to the pictures, why was she walking in the direction of her own home, and away from the locality of the cinemas in the Anfield district?

Here, Goodman has become confused. What Lily Hall actually said was:

I had arranged to go to the pictures that night if I got home in time and when I got off the tram, I looked at Holy Trinity Church clock, which is near the tram stop, and saw that it was then 8.35 p.m. by that clock.

Lily Hall was more than likely hoping to get out in time for a 9.00 p.m. performance at a local cinema (possibly at the Cabbage Hall Cinema). In checking the Holy Trinity church clock, she was gauging how much time she had to get ready in order to be at the cinema on time.

> iv. Although she could not have been more than ten yards away from the two men when they parted (compared with the distance of thirty or forty yards at which, she said, she first saw Wallace), and although she was interested enough to be looking over her shoulder at them, she was unable to identify one man from the other. She was sure, though, that 'one went down the entry by the Parish Hall, and the other along Richmond Park, walking in the direction of Breck Road'. In order to accept her testimony, it was necessary to believe the almost unbelievable – that Wallace had walked from the tram stop at St Margaret's Church to within a hundred yards of his house, and then, instead of simply crossing the road to the entry leading to Wolverton Street, had either turned round and walked back the way he had come, or turned sharp left and walked in the direction of Breck Road.

Here, when Lily Hall was passing the entry 'leading from Richmond Park to the middle of Wolverton Street', she was almost directly opposite Wallace when she saw him (a matter of feet away), a man she had known by sight for four years. Miss Hall was in a rush to get home and, as she turned into Letchworth Street, she more than likely merely took a brief glance over her shoulder and saw two dark shapes making their way down Richmond Park before she passed the corner of her street. Regarding Goodman's account of the direction the men took after their conversation, he, unfortunately, had misunderstood Lily Hall's statement. Goodman asserts that one of the men walked down Richmond Park to Breck Road, whilst the other took a route up the entry at the side of the Parish Hall. If either were to be Wallace, why would he have done this? What Lily Hall actually said at the committal trial was, 'One went down the entry and the other down Richmond Park but I do not know whom.' When Scholefield Allen (Wallace's defence counsel) asked her to clarify this, Lily Hall said, 'The man went down the entry opposite the institute.' The entry opposite the 'institute' (Parish Hall) was the entry leading from Wallace's back door into Richmond Park: the entry Wallace had used upon leaving his back door to begin his journey to Menlove Gardens East earlier that night – and the entry he had told Inspector Gold he had used upon his return.

If we accept that this meeting took place, there are some interesting points one should consider:

- If this man was an accomplice (no matter how unwilling) why have the conversation on a street pavement where anybody (like Lily Hall) might see them? The alternative would be the possibility of being witnessed having a conversation with another man in a darkened entry way – this being far more suspicious, and more memorable, than having it in public view.
- If the mystery man was the man who had just murdered Julia Wallace, why would he saunter on down a street? Surely, he would be desperate to stay in the shadows and remain unseen? Not unless he had a preconceived plan of escape – such as a car and a

driver waiting, ready to whisk him out of the vicinity, which would be far more practical than rushing about through the back entries in the dark.

• According to Lily Hall's statement, no sooner had she begun to cross the road than the two men parted company. By the time she had reached the corner of Letchworth Street (this would have taken a matter of seconds to accomplish), one man was already heading to Breck Road, the other was on his way down an entry into Wolverton Street. Was it because of her unexpected arrival on the scene that their conversation had immediately come to an end?

Monday 26 January 1931

On the afternoon of Monday 26 January, detectives were dispatched to Clubmoor in order to corroborate Parry's statement. Upon arriving at 43 Knoclaid Road, they took a statement from Olivia Alberta Brine (whose father-in-law, William Brine, lived at 21 Auburn Road, off Lisburn Lane – only four doors away from telephone operator Lilian Martha Kelly, who lived at 13 Auburn Road, and, the previous year, nine doors away from Superintendent Hubert Moore, who had lived at 1 Auburn Road). A statement was also taken from Olivia's nephew, 15-year-old Harold Denison.

Olivia Alberta Brine says:

I am a married woman, my husband is away at sea. I have known R. G. Parry about two years. Just before last Christmas he commenced calling with my nephew William Denison, 29, Marlborough road. At about 5 p.m. to 5.30 p.m. on Tuesday the 20th inst Parry called at my house. He came in his car. He remained till about 8.30 p.m. when he left. Whilst he was here a Miss Plant, Gloucester Road called. My nephew Harold Denison also called.

[Signed] O. A. Brine.

Harold English DENNISON [*sic*], 29 Marlborough Road says:

I have known R. G. Parry for two years. I called at 43 Knocklaid [*sic*] on Tuesday 20th inst about 6 p.m. My aunt Mrs Brine lives there. When I called Mr Parry was there. He remained till about 8.30 p.m. when he left.

[Signed] H. E. Denison.

Mrs Brine's husband, James Frederick Brine, a ship's steward, was 'Linen Keeper' on board the Cunard Line's *Lancastria*, travelling from London to New York; having sailed on 15 January, his ship would not arrive in New York until 26 January. In corroborating Parry's alibi for the night of the murder, both Mrs Brine and Harold Denison disqualify him from having any involvement in the actual murder itself. Whether we use the police time frame of between 6 and 7 p.m., or the time between Parry leaving Mrs Brine's house, 8.30 p.m., and the time Wallace entered his house upon his return, approximately 8.45 p.m., it is patently obvious that Richard Gordon Parry could not have murdered Julia Wallace.

Parry had been introduced to Mrs Brine and her husband sometime around the Christmas of 1929 through his acquaintance with their nephew, Harold English Denison's brother,

William Samuel Albert Denison, who was three years younger than Parry. At the time, the Denisons lived at 29 Marlborough Road, Tuebrook, Liverpool. Their mother, Amanda Matilda Alexandra Claus, was Mrs Brine's sister. The Claus family had originated in Frankfurt am Main, Germany, arriving in Liverpool when Olivia's grandfather, John Adam Claus, a clerk, arrived sometime around 1840, marrying Margaret Smith in 1843. The Denisons' father, William English Denison, born in Leeds in 1888, was the great grandson of Samuel Denison, founder of Samuel Denison & Son, the prominent Yorkshire iron founders and weighing machine manufacturers. During the 1880s, William's father, Henry Dean Denison, lived at 2 De Grey's Road, Leeds – a few doors away from the then Chief of Police of Leeds (soon to be Chief of Police of Liverpool), John William Nott Bower, who was living alone at 37 De Grey Terrace, just around the corner. William English Denison and Amanda Matilda Claus were married at St James's church, West Derby, Liverpool, on 12 August 1909. The following year, whilst living at 7 Windsor Road, Tuebrook, Liverpool, the first of their three children was born, Violet Elizabeth. After the family's move to 29 Marlborough Road, Tuebrook, William Samuel Albert was born in 1912, and Harold English Denison was born in 1914. William English Denison appears to have been quite a versatile man, his occupations including 'Optical Expert', 'Manager', 'Entertainer' and, in 1915, a 'Film Agent'. It may have been due to the latter role that Parry, the aspiring actor, got to know William Samuel Albert Denison. On 3 April 1929, William English Denison had a patent accepted concerning 'Improvements in or relating to Thermionic Amplifier Circuits': a device to prevent sound distortion in loudspeakers. In 1932, the Denisons left Marlborough Road moving to 24 Aysgarth Avenue, West Derby. Amanda Matilda Alexandra (Claus) Denison died in Liverpool, in 1943; William English Denison died in Liverpool in 1955; Violet Elizabeth (Denison) Copple died in Liverpool in 2003; William Samuel Albert Denison died in Liverpool in 1980; Harold English Denison died in Liverpool in 1992.

Since their marriage at St James's church, West Derby on 12 January 1917, James Frederick Brine and Olivia Alberta Claus had been living at 21 Auburn Road, Tuebrook, with James's parents, William[9] and Grace Anne Brine, who had been living there since 1912 (the same year that Superintendent Hubert Moore had moved into 1 Auburn Road with his family), their daughter Savona being born on 21 April 1917. James and Olivia eventually moved into 43 Knoclaid Road sometime during 1929, around the same time they first met Parry.

Upon arriving at 7 Missouri Road, Clubmoor, the police interviewed Parry's girlfriend Lily Lloyd and her mother Josephine Ward Lloyd.

Lillian [*sic*] Josephine Moss LLOYD says:
I am 20 years of age and reside with my parents at 7, Missouri Road. I am a music teacher. I am keeping company with R. E. [*sic*] Parry, 7, Woburn Hill. On Monday the 19th inst I had an appointment at my home with a pupil named Rita Price, 14a Clifton Road at 7 p.m. I cannot remember properly but either Rita Price was late or I was late. It was not more than 10 minutes. I gave my pupil a full ¾ of an hour lesson and about 20 minutes before I finished Parry called. That would be about 7.35 p. m. I did not see him and when I finished the lesson he had gone. I know he called because I heard his car and his knock at the door and I heard his voice at the door.

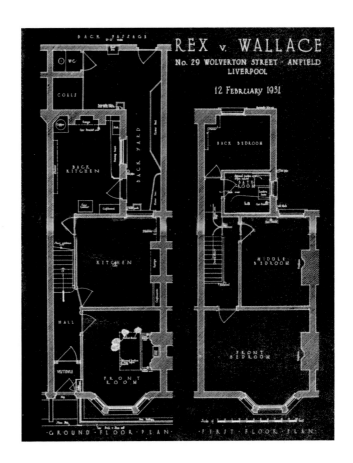

1. Plan of 29 Wolverton Street.

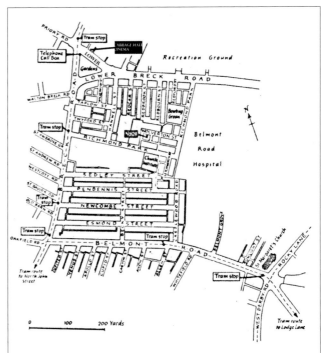

2. Diagram of the district around 29 Wolverton Street in 1931.

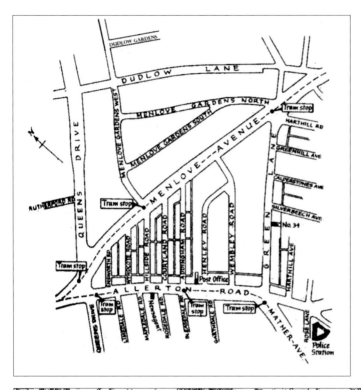

3. Diagram of the Menlove Gardens district of Mossley Hill in 1931.

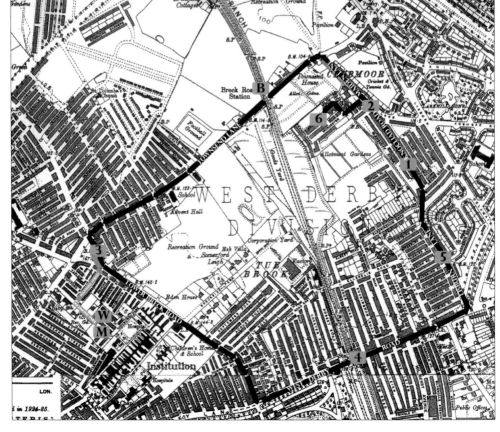

Top: **5.** William Herbert Wallace and Julia Dennis.

Middle: **6.** William Herbert Wallace and Julia Dennis' original Marriage Certificate, signed at St Mary's church, Harrogate (the 'Tin Tabernacle') on the day of their marriage.

Bottom: **7.** Advertisement from *Harrogate Herald*, 5 August 1914. (Courtesy of Tom Slemen)

	1	2	3	4	5	6	7	8
1914. Marriage solemnized at *the parish Church* in the *parish* of *St Mary in Harrogate* in the County of *York*								
No.	When Married.	Name and Surname.	Age.	Condition.	Rank or Profession.	Residence at the time of Marriage.	Father's Name and Surname.	Rank or Profession of Father.
109	March 24 1914	William Herbert Wallace	36	Bachelor	Secretary	9 Belmont Rd	Benjamin Wallace	Retired
		Julia Dennis	37	Spinster	—	11 St Mary's Av.	William George Dennis (dec)	Missionary Surgeon

Married in the *above Church* according to the Rites and Ceremonies of the *Established Church*, by *License* or after by me,

This Marriage was solemnized between us, { *William Herbert Wallace* { *Julia Dennis* } in the Presence of us, { *Jno. L. Allanson* { *Jessie Wallace* } *Ernest A. Chard* Vicar

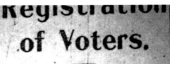

Opposite: **4.** Map showing Parry's possible route to Lily Lloyd's house after leaving Mrs Brine's house at 8.30 p.m. on the night of the murder. The black arrows show Parry's route after leaving Mrs Brine's house. The grey arrows show Marsden's possible route after leaving Wallace and making his way to Parry's car.

Key: 1. Mrs Brine's house – 43 Knoclaid Road, Clubmoor. 2. Maiden Lane Post Office, Clubmoor. 3. Cabbage Hall Cinema, Dr Dunlop's house, Mrs Smith's house – and where Parry may have parked his car whilst awaiting Marsden's arrival. 4. Position of Hignett's Bicycle Shop and entrance to Tuebrook railway station. 5. Mrs Williamson's house – 49 Lisburn Lane, Clubmoor. 6. Lily Lloyd's house – 7 Missouri Road, Clubmoor. M = Entry at side of Richmond Park Parish Hall where Wallace was witnessed talking to another man. B = Breck Road railway station. W = The Wallaces' house – 29 Wolverton Street.

Above left: **8.** 29 Wolverton Street at the time of Julia's murder. (© Merseyside Police)

Above right: **9.** Anfield 1627, from which the Qualtrough call was placed. (© Merseyside Police)

Left: **10.** Telephone similar to that in Anfield 1627. (© Merseyside Police)

11. Bank 3501 inside Cottle's City Café, where the Qualtrough call was received by Gladys Harley. The Liverpool Central Chess Club noticeboard can be seen on the wall next to the cloakroom. (© Merseyside Police)

12. Liverpool Central Chess Club noticeboard situated inside Cottle's City Café. (© Merseyside Police)

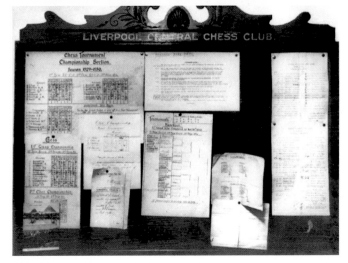

13. Liverpool Central Chess Club 2nd Class Championship notice. (© Merseyside Police)

2nd Class Championship.

1st Prize 10/- 2nd Prize 5/-

Mondays.

		NOV		DEC		JAN		FEB
		10	24	8	15	5	19	21
1	Chandler F.C.	ʎ	2ʳ	3D	4	5	6	7
2	Ellis T.	7L	1L	x	3	4	5	6
3	Lampitt E.	6W	7	1D	2	x	4	8
4	McCartney	5v	6	2	1W	2	3	x
5	Moore T.	4	x	6	1	1	2	3
6	Wallace W.H.	3L	4	5	x	7	1	2
7	Walsh J.	2W	3	4	6	6	7	1

Underlined take Black.

Above left: **14.** Sgt Harry Bailey outside the back door of 29 Wolverton Street. (© Merseyside Police)

Above right: **15.** The backyard of 29 Wolverton Street. (© Merseyside Police)

Below: **16.** The kitchen of 29 Wolverton Street. (© Merseyside Police)

Right: **17.** Harry Hewitt Cooke's crime-scene photograph taken from the parlour doorway – referred to at the Assize trial as exhibit 'WHW 6'. (© Merseyside Police)

Below: **18.** Harry Hewitt Cooke's crime-scene photograph taken from the bay window of the parlour – referred to at the Assize trial as exhibit 'WHW 7'. (© Merseyside Police)

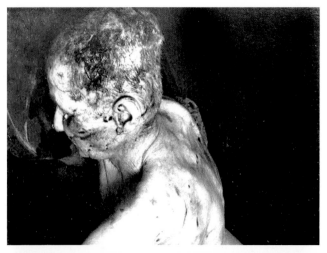

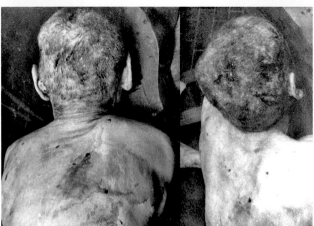

Top and middle: **19. & 20.** Julia Wallace's morgue photographs clearly show the 2-inch by 3-inch hole through her skull, the diagonal 'incised' wounding to the back of her head, and the distension of the skull toward the top of the head. (© Merseyside Police)

Bottom: **21.** Sgt Joseph Michael Breslin (front row, second right) and officers of the Anfield police station.

Clockwise from top left: **22.** Professor John Edward Whitley MacFall.

23. Superintendent Hubert 'Rory' Moore.

24. Hector Alfred Munro, Wallace's solicitor.

25. William Herbert Wallace shortly after his successful appeal.

Above: **26.** The Right Honourable Justice Wright (centre) and Assize Counsel: Roland Oliver, KC, for the defence (left) and Edward George Hemmerde, KC, for the Crown (right).

Far left: **27.** Gordon Parry, possibly taken in 1930, when Parry was 21, for the theatre poster for *John Glayde's Honour*.

Left: **28.** Police 'mug shot' of Parry, possibly taken in Aldershot in 1934 when Parry was 25.

Above left: **31.** Members of the Johnston family living at 31 Wolverton Street (along with Mrs Johnston's father Arthur Mills) on the night of the murder. Clockwise from top left: John Sharp Johnston, Florence Sarah Johnston (née Mills), Norah Russell Johnston, Amy Beatrice Johnston (née Towers), Robert Leslie Russell Johnston.

Above right: **32.** Lillian Hall.

Right: **33.** Richard Gordon Parry's list of offences for the magistrate to take into consideration of his plea for leniency after being arrested on 24 February 1932.

Opposite bottom left: **29.** James Caird and Kenneth Campbell Caird.

Opposite bottom right: **30.** Ada Cook (née Pritchard).

Richard James Qualtrough, 8
Northumberland Terrace, joiner.
At home all evening Monday
19/1/31. Does not know Wallace.
Insured with Prudential, agent
Mr. Sutton, 74 Queens Drive Walton.
Has son, William 25yrs. s/a out
with Miss Thompson, 20 Orient St.
at her house from 8.00 p.m. to 12. at
home until about 7.55 p.m.
Mr. Marsden, Adelaide Rd.
collected for Prudential for about 3 or 4 yrs.
up to about 3 or 4 years, when Sutton took it over.

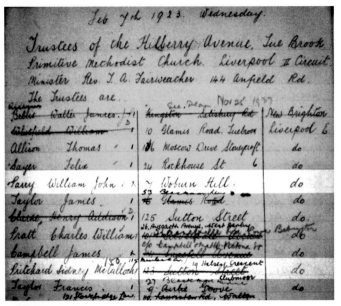

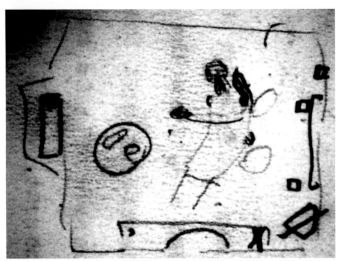

Top: **34.** Typed copy of handwritten notes taken by Sgt Harry Bailey whilst interviewing Richard James Qualtrough. (© Merseyside Police)

Middle: **35.** Page from minute book of the Hilberry Avenue Primitive Methodist church dated 7 February 1923, showing both William John Parry and Sidney McCulloch Pritchard as trustees.

Bottom: **36.** Sketch contained within Hector Munro's Wallace Case archive, showing the original position of Julia's body as stated by Mr and Mrs Johnston in their testimony at the committal trial: left arm resting over the body and right arm hidden beneath the body. There is also a depiction of the placement of the mackintosh. (© Hill Dickinson LLP)

for me I always put the money into it when they called to
pay over to me their collections. They had both seen me
take it down and put it back to the top of the book-case i
the kitchen often.   Marsden is about 28 years of age, abou
5 ft 6/7 ins. brown hair, and fairly well dressed. Parry is
about 5ft 10ins. slimmish build, dark hair, rather foppish
appearance, well, dressed and wears spats, very plausible.
Supt, Crewe, his assistant, Mr. Wood, 26 Ellersley
Rd., Mr. J.Bamber, Ass.Supt., 43 Kingfield Road, Orrel Park
employees of the Coy. would be admitted by my wife without
hesitation if they called.   There are personal friends of
ours who would also be admitted if they called. They are
Mr.F.W.Jenkinson, his son Frederick, 20 yrs?, his daughter
16, and his wife, they live at 112 Moscow Drive. Mr. James
Caird, 3, Letchworth St. Anfield, his wife and family. He

(handwritten marginal notes:) in bed wilt / in 20th / Thu 20th / at home / from 5.45pm / to 7.30pm / Syle went / parents Rd / 26 Cedar / Anlies / 20th

(handwritten inserted above 'Wood':) Albert

(handwritten inserted before 'Bamber':) Joseph

37. Extract from Wallace's second police statement, with additions penned in by police,
showing Marsden's alibi for the night of the murder – 'in bed with flu 20th'. (© Merseyside
Police)

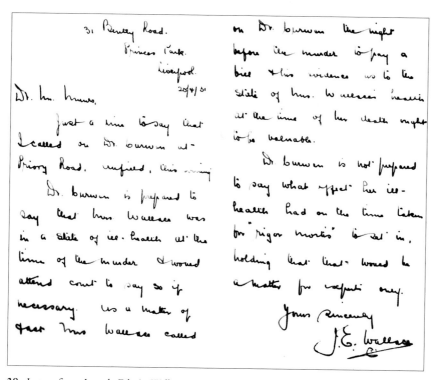

38. Letter from Joseph Edwin Wallace to Hector Munro explaining that, after visiting Dr
Curwen, he was told that Julia had visited him to pay a bill on the night before her murder.
(© Hill Dickinson LLP)

Account	I.B.	O.B.	G.B.	Total as per form 199	Total as per form 228	Date paid in D.O.
1931	£. s. d	£. s. d	£. s. d	£. s. d	£. s. d	
Jan.5	30. 0. 9	5. 2. 2	---	35. 2.11	35. 2.11	8. 1.31
12 M	77.12. 2	9.10. 7	1.18. 0	89. 0. 9	89. 0. 9	15. 1.31
19	10.11. 0	---	---	10.11. 0	10.11. 0	21..1.31
26	43.12.11	7.16. 9	1. 6.10	52.16. 6	52.16. 6	29. 1. 31
26		2. 9. 9		2. 9. 9	2. 9. 9	29. 1.31

Above: **39.** The Prudential Assurance summary of Wallace's collections showing he paid in £10 11*s* on the day after Julia's murder. (© Hill Dickinson LLP)

Middle: **40.** Harry Hewitt Cooke's crime-scene photograph of the Wallace's toilet showing the blood clot at the right and to the front of the pan. (© Merseyside Police)

Bottom: **41.** Digital enhancement of the same photograph showing that with the seat down, the right foot of the seat covers the blood clot.

FOOT OF SEAT COVERS BLOOD SPOT

42. Entrance to Tuebrook railway station. Hignett's bicycle shop would be next door, to the right.

43. Tuebrook station platform.

44. Detail of the crime-scene photograph taken from the bay window. Could this be a single fur-edged mitten belonging to Julia? Could the other have been covered in blood inside Parry's car?

Left: **45.** Detective Superintendent Robert Duckworth, MBE.

Middle: **46.** William Herbert Wallace leaving the Court of Appeal.

Bottom: **47.** Arriving back in Liverpool after his success at the Court of Appeal, Wallace and his brother Joseph thank Hector Munro.

I do not know who answered the door. He returned between 8.30 and 9 p.m. and remained until about 11 p.m. He told me he had been to, I think he said, Park Lane.

On Tuesday the 20th inst Parry called between 8.30 p.m. and 9 p.m. but I think it was nearer 9 than 8.30 p.m. He told me in answer to my question as to where he had been that he had been to a Mrs Williamsons [*sic*], 49, Lisburn Lane. I know Mrs Williamson, she is a friend of mine. He told me that he had got an invitation for myself and him to Leslie Williamson's 21st birthday party in April. I do not remember whether or not he told me he had received the invitations that night but I got the impression that he had. He remained until about 11 p.m. and then went home. He came in his car. I think Parry wore his striped trousers on Monday night and his blue suit on Tuesday and Wednesday, and I think he has worn his striped trousers every day since, but I'm not sure about Friday and Saturday.
[Signed] Lilian J. M. Lloyd.

Josephine Ward LLOYD, 7, Missouri Road, says:
I am the wife of Reginald Lloyd and I have a daughter, Lillian [*sic*] Josephine Moss Lloyd, 20 yrs. My daughter is a music teacher. She is keeping company with R. G. Parry of 7, Woburn Hill.

On Monday the 19th of January 1931 Mr Parry called at my house at about 7.15 p.m. as near as I can remember. I can fix the time as about 7.15 p.m. because my daughter has a pupil named Rita Price, of Clifton Road, who is due for a music lesson at 7 p.m. or a bit earlier every Monday. Last Monday (19th inst) she was a few minutes late and she had started her lesson when Parry arrived in his car. He stayed about 15 minutes and then left because he said he was going to make a call to Lark Lane. He came back in his car at about 9 to 9.15 p.m. and stayed until about 11 p.m. when he left.

On Tuesday the 20th January Mr Parry called at about 9 p.m. and remained here until about 11 p.m. He came in his car which he left outside. On Monday and Tuesday nights of last week (19th and 20th) Parry was dressed in a black jacket and vest and striped trousers and spats when he called. On Wednesday and Thursday or Thursday and Friday he was wearing a navy blue suit, I think it was Thursday and Friday because on Saturday he had his striped trousers again.
[Signed] Josephine W. Lloyd.

Josephine Ward Lloyd further states:
When Parry called at about 9 p.m. or a little after on Tuesday the 20th my daughter told him he was late and he said he had been to Mrs Williamson's, Lisburn Lane and to Hignetts at Tuebrook about a battery for his wireless. He was wearing his dark overcoat that night. He has a check grey tweed overcoat. He also has a brownish plus four suit and another brown tweed suit.
[Signed] Josephine W. Lloyd.

It was presumably at this point that the police knew Parry's statement, concerning the evening of the 19th January, was a pack of lies.

In the light of the previous four statements concerning Parry's movements on the night of the murder, Parry's statement is interesting on several levels. The better part of his alibi for the night of the murder concerns him going to Mrs Brine's house at around 5.30 p.m. and remaining there for three hours, until 8.30 p.m. He called at Mrs Williamson's house for only 10 minutes and yet he did not tell his girlfriend or her mother that he had been at the Brine's house. In fact, from the moment the police took his statement, up until his death in 1980, it would appear that Parry never told anybody else he was at the Brines' house. Mrs Brine stated that a 'Miss Plant' called to the house when Parry was there. Phyllis May Plant was about six months younger than Parry; if Parry was seeing Phyllis Plant behind Lily Lloyd's back, this might be reason enough for him not to mention the liaison to his girlfriend or her mother at the time. For him never to mention again the most substantial part of his alibi – in fact, the part of his alibi that would totally exonerate him of the murder – is a little strange. His one abiding alibi for the night of the murder was that he was with friends organising a birthday party. In 1966 when Jonathan Goodman and Richard Whittington Egan confronted Parry on the doorstep of his London flat, Parry referred to the incident yet again. Goodman noted that 'they [the police] finally seemed satisfied as to his innocence of the Wallace murder when he was able to produce some people with whom he had spent the evening "arranging a birthday celebration"'. Once again, he did not admit, despite it having been the better part of his alibi, that he had been at 43 Knoclaid Road for three hours. It should be noted that the police, in corroborating Parry's statement for the night of the murder, appear to have taken no statements from Mrs Brine's daughter Savona; Phyllis May Plant; William Hodgson or his wife Mary, of the Maiden Lane post office; Walter, Katie, Samuel or Josephine Hignett, nor any member of the staff of Hignett's, West Derby Road; and neither Mrs Williamson nor her son Leslie of 49 Lisburn Lane.

Later on that evening and the following evening, Tuesday 27 January, Moore had decided that the route Wallace had stated he had taken between his backyard door and Menlove Avenue would be investigated. Over these two nights, various officers, derisorily called the 'Anfield Harriers' by the locals, would set out at various times to see how long it took them to get to the tram stop at the junction of Smithdown Lane and Lodge Lane, where they ended their tests. At the committal proceedings, when asked by defence counsel Scholefield Allen why they had not tested the whole route to Menlove Avenue, Sergeant Harry Bailey admitted, 'It would have been a fairer comparison had I waited for a car at Smithdown Lane corner and boarded the car going to Menlove Avenue and then taken the time', but said, 'I did not wait for or get on to a tram going to Menlove Avenue because I was not instructed to.' Most likely, this was because the police had only Wallace's word that he had left his house at 6.45 p.m., but had tram conductor Thomas Charles Phillip's evidence that he had seen Wallace at the tram stop at the junction of Smithdown Lane and Lodge Lane at about 7.06 p.m. From this point on, Wallace's progress was meticulously accounted for. Their tests were eventually to prove that Wallace would, indeed, have had to have left the back door of 29 Wolverton Street at around 6.45 p.m. in order for him to have been at the junction of Smithdown Lane and Lodge Lane at about 7.06 p.m.

Whilst the 'Harriers' were flying around Richmond Park, a meeting had begun at the Dale Street Detective Office and would last well into the early hours of Tuesday morning.

Besides Superintendent Moore and other officers involved in the case, the Chief Constable, Assistant Chief Constable and Mr J. R. Bishop, assistant prosecuting counsel for the Liverpool Corporation, were also in attendance. The following afternoon, Tuesday 27 January, a brief meeting was held between officers involved in the case, and Mr Bishop was despatched off to London with Inspector Herbert Gold for an audience with the Assistant Director of Public Prosecutions, Mr Pierce.

At around six o'clock that evening, Wallace called into the Detective Office to ask Hubert Moore for permission to return to Wolverton Street to fetch a change of underwear. Moore took the opportunity to quiz him over Lily Hall's statement.

'Did you speak to anyone on your way home from the tram car on the night of the murder?' asked Moore.

Wallace denied it.

'Are you sure?'

'Yes,' Wallace replied.

'You told me you were in a hurry to get home. You should remember,' Moore insisted.

Wallace paused for a moment. 'I was not so alarmed that I would not raise my hat or speak to a person I knew.'

Moore explained that a Miss Hall, who had known him for some years, had seen him talking to a man by the entry near Letchworth Street at 8.35 p.m. Wallace thought for a moment, then said, 'Positively I did not.'

The following day, Wednesday 28 January, the Assistant Director of Public Prosecutions, Mr Pierce, was presented with the facts of the case. However, in his arrest report Gold stated, as though it would have been a deciding factor in obtaining a warrant for Wallace's arrest:

It was not known to us when interviewing the Assistant DPP that Wallace had denied having had a conversation with a man in Richmond Park on the evening of the 20th ultimo, as stated by witness Hall.

What made them so sure he had? Pierce told the men that, on the basis of the present evidence, he would not advise proceedings to go ahead and, if further enquiries brought no additional evidence, it should be left to the coroner to decide at the adjourned inquest.

Arriving back in Liverpool late that same evening, Bishop and Gold were rushed off to police headquarters where another meeting was held which, once again, lasted until the early hours of the following morning. Clearly, the Criminal Investigation Department were chasing a warrant of arrest for somebody. What had promoted this feverous rush to judgement? Apparently, the most recent and most damning evidence in the case had landed on their desks only sometime on the Monday evening when they received the statements from Lily Lloyd and her mother clearly showing that Parry was lying through his teeth. Were they going to arrest Parry? No – the warrant they were chasing was for Wallace. Had not his alibi been checked and re-checked and found to be sound? Had not his relationship with his wife been shown to have been, more or less, one of devotion? He had made a faux pas in grilling Beattie over the time of the phone call at the City Café – but nothing as damning as Parry's statement. Yet it was Wallace they were pursuing. Why where the police so certain

Wallace was the man they were seeking? As previously mentioned, two days after Bishop and Gold had returned from their meeting with the Assistant Director of Public Prosecutions, on Friday 30 January, PC James Edward Rothwell of Anfield police station gave his statement that on the day of the murder he had witnessed Wallace walking up Maiden Lane, Clubmoor, distraught and crying 'as if he had suffered from some bereavement'. Could this have been the 'additional evidence' the police needed in order to satisfy the Assistant Director of Public Prosecutor that 'proceedings' should go ahead? Two days after PC Rothwell gave his statement, on Monday 2 February, at 7 p.m., Superintendent Moore, Inspector Gold and Sergeant Bailey arrived on the doorstep of 83 Ullet Road.

8

Arrest!

Throughout the day of his arrest, as he had been doing ever since the day after he had found Julia battered to death on the hearth rug of their home, Wallace had been going about his usual business of collecting insurance premiums in Clubmoor. At around 4.30 p.m. he arrived back at Ullet Road, had tea and had set about his clerical duties. Then, in Wallace's own words:

On Monday night, my nephew and I were alone in his mother's house. I was sitting in the drawing-room writing letters and he in his bedroom studying. A knock at the door! My nephew answered it. I heard footsteps and voices. The drawing-room door opened. 'Someone from the police-station wants to see you, uncle,' my nephew said. Three men (Superintendent Moore, Superintendent Thomas and Inspector Gold) entered behind him, not waiting for any invitation. I rose to my feet. 'Take a seat gentleman,' I said. They remained standing, their hats still on their heads. Then the three of them approached closer to me, practically surrounding me. One inspector stood in front of me (Inspector Gold) and another to the right and left of me. The inspector looked straight at me. 'Mr Wallace,' he said. 'It is my duty to arrest you on the charge of having wilfully murdered your wife, Julia Wallace, and I have to caution you that anything you may say in reply to the charge will be taken down in writing and may be used in evidence against you.' Stunned, I looked at the three of them. My brain reeled; momentarily my body seemed detached. With an effort I pulled myself together. 'What can I say in answer to this charge of which I am absolutely innocent?' I burst out. Quite calmly the inspector noted this reply in his book. Even at that horrifying moment the stupidity and senseless formality struck me quite forcibly. Meanwhile, the other detectives were examining all the papers on the table; they collected them all, even the unfinished letter I had been writing to a personal friend. I was allowed to get my hat and overcoat and speak a word with my nephew. 'They have come to take me away,' I said, and his face grew white. I did not wish to distress him or use the word 'arrested'. Even at that moment I felt I must somehow minimise the shock to him and his mother who was out shopping. But he seemed to realise the position and what it all meant. 'I'm awfully sorry, uncle. Is there anything I can do?' He whispered. 'No. Tell your mother not to worry. It will be all right,' I replied. Thereupon, I was hustled out and into a waiting taxi. The half-suspected, wholly incredible thing had happened. I was arrested and charged with MURDER MOST FOUL!

Wallace had to have been mortified as to why his plan had failed. His alibi for the night of 19 January, his movements during the daytime of 20 January and his alibi for the evening were absolutely true. He had related them with no fear of mistake in the retelling. Every step he had taken during these two days he could solemnly account for. Even the discovery of Julia's body was truthful; the first time he had seen her devastated body was when he had left the Johnstons by the back entry door and had entered the parlour. How could Wallace have known that the one man he had relied upon to vindicate him in the light of his alibi, Professor John Edward Whitley MacFall — a man of science like himself — had failed him so incompetently? Placing the time of death at no later than six o'clock, and not nearer the true time Wallace knew it to have been, had sealed Wallace's fate: his carefully planned alibi was set quivering in its foundations. Even the possible lifeline of milk boy Alan Close's initial statement — that he had seen Julia at 7.45 p.m. — had been diluted in the mix.

Driven in silence to Cheapside police station in Dale Street, Wallace was formally charged with murder. He was asked, once again, if he had anything he wished to say, but he remained silent. Wallace was then searched and every item on his person (including his glasses) was removed from him with the exception of his clothes. He was then taken down a set of stairs and placed in an empty cell. Before the warder left him, he was brought a large tin pannikin holding about half a gallon of drinking water: 'I must confess that even in my trying condition and mental perturbation I was forced to smile. I could almost have taken a bath in that pannikin!' Later that evening, Wallace was brought a fibrous mattress and two blankets. Needless to say, he did not have a wink of sleep: 'My brain was on fire with riotous thoughts. My heart was sick with the gross injustice of it all.'

At seven o'clock the next morning, Wallace was brought a tin mug of tea and some bread and butter. At ten o'clock, he was before the stipendiary magistrate, whereupon he was remanded for eight days. At 2.30 that afternoon, Wallace was brought from the cells and, wearing his bowler hat, was placed in a line-up of nine other men: six wearing glasses, five with bowler hats and five with moustaches. After changing his position in the line-up, he was identified by Lily Hall as the man she had seen talking with another man near the entry at the side of the Parish Hall in Richmond Park at 8.35 p.m. on 20 January. Tram conductor Thomas Charles Phillips then identified him — by saying 'That resembles him' — as the man who had boarded his tram at the corner of Smithdown Lane and Lodge Lane at around 7.06 p.m. the same night. Wallace was to undertake another identification parade at Cheapside police station on 11 February, where, with Wallace presented alongside fourteen other men, Arthur Thompson, the conductor on the No. 5A tram Wallace boarded at Penny Lane, could not identify him.

The identification parade over, Wallace was allowed to retain the services of a solicitor before being taken to Walton Prison. Immediately, he contacted Hector Munro, a young partner in the firm of Herbert J. Davis, Berthen & Munro, who had their offices in the Prudential Building at 36 Dale Street. Although Munro did not know Wallace, as Munro was a keen chess player and also a member of the Central Chess Club, Wallace knew him; at the time, Munro was recovering from his own domestic troubles. Hector Alfred Munro was born at 56 Salisbury Road, Wavertree, Liverpool, on 28 September 1899 to solicitor William Hector Bryden Munro and Evelyn Fairfax Kynaston, daughter of a manufacturing chemist,

Josiah Wyckliffe Kynaston (Liverpool College of Chemistry, elected Fellow of the Chemical Society on 17 February 1859) and Martha Elizabeth Heath Hall. On 1 August 1925, Munro married 28-year-old Antoinette Grenat (a schoolmistress at the Rotrou College, Dreux, Eure et Loir, Beauce) at the Mairie of the 9th Arrondissement in Paris (the very place where, in 1873, artist Paul Gauguin had married Mette-Sophie Gadd). At the time of the couple's marriage, Munro was living at Toynbee Hall, London, where, since 1924, he held a joint practice (Berthen & Munro) with Edith Annie Jones Berthen, one of the first women in England and Wales to qualify as a solicitor, gaining much experience of working with large cases at the High Court. After joining her husband at Toynbee Hall, on 17 August 1926, Antoinette and Munro's only child was born – Donald Hector Berthen Munro. However, their marriage appears to already have been faltering. After the dissolution of the long-established Liverpool legal firm of Herbert J. Davis, McFarlane & Stockdale in 1923, in 1927 Herbert J. Davis offered the then 50-year-old Edith Berthen a partnership in the practice. Edith Berthen insisted that Munro be included in the partnership and the pair relocated to Liverpool. Returning to the city of his birth alone, Munro moved into a second-floor flat at 1 Marmion Road, Toxteth Park. Whilst living here, on 10 March 1930, his wife (by this time living at the Observatoire de Meudon) filed for divorce on the grounds of adultery, citing a Miss May Freeman, then living in a flat at 16 Forest Road, Claughton, Birkenhead, as co-respondent. Munro and Miss Freeman were married shortly after Munro received the decree nisi on 12 January 1931 (only eight days before Julia's brutal murder).

Upon their meeting at Cheapside police station, Wallace quickly signed a formal request upon a scrap of paper and handed it to Munro:

> 3rd February 1930 [*sic*]: I hereby retain you to act for me as my solicitor in the defence of the prosecution instituted against me & authorise you to take all necessary steps on my behalf. W. H. Wallace: To Mr Hector Munro.

After arriving at Walton prison in a 'Black Maria' police van along with other prisoners, Wallace was taken into the 'reception room'. Here, all the prisoners stood in line and identified themselves – name, occupation, religion – whilst the charge against them was read out. Placed in 'open cells', the men awaited the arrival of the prison doctor, whereupon they were stripped naked and compelled to take a hot bath before being medically examined. Given the blue suit of a remand prisoner to wear, Wallace protested that

> the officer in charge had no instructions from his superior and I was forced to wear this common clothing until the following day … Being made for what one may term an average man and I being six feet two inches, I felt and probably looked as if I were wearing the clothes of a schoolboy.

So began Wallace's incarceration – an incarceration that would last for 105 days. After a further eight-day remand, Wallace's committal trial began on 19 February 1931 and lasted for ten days, ending on 4 March 1931, when the stipendiary magistrate (Mr R. J. Ward) declared, 'You must go for trial at the next Liverpool Assizes.'

Soon after newspaper reports of Wallace's arrest had been circulated about the city, garage hand John Parkes asked his boss, William Atkinson, to inform the police of his encounter with Parry on the night of the murder; and it was not long before Superintendent Moore arrived at Atkinson's garage. Parkes told Moore his story of the night he had washed down Parry's car, about the bloodstained mitten and Parry telling him of the bar he had thrown down a drain. Moore's reaction was decisive. As with Alan Close's testimony, he dismissed it, saying, 'Pooh, pooh; I think you've made a mistake.' Why had Superintendent Moore not acted upon Parkes's statement? Why had the benzidine test not been applied at Atkinson's Garage? Could Moore have known that to have officially acknowledged Parkes's statement would surely have meant that a benzidine test would have to be applied? Had it shown a positive result, Parry would have to have been the subject of intense official scrutiny. He would then have to officially account for the disparities in his statement regarding the night of the Qualtrough phone call – and may have revealed the true identity of Marsden.

Hector Munro was now faced with a problem. He estimated that the costs for Wallace's defence would reach in excess of £1,000. Wallace had only £150 in his bank account and, though he offered to cash in two endowment policies, an awful lot more would be required. The only option that seemed viable was to approach Wallace's colleagues at the Prudential. With the offices of Herbert J. Davis, Berthen & Munro being within the Prudential Assurance building, Munro was familiar with James Wild, the Prudential's Chief Clerk for the Liverpool district. Tentatively approaching Wild, he was relieved to hear that he was more than happy to help. In fact, the day after Wallace's arrest, Wild had approached Arthur Evans, the local secretary of the Prudential Staff Union, and asked him if he would organise a collection from all union members nationwide to help Wallace with his costs. As Wallace had been a union member since early on in his career with the Prudential, and had also been chairman of the Liverpool branch in 1919, Wild also asked if Evans would contact the union headquarters in London with a view to them seriously considering contributing toward Wallace's costs with financial aid from the union funds. Wild produced a letter received from the joint national secretaries stating that 'you may rest assured that the Executive Council will consider ways and means of helping our brother member'. Munro was elated. On 10 March, Munro contacted the Liverpool Police with a request to supply him with copies of all statements taken from persons who were not called at the police court (this should have included statements taken from Parry, Marsden and any statements taken to corroborate their statements). This would allow the defence team a chance to investigate the lines of inquiry taken by the police which, as far as they were concerned, did not yield results or were not worth pursuing. The request was ignored. Munro renewed the request on 31 March – but once again, Liverpool Police failed to supply the documents. Had they been far too busy to comply with these requests? Had the requests fallen on deaf ears? Ultimately, these documents were never to be produced.

A fortnight before the committal trial, Wallace's defence fund was a mere £650: £150 from Wallace, £300 donated by his brother Joseph, £50 received from local Prudential Staff Union members and a cheque for £150 received from the Prudential Assurance Company. In order to boost confidence in their members and impress upon them the urgency for Wallace's much-needed fiscal support for the upcoming Assize trial, the Prudential Staff

Union joint secretaries had come up with a plan – they would stage a mock trial to be attended by union officials from all over the country who would act as jury. As in a real trial, both sides of the case would be heard: that presented by J. R. Bishop at the committal trial and Hector Munro's defence arguments. The 'jury' would then be asked for their verdict on the case. It was a gamble. If Wallace was found guilty here, there could be little hope of receiving any assistance at all from union members and the defence fund would be left vastly short of its target. Munro, confident of Wallace's innocence and, no doubt, of his defence arguments, embraced the scheme. There would, of course, have to be certain precautionary measures in place to both protect Wallace from any adverse prejudicial effects in the public eye should a guilty verdict be reached and leaked out and to protect the strength of Munro's defence from getting into the hands of the prosecution counsel before the start of the actual trial. To accomplish this, the mock trial would be held in total secrecy behind the closed doors of the union headquarters at Holborn Hall, Gray's Inn Road, London.

At 10.30 a.m. on Thursday 26 March, the 'trial' began and lasted for the whole of the day and well into the evening. When a vote was eventually called for, the voting slips were issued and collected. A space was cleared on a desk large enough to house two piles of papers – guilty and not guilty – and the count began. Munro knew that not only were they voting for much-needed funding, but also on the strength of the very strategy he would be using to save Wallace's life at the actual trial. By the end of the count, as every single slip of paper only served to increase the pile on the right-hand side of the desk, a tortuous moment in the life of the young Hector Munro turned into unbridled jubilation as the previously anxious, apprehensive and troubled room turned into a chaotic and riotous melee of stamping feet, clapping hands and cheers of 'Yes! Yes! Yes!' Forgoing any redundant overtures, the president of the union announced that the whole assembly had found William Herbert Wallace *not guilty*. The Executive Council would guarantee the *whole* of the cost of the defence.

William Herbert Wallace's trial at the Liverpool Spring Assizes began on 22 April before the Right Honourable Mr Justice Wright, with Mr Edward George Hemmerde, KC (Recorder of Liverpool) and Mr Leslie Walsh (instructed by Mr Walter Moon, Town Clerk, on behalf of the Director of Public Prosecutions) for the Crown, and Mr Roland Oliver, KC, and Mr Sidney Scholefield Allen (instructed by Messrs Herbert J Davis, Berthen & Munro) for the Defence. Throughout the trial, Wallace appeared impassive, emotionally dislocated from the gravity of the occasion – as interested an observer as the hundreds who had sat in the public gallery. Could this detachment have stemmed from his knowledge of his own guilt? If he was found guilty, he knew it was justifiable, the consequence merely a hastening of his premature demise due to his failing kidney. If he were in that frame of mind, having nothing to lose, why would he not have played the system? If he was found guilty, he had simply played the game and lost – if he got away with it, he had beaten the system and could live what remained of his life in contentment, congratulating himself upon his accomplished game-playing skill. Describing Wallace's demeanour throughout the trial, the *Liverpool Echo* commented:

Never once during the trial did it appear to those who watched him closely and continuously that Wallace could be brought to display the slightest sign of emotion.

His outward attitude was that of a man resigned to whatever fate might have in store for him. His customary attitude – his arms folded, his head slightly on one side as though with weariness – remained unchanged. The many references to his dead wife – the woman who, as counsel had remarked, had been everything to him throughout their married life – left him completely unmoved. The details of her death appeared to affect him not a whit; even the little human references to intimate details of their family life, even to the little sum of money they were saving for their holiday together.

Only when Mr Justice Wright commenced his low-voiced summing up, which could not be heard from the public gallery, did Wallace betray any sign that he was more than an ordinary spectator of the drama. He leaned forward more intently, his right arm doubled up beneath him on the rail of the dock, his fist clasped beneath his chin, listening closely to all that the judge said. The low voice ceased; there was an audible sigh in the court; the jury retired. Counsel for the prosecution, and for the defence, left the places into which they had sunk, exhausted, after their long addresses; the prisoner's white head disappeared down the narrow stairway leading to the cells beneath …

The trial lasted for only four days, at the end of which Mr Justice Wright, realising that the evidence against Wallace, as presented, was not sufficient to warrant a verdict of guilty, gave a closing speech that was decidedly in favour of clemency for Wallace:

However you regard the matter, the whole crime was so skilfully devised and so skilfully executed, and there is such an absence of any trace to incriminate anybody, as to make it very difficult to say, although it is a matter entirely for you, that it can be brought home to anybody in particular. If there was an unknown murderer, he has covered up his traces. Can you say it is absolutely impossible that there was no such person? But putting that aside as not being the real question, can you say, taking all this evidence as a whole, bearing in mind the strength of the case put forward by the police and by the prosecution, that you are satisfied beyond reasonable doubt that it was the hand of the prisoner and no other hand that murdered this woman? If you are not so satisfied, if it is not proved, whatever your feelings may be, whatever your surmises or suspicions or prejudices may be, if it is not established to your reasonable satisfaction as a matter of evidence, as matter of fact, or legal evidence and legal proof, then it is your duty to find the prisoner not guilty. Of course, if you are satisfied, equally it is your duty to find him guilty. But it is your duty to decide on the evidence which has been given before you during these three days and whatever your verdict is that is the acid test which you must apply. Will you consider your verdict and say whether you find the prisoner guilty or not guilty?

At 1.20 p.m., the jury filed out of the court. At 2.25 p.m., they returned to shock the court with their verdict:

The jury filed in; only one member of it stole a furtive glance at the tall, slender, white-haired figure in the dock. What was their verdict? The foreman of the jury, in reply to the usual question from the Clerk of Assize, said the jury had found the prisoner guilty. Immediately the tense atmosphere was broken by the gasp that approximated almost to a roar from the spectators who crowded the court. It was promptly suppressed by court officials.

In Wallace's own words:

Even at that awful moment I could hear a tone of grim satisfaction, almost pride in that foreman's voice; a note of jubilance … Then throughout the court, before and behind me, rushed one great gasp of absolute amazement. Even the Clerk of Assizes looked dumbfounded. I have since learnt that all those sitting on the bench, sheriff, chaplain, clerks and even the judge, were shocked at the unexpected verdict.

The Clerk of Assize turned to Wallace. 'William Herbert Wallace, you have been convicted of murder upon the verdict of the jury. Have you anything to say why sentence of death should not be passed according to law?'

Wallace hopelessly uttered, 'I am not guilty. That is all. I cannot say anything more.'

Mr Justice Wright had no choice in the matter; after his steward had placed the square black silk on the crown of his wig and the chaplains had risen and moved toward his right hand, he faced Wallace:

William Herbert Wallace, the jury, after a very careful hearing, have found you guilty of the murder of your wife. For the crime of murder by the law of this country, there is only one sentence, and that sentence I now pass upon you. The sentence of the Court upon you is that you be taken from this place to a lawful prison and thence to a place of execution, and that you be there hanged by the neck until you be dead, and that your body be afterwards buried within the precincts of the prison in which you shall have been last confined before your execution; and may the Lord have mercy on your soul.

Wallace was taken back to Walton Prison that afternoon and left to reflect upon his dire position over the rest of the weekend. During the afternoon of Monday 27 April, the governor of the prison came to see Wallace and told him the date of his execution had been officially fixed for Tuesday 12 May. On the same day, however, plans were already under way to lodge an appeal. For Wallace, news of this could not come too soon:

Hope sprang to life again when my solicitors brought me the news that an appeal was to be formulated and sent in. There is no anodyne in all the science of narcotics quite so satisfying as hope; it gave me at least much peace and quietness of mind. It seemed to be totally impossible that three great wise judges, learned in the law, with only the bare facts of the case before them, and free from any trace of rancour, prejudice or evil rumour, could do otherwise than set me free.

As before, funds would be needed to pay for the appeal. Munro, once again, turned to the Prudential Staff Union. On 1 May, he received their reply:

> We are all staggered by the verdict, and whilst appeal in all such cases seems such a hopeless procedure, we are bound to concur in exploring every possibility of saving Mr Wallace from such a cruel fate.

On 28 April, and over the next five days, Munro and Scholefield Allen began dissecting all of the evidence from the recent trial. Between them, they came up with ten grounds of appeal, the core of which was based upon the fact that:

> The verdict was unreasonable and cannot be supported having regard to the evidence. The whole of the evidence was consistent with Wallace's innocence and the prosecution never discharged the burden of proving that he and no one else was guilty.

After having had Wallace sign the document and hand it to the governor of the prison, the Notice of Appeal was delivered to the Registrar of the Court of Criminal Appeal on Monday 4 May. All they could do now was to wait.

On the morning of 18 May 1931, Wallace's appeal trial began before the Lord Chief Justice, Viscount Gordon Hewart of Bury, Mr Justice Branson and Mr Justice Hawke. Once again, he was standing in the dock awaiting a decision on his life:

> I cannot recall what my sensations were when I was ushered into that final court of all. I knew it was to be all – or nothing.
>
>   There was a great difference in the atmosphere of this court than that of the assize court in Liverpool. What I did feel was that here, if nowhere else, my case would be fairly tried, without prejudice, without conflicting rumours, without the dramatic witness box or the forensic melodrama of the prosecuting counsel. I knew that the evidence for and against me would be weighed with studied accuracy and impartiality on the scales of justice … And with thoughts like these I entered my railed-off gallery, tense and expectant.

The whole of that first day was devoted to the case for the defence, passionately put by Roland Oliver. The following day, Edward Hemmerde gave the case for the prosecution for over four hours, then, eventually, sat down. In hushed tones, the three judges conferred for a short time; then the Lord Chief Justice announced they were to retire for a short time to consider their verdict. Wallace was ushered out into a back corridor to await their return. After 45 minutes, Wallace was recalled, and the judges delivered their verdict:

> The Lord Chief Justice [Lord Hewart] giving the judgement of the court, said that three things were obvious. One was that at the conclusion of the case for the Crown no submission was made on behalf of Wallace that there was no case to go the jury … A second thing was that the evidence was summed up by Mr Justice Wright with

complete fairness and accuracy, and it would not have been at all surprising if the result of the trial had been an acquittal. Thirdly, it was obvious that the case was eminently one of difficulty and doubt.

The whole of the evidence had been closely and critically examined for two days, and it was not necessary to discuss it further. Suffice to say that the Court was not concerned with suspicion, however grave, or with theories, however ingenious.

Section 4 of the Criminal Appeal Act, 1907, provided that the Court of Criminal Appeal should allow an appeal if they thought that the verdict of the jury should be set aside on the ground that it could not be supported having regard to the evidence.

According to Wallace:

With what seemed callous deliberation, the Lord Chief Justice of England began to speak. I know now that every sentence had to be taken down for the purpose of reference in future cases. The judgement of that Court of Appeal may be quoted a century from now. But at the time, the careful weighing of words and sentences, the long pauses, the unemotion of that even voice, the almost icy mechanism of his dictation, kept all hearers strained and tense. To almost his Lordship's last word, the issue seemed to be in doubt ... 'We are not concerned with theories however ingenious or with suspicions however strong ... We do not find that the evidence ... was ... sufficient. Therefore ... this appeal ... must be ... upheld ... and the conviction ... quashed!'

Wallace was a free man. After being led from the dock to an open door to signify his freedom, Wallace left the Court of Appeal to be greeted by his brother Joseph, Hector Munro and Munro's wife – along with a swarm of pressmen. Hector Munro said of greeting Wallace on the steps of the Royal Courts of Justice, 'Mr Wallace met his brother, my wife and myself with a quiet smile. I am not going to repeat what Mr Wallace said as he accepted our congratulations.' Rushing from the building with his brother, the half-dazed Wallace was whisked off to the Strand and into a taxi.

The following day brought a morning of many thank yous. Wallace visited the Prudential offices and was given a month's paid leave. Arriving at the Prudential Staff Union headquarters, he thanked them all for their most generous support. During the afternoon, Wallace and Joseph had decided the time had come for relaxation; desperately needing a true sense of his newly found freedom, Wallace chose to visit Kew Gardens. Later that afternoon, the pair relaxed at a club cricket match. That evening, whilst staying at a boarding house with Joseph in Turnham Green, Chiswick, Wallace received an invitation from comedian Laddie Cliff to the premier of his new comedy musical *The Millionaire Kid* at the Gaiety Theatre. 'If only you knew how amazingly thrilling it is to laugh again,' Wallace said, 'you would realise how every moment of tonight's entertainment has been to me a joy.'

On Thursday 21 May, with less than a dozen people in the court, Julia's inquest resumed. Proceedings lasted less than two minutes. No sooner had the Liverpool Coroner, Mr Cecil G. Mort, taken his seat than he said:

In accordance with Section 20 of the Coroner's Amendment Act, I have to say that I received yesterday a notice from the Court of Criminal Appeal, with regard to proceedings in that court. That notice intimates that a conviction has been quashed with regard to the murder of one, Julia Wallace. The notice is signed by Mr N. W. Kershaw, Registrar of the Court of Criminal Appeal, and therefore I formally close this inquest in accordance with that notification.

When the proceedings concluded, the coroner gave no verdict. On the same day, the Liverpool *Evening Express* stated that 'the investigations by the Liverpool police into the death of Mrs Wallace will not be closed until a conviction has been secured. The case will remain on the books, and should any new facts or details come to light they will be subjected to the closest examination. The following day *The Times* reported, 'The Liverpool police stated officially yesterday that they would not reopen investigation into the circumstances of Mrs Wallace's death.'

9

The Price of Freedom

During the afternoon of 21 May, Wallace returned to Liverpool. Paying a visit to the Prudential offices in Dale Street, he called in on Hector Munro and attended a celebration party given by his Prudential colleagues. He was eventually whisked off in a car amid crowds of spectators who, having heard Wallace was back in Liverpool, had gathered in Dale Street. Upon being asked by reporters where he had gone, Munro told them he was off to Wales for a much-deserved holiday. In fact, he and his brother were heading north, to Latham House, a guesthouse in Broughton-in-Furness. Whilst here, thoughts of Julia were, apparently, never far from his mind. On 6 June, he wrote in his diary:

> My dear Julia is seldom out of my thoughts, and now I am on my own I realize the fight I am going to have in this battle against loneliness and desolation. Julia, Julia, how can I do without you! The anguish in my soul rises up and distils itself in tears which not all my resolution can hold back. Little did I ever think that grief and sorrow would so utterly unman me, and, yet, I must fight it down? Nothing can bring her back, nothing can undo the past. Even if he who did that foul deed is caught, it cannot bring consolation to me. The only consolation I can find is in the thought of our happy life, and the realization that she at any rate did find a large measure of happiness and content in her life.

On 7 June, his thoughts on the possibility of an afterlife resurface:

> After tea had an enjoyable ramble through the park to the woodland. I could not keep my mind off Julia, thinking how she would have enjoyed it. I am afraid these lovely walks will depress me for some time. My heart is in tears as I go along, and all the real pleasure of the walk vanished. If I could only believe in existence after death, then I could be more content. If, as the spiritualists assert, this is true, then my dear Julia will know that she is seldom out of my thoughts.

Whilst still on holiday, Wallace received Munro's bill of costs covering the period from 3 February to 1 June 1931. Along with the expected fees for correspondence, telephone calls, taking of witness statements, attending him in prison, and so on, there are two intriguing items: 'attending … on private detective, giving him full confidential instructions' and 'attending on private detective'. The actual charge for this service is simply listed as 'Paid private detective … £2 2s 0d'. Not one single document from the vast archive of Hector Munro's personal records concerning the case contains a single reference to identify who this detective was, nor what service he was providing. Was he shadowing Parry or Marsden? Unfortunately, we will never know.

On 9 June 1931, Wallace attempted to return to Wolverton Street and continue running his agency around Clubmoor. Eventually, this proved hopelessly untenable. With rumour and conjecture running rife around the Anfield district, between the sneers, taunts, constant second glances and the torrent of poison-pen letters, Wallace eventually succumbed. On 15 June, he wrote in his diary, 'I think I must definitely abandon the idea of returning to a Liverpool agency as the ill feeling against me is evidently stronger than I expected.' Again, on the 16th: 'Find all the neighbours up against me. They are the rottenest crowd I ever struck. Mean and paltry brained. I feel it a wicked insult to Julia. How she would have scorned the whole thing!'

Forced to relinquish his agency, Wallace took up a clerical position in the Prudential offices. Interviewed for Roger Wilkes's radio programme *Who Killed Julia?*, Hal Brown, an 18-year-old clerk at the time, recalled:

> Part of my duties were, on the one day in the week that some two to three hundred local agents came in to pay in their collections, I had to run up and down cellar steps dispensing stationery to them … The Prudential returned him [Wallace] to a job in the office, instead of an agency. He was with me in an office to the rear of the Prudential building. We worked together and we got to know each other a lot better. He received loads of scurrilous letters, and he'd say, 'Brownie, read through these for me will you; and just give me the ones you feel I should see.' And I used to open those letters, and some of the vile rubbish that people wrote. And whilst one or two of those letters were sympathetic, the rest were vindictive and nasty.

By the end of June, Wallace had had enough. With Hector Munro's assistance, he took out a £375 mortgage on Summer House, Meadowside Road, Bromborough, across the River Mersey on the Wirral peninsula (upon leaving 29 Wolverton Street, Patrick Stephen Devine, a druggist's packer, and his wife Lilian moved in). In contrast to the reception he had had upon his return to Liverpool after his success at the Court of Appeal, Wallace noted in his diary on 25 August:

> Quite a fine experience this morning. As I was going to catch my train I passed a man, and to my great surprise he said – 'Good morning Mr Wallace,' and introduced himself as a Mr ——. He had heard of my coming to live in Bromborough and, believing me to be an innocent man, desired to be friends. It was a kind action for which I am immensely grateful. To know that I am not an object of scorn and suspicion to everyone is something. And to go about feeling that one is shunned by nearly everyone is a terrible ordeal, and though I try to fight it down and ignore it, the whole business depressed me beyond words. Perhaps, after a while I may get immersed in some new

hobbies to take my mind off the terrible tragedy. What I fear is the long nights. But, perhaps the wireless will help me to overcome the desperate loneliness I feel.

It would not be long, however, before the past would rear its unforgiving head, on 14 September:

> Just as I was going to dinner, Parry stopped me, and said he wanted to talk to me for a few minutes. It was a desperately awkward position. Eventually, I decided not to hear what he had to say. I told him I would talk to him someday and give him something to think about. He must realize that I suspect him of the terrible crime. I fear I let him see clearly, what I thought, and it may unfortunately put him on his guard. I wonder if it is any good putting a private detective on to his track in the hope of something coming to light. I am more than half persuaded to try it.

Wallace knew that Munro had already employed the services of a private detective (Wallace had eventually footed the bill for his services) and, apparently, nothing had come of it. Yet, it would appear that Wallace expected that his diary entry would be read – and that the reader would be unaware that this undertaking had already been performed. Could this also be said of his other post-murder diary entries – and possibly some of the previous ones? Despite the new location, and the much-relished tranquillity Wallace found there, it would appear he was still apprehensive. On 6 October, he wrote:

> I cannot disguise from myself that I am dreadfully nervous about entering the house after dark. I suppose it is because my nerves are all so shattered after the ordeal, and this, together with the recurring fits of grief and anguish over my dear Julia's end make me horribly depressed and apprehensive … Left to myself I am for ever trying to visualize what really did happen. Although I am convinced Parry killed her, yet it is difficult to get proof. It would be a great relief if he could only be caught, and the foul murder brought home to him.

For some reason, the January of 1932 saw the beginning of Richard Gordon Parry's documented criminal career after his apparent run-in with the law as a juvenile offender. What had brought about this turn of events? After Parry's involvement with the police concerning Julia Wallace's murder, had his father eventually arranged for him to leave the city until things had quietened down? In doing so, Parry would have had to have terminated his employment with the Standard Life Assurance Company. Upon his return to Liverpool, he would have, for possibly the first time, found himself without a job. Being somebody who seems to have spent the majority of his time in constant search of money and having no employment, could this have been his motivation for turning to petty crime? Having no discernable talent for this chosen path and being no criminal mastermind, Parry was arrested on 13 January (the day after his 23rd birthday), by Police Constable H217 Jones, for 'Taking and driving away motor car FV207 without consent of the owner, or other lawful authority, from Sir Thomas St'. (What had now happened to the car he was driving at the time of

Julia's murder?) On 30 January, he was arrested twice on the same day: loitering with intent to commit a felony in North John Street, Liverpool (where the City Café was situated), and later that same day for stealing a car from the same street. The car belonged to Herbert Owen, a councillor from Cardiff; in returning to his car, Owen found Parry sitting in it. Asked what he thought he was doing, Parry replied 'Sorry, that's my car in front', and got out. Parry approached the other car with a set of keys; failing to open the door, he crossed over the road. Owen informed a policeman. In talking with Parry, the officer was told he was waiting for a friend. Asked to accompany the officer back to the car, Parry ran around the corner into Dale Street, where he was tripped over by a tram inspector, whereupon he was escorted to Cheapside police station. Outside the station, Parry threw himself onto the ground and had to be carried inside. His defence counsel said that Parry had had to meet his girlfriend but had been held up; he was tempted to get in the car in order to keep his appointment. Once in the car he had realised the seriousness of his action and was about to exit the car when Councillor Owen turned up. His subsequent actions were due to fear of the consequences. On 18 February, he was arrested for stealing one shilling and sixpence from a telephone kiosk in Crane Buildings (where, as an aspiring actor, he had appeared in *John Glayde's Honour* on 17 November 1930). On 24 February, he was arrested for stealing two shillings from a telephone kiosk in the Liverpool department store Owen Owen's, Clayton Square; later that same day he was re-arrested for stealing two shillings and twopence from Reece's Café in Clayton Square – by the same police officer. Whilst Parry was before the magistrate answering for these offences, his solicitor asked for leniency and asked for four other offences to be taken into consideration:

- 25 January 1932: Taking and driving away motorcar KD 2301 without the consent of the owner or other lawful authority from School Lane.
- 27 January 1932: Taking and driving away motorcar KD 8605 without the consent of the owner or other lawful authority from North John Street.
- 10 February 1932: Stealing seven shillings from the telephone kiosk, the monies of Messrs S. Reece & Sons Ltd, from 14 Castle Street.
- 24 February 1932: Stealing one shilling, the monies of Moss Empires Ltd, from the kiosk at the Empire Theatre, Lime Street.

After this, Parry appears either to have turned over a new leaf, or to have gone into hiding. Though, in talking to Jonathan Goodman whilst he was researching the book *The Killing of Julia Wallace*, Parry's father, William John Parry, told Goodman that his son 'was in the army after 1931' (he had become a conscript at Aldershot). This might have occurred sometime during 1932. Coincidentally, during the summer of 1932, *John Bull* magazine printed a series of articles, reputedly penned by Wallace, entitled 'The Man They Did Not Hang'. These articles have long been considered to have been totally ghostwritten, Wallace having nothing to do with them at all. Hector Munro's archives, however, contain a draft copy of the original document ('The Life Story of William Herbert Wallace'), edited, signed and approved by Wallace himself.

In one of the last diary entries to be made by Wallace, on 31 March 1932, he states:

Got —— book on ——. I see I am included in the list of great criminals. The thing is too hideous to think about. I, who could not have hurt any living thing, I am supposed to have most brutally murdered Julia – Julia who was the whole world to me, my only companion with whom I could have trusted my life. If there is a God in Heaven, why, oh, why! Has she solved the great mystery of the beyond, or is it utter extinction? Does she know how I grieve for her, or is it the end? I am tortured by doubts.

With Wallace still seemingly tortured by the ignominy of being branded a murderer and devastated by the loss of his wife, his relentless obsession with the question of life after death is still dominant. Little did he know, it would not be long before his questions would be answered. Could he have been hoping that if Julia was waiting for him 'on the other side' even she would not know it was he who had orchestrated her murder? Sometime around Christmas of 1932, his persistent kidney trouble had worsened and he was in great pain. Prudential clerk Hal Brown remembered that:

The last time I saw Wallace, it was necessary for him to go to hospital for a check up on his remaining kidney; and I remember seeing him standing by the door looking rather bewildered and lost, and I said, 'Hello Mr Wallace', and he said, 'Just a moment Brownie', and I went over to him and he said, 'They told me, these specialists, that if I have an operation on my one kidney, I could live for a couple of years; and that if I don't have the operation, I won't last more than six weeks: what would you do, Brownie?' And I said, 'You can't ask me to make a decision like that Mr Wallace'. He said, 'No, no – I'm sorry, I didn't meant to give you that job'. But, he said, 'I've decided, I've got nothing to live for now, I'm not going to bother about an operation'. And that was the last I saw of him; just a very short time after that, he died.

Wallace's housekeeper at Summer House, Annie Mason, recalled that he had no wish to remain alive: 'he was committing slow suicide'. On Thursday 9 February, Wallace was taken by ambulance to Clatterbridge Hospital, Cheshire. Upon his arrival there, he made out his will, witnessed by Clatterbridge staff members Dorothy Ellison and George Cecil Reginald Watts. In this will, the only beneficiary was to be his housekeeper, Annie Catherine Mason, to whom he left £100 (a present-day equivalent of just over £5,000) 'for her kindness and care during my illness'. The residue of Wallace's will was to go to its sole executor, his brother Joseph. After a re-sworn assessment of the gross value of Wallace's estate, this came to £1,672 14s 7d. After deducting debts and funeral expenses, the net value dropped by a staggering £1,051 19s 9d – leaving only £620 14s 10d.

What had happened to all this money? When Wallace bought his house in Bromborough, he had taken out a mortgage for £375; this was to be paid off at £1 4s 10d a week, beginning on Monday 7 September 1931. At the time of Wallace's illness, on the day he was taken into hospital, he had paid £90 9s 9d off his mortgage – leaving £267 8s 6d still to be paid. If we deduct this, along with the £100 left to Annie Mason, this leaves £1,305 6s 1d (a present-day equivalent of over £66,000) still to be accounted for. If we then deduct the residue of the estate, £620 14s 10d, this leaves £684 11s 3d unaccounted for. What other debts could

Wallace have acquired that would have required this large amount of money to have paid them off? Joseph Edwin Wallace, the executor of the will, was in Malay at the time of his brother's death and so his son, Edwin Herbert, was given power of attorney until his father's return to England, with two of Wallace's oldest friends, Frederick William Jenkinson and James Caird, standing surety.

During that week, an unsuccessful emergency operation was performed. From that point on, Wallace was hardly conscious; on the occasions he was, he was in a high fever. On 25 February, he was visited by his nephew Edwin. The pair talked for around quarter of an hour. When Edwin left his uncle, Wallace told him, 'Do good with your life.' At 3 a.m. on Sunday 26 February 1933, William Herbert Wallace died of uraemia and pyelonephritis. Pyelonephritis is caused by a bacterial infection contracted either internally or, more commonly, externally, entering the body through the urethra and travelling up the urinary tract to the bladder and on to the kidneys. It is not uncommon for patients with chronic pyelonephritis to have acute symptoms such as fever and tenderness beneath the ribs; as the kidney becomes more inflamed, the pain increases and there is loss of appetite and headaches. However, in some patients, there are no symptoms, or the symptoms are so mild as to be missed. This causes the disease to progress slowly, often undetected, over many years until there is enough deterioration to produce kidney failure. According to Wallace's diaries, as far back as 1928 he was complaining constantly about severe headaches and trouble with his kidneys; could these have been early signs of the onset of pyelonephritis?

William Herbert Wallace was buried, along with Julia, at Anfield cemetery on 1 March 1933. To avoid the prying eyes of morbid onlookers and pressmen, two gravediggers had opened the grave in the late hours of the previous evening, finishing up in the early hours of the next day. At 9 a.m. that morning, the cortège arrived. In contrast to Julia's burial, there were ten mourners present; among them were his nephew Edwin Wallace and his lawyer Hector Munro, the rest being largely made up of Prudential colleagues. A full committal service was given by the Reverend C. H. Startup.

Edwin Herbert Wallace graduated from the University of Glasgow in 1935 as a Bachelor of Medicine and a Bachelor of Surgery. That same year, he became a probationary lieutenant with the Indian Medical Service (IMS). Remaining with the IMS until its disbandment in 1947, Edwin eventually rose to the rank of major. During the Second World War, whilst taking part in the Malaysian Campaign, he was taken captive by the Japanese and was a prisoner of war in Singapore and Siam, where he was forced to work on the infamous Siam–Burma Railway (which included the famous 'Bridge over the River Kwai') – also known as the Death Railway. Here, an estimated 90,000 Asian labourers and 16,000 Allied prisoners of war died as a direct consequence of the project. After the disbandment of the IMS, Edwin joined the Sarawak government service as a general duties medical officer. During 1955 and 1956, he became honorary secretary of the Borneo and the Sarawak branches of the British Medical Council. During 1957 to 1959, he became chairman of the Sarawak division of the British Medical Council. Specialising in ophthalmology, in 1957 he was appointed to the post of ophthalmologist. This appointment covered all three Borneo territories: the Indonesian provinces of East, West, South and Central Kalimantan; the Malaysian states of Sabah and Sarawak; and the independent country of Brunei, through which, in connection with his position, he would travel extensively.

Edwin Herbert Wallace died on 22 December 1960, aged 49. He left behind a widow, Anne, and three children, Elizabeth, Susan and Josephine. Not only was 'Dr Wyn' Wallace both highly esteemed and well respected during his time in Borneo, he was also well loved by his patients. In a Kuching newspaper, printed shortly after his death, this tribute was made:

> No man or woman who sought treatment or advice from Dr Wallace had ever any cause for complaint, for to him they were all alike – be they rich men from an urban centre or farmers in the interior … And thus, no matter how busy, over-worked and strained he might personally be, Wyn Wallace always had time for 'the next one please'. It was partly his selfless devotion to humanity which kept him on the move all the time in Sarawak, North Borneo and, until lately, in Brunei also, and, though he himself must have known perfectly well the strain that was bearing down on him in this one-man job, he still 'kept on' to the great benefit of many, but, alas, at what great sacrifice. In the death of Wyn Wallace, Sarawak and North Borneo have lost a truly good and respected man and doctor.

It would appear that Edwin had certainly taken his uncle's last words to heart – 'Do good with your life.'

Shortly after William Herbert Wallace's funeral, Parry broke up with childhood sweetheart Lily Lloyd. 'Terribly upset when the relationship ended', she had, apparently in a rage of resentment, taken herself off to see Hector Munro, telling him she had lied in her police statement: she had seen Parry on the night of the murder, but it was not until later on that night. In 1981, Roger Wilkes approached Hector Munro to see if he could recall the event. However, he had no recollection of the incident:

> My recollection at this age is very feeble about this sort of thing, and I don't remember that at all – I doubt if that occurred. If it had occurred, I can't tell you what steps one would have taken. I've got to impress that Wallace was dead at that time, and I had no client. A solicitor in England doesn't act without instructions or just out of the blue, so to speak. It's very unlikely an English solicitor of any character would … begin to investigate on his own volition without instructions.

Though Miss Lloyd's statement is corroborated by her mother's statement and it does not furnish Parry with an alibi for the time of the murder – whether that be around 6.45 p.m. or between 7.30 and 8.30 p.m. – it would not have been needed since, for both these times, Parry already had two witness statements confirming he was at 43 Knoclaid Road between 5.30 p.m. and 8.30 p.m. Regarding 19 January, the night of the phone call to the City Café, Lily Lloyd does not corroborate Parry's statement at all. So, in which part of her statement was Lily Lloyd supposed to have lied?

On being contacted by Roger Wilkes for his Radio City programme, Lily Lloyd – at that time not long turned 69 and a widow, having married butcher Charles William Alway (who, at the time of their marriage, lived yards away from Joseph Caleb Marsden in Childwall), at St Mary's church, West Derby, on 7 October 1937 – said of the incident:

I gave a statement to the police investigating the Wallace murder, but it was only partly true. This was because I only saw Gordon [Parry] later on the night of the crime. I can't remember how much later.

She did not say if she later went to Hector Munro or the police to retract this. Had Parry simply asked Lily to agree that he was with her on the night of 19 January? Had she had given him the gist of what she had done that evening, and Parry had forgotten or become confused over the detail, and had given the police the detail as he could remember it? If Lily Lloyd was going to reveal anything to police in 1933, might it have been this? Not that she had lied in her statement, but the fact that she had complied when Parry had asked her to provide him with an alibi by telling him what *she* was doing that evening? Where had this questionable piece of information concerning Lily Lloyd's retraction originated?

The first revelation of this came in Roger Wilkes's book *Wallace: The Final Verdict*. Here, whilst recounting his endeavours to retain Goodman's assistance as consultant for the Radio City programme, he eventually received a letter from Goodman:

On 7 November, I received from Jonathan Goodman a letter confirming his acceptance of the consultancy arrangement for the radio documentary … I knew of Parry's reported romance with Miss Lloyd of Missouri Road, but I did not know that two years after the murder and after Wallace's death, Parry jilted the young lady … Then came Goodman's knock out blow. Miss Lloyd, jilted by Parry, 'went to Hector Munro offering to swear an affidavit saying that the alibi she had given Parry for the night of the crime was a fabrication: quite untrue – and, indeed, quite impossible (as police could have discovered if they had taken the trouble), as she worked as a pianist in a Clubmoor cinema and was there the whole of that night'.

From where had Goodman received this information? Hector Munro had told Roger Wilkes 'I don't remember that at all – I doubt if that occurred', so it cannot have come from him. In Goodman's book *The Killing of Julia Wallace*, referring to Parry's police statement, he states:

Regarding his alibi, when interviewed by the police (less than forty-eight hours after the murder) [it was, in fact, three days after the murder] he said that he had spent an innocent Tuesday evening in the company of friends, one of whom was named. Separately interviewed, the friends confirmed that his alibi was so. But two years later it was admitted that this was a mistake. If the police had investigated properly they would have discovered that it was quite impossible for them to have been together.

Where had he got this information? This also cannot have come from Hector Munro. During the building of his defence case for Wallace, he had approached both Hemmerde and the police, requesting them to send him copies of all statements they had taken that had been considered of no value to their case, but neither had acquiesced. Munro had never seen Parry's statement. It must be remembered that neither Jonathan Goodman nor Roger

Wilkes had seen Parry's statement either. Until the excerpt printed in James Murphy's book *The Murder of Julia Wallace*, in 2001, it appears that, apart from the police, nobody else had seen the statement. In researching his book, Goodman had spoken to Harry Bailey, Herbert Gold and William Prendergast – all officers involved in the Wallace murder case. Could one of these ex-police officers, in talking with Goodman, have amassed all of the people in Parry's statement (which they would have seen) referring to the night of the murder (Mrs Brine, Harold Denison, Lily Lloyd and her mother), and simply described them as 'company of friends'? 'Two years later it was admitted that it was a mistake. If the police had investigated properly they would have discovered that it was quite impossible for them to have been together' could be referring to his sources' unverifiable claims that Lily Lloyd was working at the Clubmoor Cinema that night and in 1933 had wanted to admit this. If this is true, why would his sources also claim that she had approached Hector Munro with this information? Munro had, apparently, never seen nor spoken to Lily Lloyd or Parry. If Lily Lloyd had wanted to make a clean breast of things, would she not have gone straight to the police? If this had been the case, serious questions immediately arise. The case, being a fairly recent unsolved murder, would still have been open to investigation so why would police not have investigated Lily's claim? Her retraction being two years after the fact, did Miss Lloyd have witnesses to corroborate her being at the Clubmoor Cinema on the night of the murder? If so, who were they? During the phone-in after Radio City's airing of *Who Killed Julia?*, one of the callers was Ted Holmes; Mr Holmes was the House Manager at the Clubmoor Cinema at the time of the murder. When questioned by Goodman and Wilkes about the likelihood of Lily Lloyd having worked on the night of 20 January 1931, Mr Holmes's recollection of the event was extremely vague: 'That I couldn't tell you ... we had an orchestra, and she simply did the relief pianist work to help out whilst they went to the pub for a drink'. Mr Holmes went on to say that it was Parry's practice to pick Lily Lloyd up after work. When pressed about Lily Lloyd's starting and finishing times when she was working at the cinema, he was equally vague: 'I'd say [she started work] around half seven, eight o'clock ... [She would finish work] somewhere about nine-thirty to ten ... or eight thirty to nine o'clock, I'm not quite certain – it was a long time ago'.

In 1986, two years after the release of Roger Wilkes's book *Wallace: The Final Verdict*, an ex-member of the orchestra that Lily Lloyd would stand in for during their breaks, George P. Johnston (no relation to John Sharp Johnston) wrote to Wilkes stating that it was almost a certainty that Lily could *not* have been working at the cinema at the time of the murder:

> In 1926 (as a young man of twenty) I was told by my old Liverpool Collegiate School friend Charlie Olden (later to become Ted Ray and my brother-in-law) that there was a vacancy for a pianist at the Clubmoor Cinema. I saw the manager (Frank Prendergast), secured the job and remained with the orchestra a pianist until the 'talkies' took over in 1929. There was a matinee and two separate performances during the evening. Between the shows the band had a 'break' – usually at the Farmers Arms, a nearby pub, and Lily Lloyd was the 'relief pianist' and played during the interval ... When, in 1929, the band was dissolved I can't remember whether Lily left with us as there was no further need for a band relief ... mechanical music has also been

installed so I find it difficult to accept the assumption that at the time of the Wallace affair she was still engaged as a relief for an orchestra that no longer existed. Not since September 1929 …

The first talking picture to feature at the Clubmoor Cinema was William C. DeMille's (older brother of Hollywood director, Cecil B. DeMille) *The Doctor's Secret*, starring Ruth Chatteron and H. B. Warner. Opening on Monday 19 August 1929, it was billed as 'Grand Opening – All Talking Feature – 100% All Talking Programme'. It would appear from George P. Johnston's letter, that not only was Lily Lloyd *not* working at the Clubmoor Cinema on the night of the murder – but also she may not have been working there since the end of 1929. On the night of Julia's murder, the Clubmoor Cinema was showing William C. DeMille's spy thriller *This Mad World*, starring Basil Rathbone, advertised as using 'Western Electric Talking Equipment', thus bearing out George P. Johnston's recollections.

If Goodman had received this unlikely scenario from his police sources, Lily Lloyd's motive appears to have been put forward as one of revenge: payback for Parry unceremoniously dumping her. How conceivable is this? After Parry's parents had failed to have their son smuggled out of the country by their friend Sidney McCulloch Pritchard, Parry's official criminal career had begun with vigour at the beginning of 1932 and, during that summer, Wallace's *John Bull* articles, under the title 'The Man They Did Not Hang', were published. Had this rattled a few cages within the Lloyd family and Parry families? Just when they thought all had quietened to a low whisper concerning Julia Wallace's murder, up it comes again – this time with Wallace saying he knew who had really killed his wife. Wallace died in February 1933; during 1933, the Lloyds moved from 7 Missouri Road, Clubmoor, to 50 Almonds Green, West Derby. During the same year Wyndham Brown's much-acclaimed book *The Trial of William Herbert Wallace* was published. It was also during this year that Parry became a conscript at Aldershot (as discussed below). Could it not be the case that, due to the above, both Parry's and Lily's parents had had enough of Richard Gordon Parry. *They* had broken off the relationship, not Parry himself – shipping Parry off to Aldershot.

All things considered, whilst being interviewed by Jonathan Goodman, had these ex-police officers simply been 'unofficially' emphasising their knowledge of the involvement of Parry in the murder of Julia Wallace? Obviously, in using this particular tack, they would also have had to absolve police of all accountability for their non-involvement.

In the July 1933, whilst still a conscript at Aldershot, Richard Gordon Parry was up to his old tricks yet again, and was arrested for taking and driving away a motor car without the consent of the owner. The case was eventually dropped when the owner of the car could not be located and Parry offered no evidence. On 5 November 1933 (soon after the publication of Wyndham Brown's *The Trial of William Herbert Wallace*) the *Empire News* – a Manchester-based Sunday newspaper that eventually became merged with the *News of the World* in 1960 – printed an article entitled 'Wallace Accused Me!' Apparently 'narrated' to journalist Paul Trench, the article was pre-empted by a declaration from the 'accused' man:

> Wallace always suspected me of the murder of his wife. I am not the man who was detained by the police and questioned. That man proved his absolute innocence, and

he will not enter this narrative. I am the man Wallace suspected, and even accused. And I feel it is up to me to come forward with my version.

Long thought to have been penned by Richard Gordon Parry, this initial statement already rules him out as its author.

According to the article, Wallace had three grievances against the man he had apparently accused, and so believed it was he who had murdered Julia. His first grievance was that the man knew too much about Wallace. Apparently, knowing of Wallace illness, he had recommended certain specialists to Wallace. Upon consulting these specialists, Wallace had been given 'certain serious advice'. Presumably, this refers to Wallace's renal problems. In what capacity could Parry have had any association with renal specialists that he could recommend Wallace to them?

Secondly, the writer had apparently 'told Wallace on a certain occasion that I would let him know when certain stocks would be a profitable investment and called around to his house to give him some useful information'. On this occasion, upon Julia eventually allowing him into the house,

> the first thing that struck me was an unpleasant smell. I stood and could not help sniffing, and Mrs Wallace explained that it was 'the drains'. However, after I had explained that I was a friend of her husband and one also interested in insurance, I got as far as the parlour. Here I took a seat, and here I discovered that the smell I got at the door was more pronounced. I said nothing, but used my eyes. The result was that I knew immediately that the smell was not altogether connected with the drains. The woman herself was, to my mind, untidy. The house was without doubt neglected. Piles of dishes lay all over the room – unwashed [presumably he meant the kitchen and not the parlour].

After around 15 minutes, Wallace returned to find Julia lying on the settee in the kitchen (on which she had apparently been lounging throughout the whole of the visitor's stay):

> There was a look of sneering discovery in the eyes of the man and my reply was a glance at the untidy figure on the couch. I spoke of the business I had called to discuss and after a while he covered up his temper and we talked of the matter in hand.

This obviously describes the writer's first visit to Wolverton Street (and it would appear from the whole article, his only visit). As we now know, Parry had first met the Wallace in 1926 when he was only 17 years old and had been there on many occasions. If uninvited and unexpected visitors were ever allowed into the house, Julia's habit was ostensibly to invite them into the parlour, not the kitchen. The writer explains this visit was to advise Wallace that 'certain stocks would be profitable'. Parry was *not* a successful speculator in any capacity. He was continuously on the lookout for money.

Wallace's third grievance was apparently 'because I was successful in business where he failed … My success added fuel to the fire of his hatred, and he never tried to hide this from me.' Richard Gordon Parry was a petty thief, a ne'er-do-well and a delinquent – not even successful in the 'businesses' of stealing cars and pennies from telephone boxes. I feel the crux of this article lies in its opening paragraph:

'Now let me say this, I know the murderer … He must realise I suspect him … I fear I let him see clearly what I thought … Although I am convinced —— killed her, yet it is difficult to get proof'.' Extracts from the Diary and last writings of William Herbert Wallace. These terrible disclosures appear in the new book, *Trial of William Herbert Wallace*, just published by Victor Gollancz Limited.

Either its author, Paul Trench, had recently read the book and had extrapolated this fictitious suspect from within its pages or – more likely, I feel – the whole thing was dreamt up by Wyndham Brown, his agent or his publishers in order to create a sensational advertisement for the book – a not too uncommon device today (Max Clifford would have been proud of its deviser). Wyndham Brown had been in close contact with Hector Munro whilst preparing the book; Munro had access to all aspects of the case including crime-scene photographs, trial transcripts – even Wallace's diaries themselves. The description given of the Wallaces' kitchen appears to have been taken straight from official police photographer Harry Hewitt Cooke's photograph of it. The opening paragraphs' discreet 'disclaimer', whilst not mentioning Parry by name, protects the newspaper from a possible libel action being taken out by him. Though not publicly known until at least 1981, when revealed by Jonathan Goodman and Roger Wilkes on Wilkes's series of Radio City programmes concerning the case, Richard Gordon Parry had been a police suspect and had made a statement. Hector Munro, in his capacity as Wallace's solicitor would, at that time, undoubtedly have known this. By this time, however, Wallace was no longer around to embrace or denounce the article.

The following year, Parry's name hit the headlines once again when, on Monday 24 September, he, along with two other men, was charged at Aldershot police court with taking and driving away a motor car without the consent of the owner. The three men were eventually located by the owner of the car outside the Victoria Hotel, Aldershot – the men were still in the car and Parry was at the wheel. The 'criminal genius' had taken a car that contained only enough petrol to take them a short distance from where it had been stolen. At the court, the chairman, addressing Parry, said:

Your fortune appears to have deserted you. This time you are going to meet just punishment for your conduct [as the chairman had Parry's 'rap sheet' to hand, was this meant as a slap on the wrist for the court system in Liverpool consistently dealing out light sentences to Parry?]. You will go to Prison for 3 months with hard labour.

Discharged from the Army because of this conviction, he was released on 9 December 1934. Moving on to Ealing, Greater London, he found work as a labourer. Sometime around the June of 1935, Parry was working at Steven's Valet Service as a van man. Only the following month, on Thursday 18 July, whilst living at 44 St Augustine's Avenue, Parry was arrested for fraudulently embezzling £2 7s 6d from his employers. After telling Detective Jack Robinson that he would reimburse his employers, Parry pled guilty at Willesden police court and was bound over for one year.

By 1936, Parry was back in Liverpool, living with his parents at Woburn Hill, and was a shop manager – and back in trouble again. This time, however, it was no trivial misdemeanour: he was being accused of assaulting a young woman, whom he had, allegedly, threatened to murder. The young woman alleged that at 10.30 p.m. on the night of 23 April 1936, she had met Parry in a shop in Green Lane (described as 'The Temperance Bar'), Stoneycroft, Liverpool. He spoke to her, but she did not recognise him. Parry told her they had met about six months previously when he had taken her out and offered to give her a lift in his car to her home in Knotty Ash. During cross-examination, she admitted, 'Prisoner was well known to me, and I had previously been out with prisoner in his car.' The pair left the shop at about 10.45 p.m. Upon arriving at the road where the young lady lived, she pointed out her house, but Parry drove on a couple of doors away. She asked him to back up, but he drove the car further on down the road and stopped. She then alleged that Parry kissed her and acted improperly towards her. Pushing him away, she opened the car door and told him she was going home. Parry said 'No you're not' and dragged her back into the car. She was struggling to get out, when Parry started the car and took off down Prescot Road, towards Queen's Drive. When he reached Muirhead Avenue, he swung the car around, drove her back down Prescot Road and on to Rainhill, Prescot, ignoring her requests to stop the car. Arriving at Warrington Road, Rainhill, Parry stopped the car between two houses and told her to get out; refusing, she started to cry. Parry caught hold of her hair and pulled her back. This is when she alleged, despite her struggles and screams, the assault occurred. After the assault, Parry drove her to a garage in Knotty Ash, where she saw a telephone box. She told him she would telephone her mother to tell her where she was. In reply to questioning by Mr A. J. Behn, Parry's defence counsel, the young lady denied that she had told Parry that she had 'misconducted' herself with 'men' but had misconducted herself with 'one man'.

According to Parry, on that evening he was with friends until about 10.45 p.m., when he drove to Liverpool Landing Stage, staying there for some time. He then drove up to the shop in Green Lane, arriving there at about 11.10 p.m. (he cannot have been at the Landing Stage for very long). The young lady entered the shop about half an hour later. Parry said that for five years he had seen her from time to time (despite being in Aldershot and London, he had seemingly been back and forth to Liverpool) and knew her well by sight; about three months earlier he had driven both her and her friend to Bowering Park (an area just outside of Knotty Ash) in his car. On the night of 23 April, she had walked into the shop and asked him about his car. He asked her if she was going straight home and she allegedly replied that she was not particular, but she must not be home late. They left the shop at about 11.45 p.m. (she cannot then have walked into the shop half an hour after he arrived; that would have made it 12.10 a.m.). Whilst driving his car, he asked the young lady where they should go. She replied, 'Please yourself, but I don't want to be home late.' He admitted stopping the car two doors away from her house, but said that this was because he did not know where she lived. Driving along Prescot Road, he had made his first attempt to pull up and even turned the car shortly before arriving at Brook Bridge (presumably Tuebrook railway bridge in

West Derby Road). The young lady said that she did not want to stop there and asked him if he were not 'a bit of a devil' with the women; she had been told that he was in the habit of taking women out and giving them a good time. She had allegedly told him that she had often wanted to go out with him. Up until that night, Parry said he had no knowledge of the young lady's habits (had there been an implication that she was a prostitute?).

He drove the car to Warrington Road, Rainhill, and pulled it across a footpath close to a gate. According to Parry, not a cross word was spoken between them for the whole of the drive to Rainhill and the young lady had never asked him to let her out nor had she screamed, and he described what transpired between them at that point (what she had considered to be the assault). They left Rainhill at around 1.25 p.m. and, during the journey back, the car had a puncture and he had asked the young lady to assist him with the jack. She had allegedly become angry. Parry suggested they wait for a lift and she became more angry, telling him she wanted to go home. Parry told her, 'All right, I will drive on the punctured wheel for you', and drove to Knotty Ash. Arriving at a garage in Knotty Ash, he found there were two mechanics there, but the young lady never said a word of complaint to them. Apparently, whilst at the garage, the young lady spotted a telephone box across the road and told Parry she was going to call her mother and tell her where she was. Instead, she pressed the emergency button and spoke to the police. The pair were taken to Old Swan police station, where, pointing to Parry, she told an officer, 'I have been insulted and assaulted by that man.' Upon being asked what he had to say, Parry said, 'There's nothing in it; I demand her to be medically examined by a doctor.' That night the pair were examined by Professor James Henry Dible (one of the experts used at Wallace's trial in relation to the blood clot found on the pan of Wallace's toilet). On Monday 18 May, the *Evening Express* reported that at Prescot Magistrates that day,

Professor Dible, of Liverpool University, in answer to Mr R. S. Trotter, prosecuting, said that on April 23 he examined Parry and found him suffering from bodily injuries and scars. About three-quarters of an hour after he had examined Parry he examined Miss ——. In reply to Mr J. A. Behn, for the defence, Professor Dible said that his examination of Miss —— led him to believe that there had been interference.

However, four days later, on 22 May, the *Evening Express* printed 'Corrections':

In the report in The Evening Express on Monday last of the case, at Prescot police court, in which Richard Gordon Parry was accused of having committed an assault … there were some misstatements concerning the evidence tendered to the magistrates … Professor J. H. Dible did not say that his examination of Miss —— led him to believe that there had been interference. Further in the evidence of Professor Dible it was reported that when he examined Parry he found him suffering from bodily injuries and scars. This was not so. Professor Dible stated that he found no marks or scars on Parry and Professor J. E. W. Macfall [John Edward Whitley MacFall, the very man who, after examining the crime scene at 29 Wolverton Street, had pronounced Julia Wallace to have been murdered no later than 6 p.m.] said that he agreed with the whole of Professor Dible's evidence and said that the girl bore no marks or scratches or an evidence that violence had been used.

Upon being questioned by Mr Trotter, prosecution counsel, Parry denied he had assaulted the young lady in the car, and said that her claim that he had threatened to murder her was 'ridiculous'.

This important case has an enigmatic outcome; no official record can be found of the verdict. Had Parry been found guilty or not guilty? Had the young woman withdrawn the charges? Parry, as mentioned above, was bound over for one year on 18 July 1935, for embezzlement. This new charge coming only nine months later, if he had been found guilty of the assault charge he would have received quite a long sentence. The following year, when living in St Helens, Lancashire (only 40 miles to the north of Liverpool), on 7 March 1937, Parry married Miriam Traverse. Either he must have been found not guilty, or the charge was dropped. It was here, sometime after his marriage, that Mrs Ada Cook (whose father Parry's parents had begged to smuggle Parry out of the country at the time of Julia's murder) had her uncomfortable encounter with Parry in a St Helens fish shop during which he had attempted to 'chat her up'.

Parry and his wife had only one child, Barbara. The marriage, however, was doomed to fail and the pair eventually divorced. Returning to London, Parry was living in Camberwell, and working, ironically, as a telephone operator for the GPO when, during December 1947 (when he was almost 39), he was married again to 27-year-old Doris Florence Howes. After moving to Lambeth, the couple had one child, Ursula Lilian Parry, who was born a year later. It was whilst the family were living in a ground-floor flat at 39 Grove Hill Road, Brixton, on 30 March 1966, that Jonathan Goodman and friend and writer Richard Whittington Egan (accompanying Goodman 'as much as a bodyguard as anything else') knocked on Parry's front door and quizzed him over Julia Wallace's murder. Goodman said of the meeting:

> Parry, who now works for 'the government' (telephone operator) and was about to go on night duty, is married to a plump woman who appears some years younger than himself (he is fifty-seven), and has a daughter who is just about to go to university.
>
> We found him a bland, plausible man who was not made in any way uncomfortable by our questioning. He had grey hair, smoothed sleekly back, and a neat-clipped military style moustache. He is of medium height and is neither fat nor thin. He appears to be in very robust health, wiry and well-preserved for his age. He is of reasonably powerful build, has noticeably large hands, and a loose, damp and rather fleshy handshake. His eyes, which are of that bold blue which is traditionally associated with 'sex maniacs', are penetrating and alternately shifty and too-candid. He exhibits a certain lack of affect. He engenders an air of spurious authority of the kind that one encounters in the knowing, self-possessed and self-satisfied kind of a jailbird. It was an air of authority that made us think of the type of ex-army non-commissioned officer who becomes a commissionaire.
>
> He also exudes a false trowel-layed-on [sic] charm, which can easily beguile, but is as bogus as the bonhomie of a car salesman. This manner masks, in our opinion,

considerable firmness – even ruthlessness. He would be a nasty man to cross. Despite an obvious, and quite attractive sense of humour, one suspects that just below the surface there lurks a considerable capacity for unpleasantness. We would sum him up as a tricky, position-shifting individual of the con man type. He is evasive, manipulative, sharp, on-the-ball and very clever. He is quite well-spoken, and throughout the interview kept a self-satisfied and inappropriate smile on his face.

During this interview, Parry admitted that there had been a surreptitious relationship between himself and Julia that was unknown to Wallace: 'Parry said that he used to sing as a young man, and would often go to tea at Wallace's where Julia would accompany his singing on the piano or the violin – Wallace knew nothing of this.' This statement has many flaws within it. If Parry went for tea during these meetings, Wallace had usually finished his collections by this time and would have been there. Julia, though an accomplished pianist, did not play the violin – Wallace did. During the Radio City phone-in, Russell Johnston had said of his mother (who was living next door, and would be home during the afternoons), 'As far as she can recall, she did not hear any piano playing or singing in the afternoons of the period leading up to the murder.' In making this incredible statement, had Parry (as all con men do) simply been embellishing a fact he knew to be true? In her statement to Thomas Brady, Mrs Cook had said of Parry's mother, 'My father and Mrs Parry sang duets together with my mother accompanying them on the piano.'

Two years after this encounter, Parry and his wife left London and moved to Llangernyw, Abergele, North Wales. After his wife died during the autumn of 1976, Parry lived there alone. A friend of Parry's from Colwyn Bay recalled of Parry:

> I called him Dick. He worked as a switchboard operator, first at Abergele Hospital and then at Colwyn Bay Hospital … I knew him because we both drank in the same pub, The Marine Hotel Old Colwyn. In Langernyw, he drank in the Bridge Inn. Dick used to get a lot of people's backs up because he had an arrogant manner on the telephone. He had been very ill during the winter of 79/80 and had been in Abergele Hospital. He had recovered and I had spoken to him two days before he died.

Richard Gordon Parry died on 14 April 1980. He had apparently collapsed in a field near to his home and had lain there for two days before being found. After neighbours were alerted by the presence of milk bottles on his doorstep, they had informed the police and he was subsequently found by one of their officers. He had died of a myocardial ischemia leading to a coronary arteriosclerosis – a heart attack. Parry was cremated on 21 April 1980 at Colwyn Bay.

10

Motive

Generally, we find that all murders have a motive: whether it be a personal motive or a more general motive to be found in the demented mind of a psychotic, random killer. Ever since the night of Julia Wallace's murder, the motive, like many other aspects of the case, has been a mystery. Even at Wallace's trial, Crown Prosecutor Edward Hemmerde had to warn the jury not to allow this 'minor' detail to cloud their judgement:

> You start here with the fact that I tell you quite frankly the Crown can suggest no motive. It would be most unsafe for you or any jury to pay too much attention to motive. Motive may be of great importance in helping you to find out who is the likely man to have done something, but supposing, to take an extreme case, you saw a murder committed, you would be unimpressed if somebody said to you afterwards, 'But there was no motive for his doing it'; you would say, 'I cannot help that; I saw it.' So if, although there is no motive apparent to the Crown or apparent to you, the facts seem to you to point irresistibly to the conclusion that he did it, motive has nothing to do with the question.

Generally, motives for domestic murder come down to three reasons: hatred, jealousy or greed. None of these have ever been shown to have been a viable factor in this case. If, as I argue, Wallace was party to Julia's murder, what could possibly have driven him to have orchestrated this terrible deed? As previously outlined, at the time of the murder, Wallace was suffering from the very ailment that would soon claim his life – pyelonephritis. He had been a patient at the Southern Hospital from 9 June 1930 to 10 July 1930. In a statement to Hector Munro, Wallace explains the reason for this: 'early in 1930 the trouble became more severe, and under the advice of Doctor Curwen, I went into the southern Hospital, Liverpool'. In a report sent to Hector Munro by the Southern Hospital's Surgical Registrar, Stanley V. Unsworth, he states that Wallace's condition

> is known technically as 'Pyonephrosis' [sic] and is all the more important in that it affected his sole remaining kidney … The absence of the left kidney was confirmed beyond reasonable doubt and a blood test showed that the diseased right kidney was not functioning satisfactorily. This precluded any surgical procedure, and the treatment adopted was medicinal and of a purely palliative nature … The condition … is one

which is not likely to have been much altered by treatment in the direction of restoring the kidney function … any improvement was likely to be only temporary.

After Wallace's discharge from the hospital, Dr Curwen warned him that his condition was serious and told him to be careful. Indifferently, Wallace had told him he would just have to carry on. Wallace's remaining kidney was rapidly failing and nothing could be done to stop it: Wallace was dying. In the light of his diary entries concerning his constant ailments and the afterlife, had the possibility of an early death been on his mind for some time? In the same report, a Dr Unsworth states:

CONDITION WHEN ADMITTED TO HOSPITAL. He was admitted on 9th June 1930, complaining of pain in the right loin and the passage of pus ('matter') in the urine, which latter was verified on microscopic examination of the urine.

It took a *microscopic examination* of Wallace's urine sample to verify his assertion that his urine contained foreign matter, so how had Wallace known his urine was contaminated with these minute particles? He had to have been examining his samples himself, using his own microscope, showing that Wallace (understandably) took a great interest in his condition and knew a great deal about its symptoms and progress. There is, therefore, every reason to believe that after leaving the Southern Hospital (if not before) he had known exactly what position he was in. During Russell Johnston's telephone call during the phone-in for Roger Wilkes's Radio City programme, he voiced his mother's opinion that 'possibly he knew he had a terminal illness'.

Finding himself in this condition, had Wallace taken a step back and contemplated his life thus far? Had he allowed his private life and domestic affairs to get uncontrollably out of hand? With his own mortality on the horizon, did he want to rectify this situation? Could his and, indeed, Julia's apparent unhappiness and disappointment with their lot in life have caused him to relish the idea of spending his remaining time leading a quiet life alone with his hobbies and pursuits? If this was the case, divorce would certainly not have appealed to him. At that time, divorce was far less readily available than it is today, the petitioner being presented with quite few hurdles to overcome. If the divorce were to be defended, the case had to be heard in the High Court in London, incurring not only the costs of the divorce itself, but also those of travelling and accommodation. If the petition were undefended, this could be heard before an assize judge, though a barrister would be required to represent the petitioner. The fees for this during the 1930s were, proportionately, a lot more costly than today. Add to this the fact that divorce cases at this time were essentially judged on a fault-based system: if you could not prove that your spouse was guilty of some matrimonial offence, you could not divorce. What grounds could Wallace have viably presented? Given the upset, the costs, the legal wrangling, the highly likely scandalous press coverage if anything embarrassing regarding his private life were to be disclosed in court – if his home life was untenable to him now, it would be a lot more untenable after a failed divorce petition. A more immediate solution may have occurred to him.

This particular scenario is by no means unique in the annals of crime. Laura C. Richards BSc, MSc, FRS is a criminal behavioural psychologist who, after ten years working on violent crime at the Metropolitan Police Service, New Scotland Yard, left in 2007 to take up the role of advisor on violent crime to the British Police Force, the Association of Chief Police Officers (ACPO) and the Home Office. Having previously set up the first Homicide Prevention Unit in the United Kingdom, and having trained at the National Centre for the Analysis of Violent Crime at the FBI, she worked in partnership with Co-ordinated Action Against Domestic Abuse (CAADA) and created the Domestic Abuse, Stalking and Harassment and Honour-based Violent Risk Checklist (DASH, 2009). Within this checklist, Richards highlights certain traits that may indicate the high probability, within a family unit, of the occurrence of what she terms the 'Family Wipe Out', where a member of a family (usually the husband) shows a high risk of murdering their entire family. Richards notes that, to the outside world, the family appear to be 'normal' and 'average' – their problems being kept inside the home. The men who carry out the 'Family Wipe Out' are typically self-centred, remote, socially awkward and have feelings of inadequacy; they are often seen by the outside world as 'not a people person' or a 'closed book' – unable to express any form of emotion. They lack any close friends or other family, are isolated, and lack a support structure. In such cases, Richards says that where anger and resentment build up in a man towards his wife, there develops a desperate need for him to terminate the problem for good. This is when a man can turn to the 'Family Wipe Out' as a solution.

A more recent incident than the murder of Julia Wallace bears uncanny parallels to the above scenario, the perpetrator and circumstances of the crime displaying many, if not all, of the traits used by Laura Richards in her assessment of 'Family Wipe Out'. Like Wallace, the case involved a man who had no criminal history, and, as he was an accountant, his business also involved dealing with other people's money. He was described as an attentive parent and, like Wallace, was described as being mild-mannered, courteous, soft-spoken, very precise and very exact – a man you would not mind having as a next-door neighbour. Yet, this 'average' man went on to execute his whole family – his mother, his wife and his three children. In the seventeen years it took to bring him to justice, this man committed no other crime. He changed his name, had remarried and was pursuing a quiet, average life as an accountant.

John Emil List

On 7 December 1971, New Jersey's Westfield Police were called to 'Breeze Knoll', 431 Hillside Avenue, the nineteen-roomed, palatial home of 45-year-old John Emil List and his family. Neighbours were aware that the List family had left the area a month earlier to care for an ailing relative and, during that time, the windows of the house had been brightly lit and a radio had been playing. They assumed Mr List's 84-year-old mother, Alma, was still at the house. As the month wore on, and the light bulbs in the house began to burn out, fearing that Mrs List might need assistance, the police were called. Having knocked at the door and received no answer, two officers checked around the property – all seemed in order. Neighbours insisted that elderly Mrs List may not have gone with the family and may be in difficulty, so the two officers entered the house via an opened downstairs window. As they began searching through the darkened rooms, soothing classical music could be heard playing from the other side of the house. Eventually reaching an archway covered by two large, heavy curtains, the officers moved them aside and shone their torches into what was the Lists' ballroom. Lying together across the floor, in a close arrangement, were four figures. The officers shouted to the figures to get up from the floor. There was no response. Upon entering the ballroom, the grisly truth was all too plain to see – the four figures were the badly decomposing bodies of John List's wife, Helen (45) and his three children, Patricia (16), John (15) and Frederick (13). All had been shot through the back of the head, except for John, who also showed evidence of having been shot multiple times. With police backup on the way, the two officers split up and searched the house for the father of the family, John Emil List, and his mother. After backup had arrived, and after a 45-minute search, Alma List's body was found on the floor of the back room of her third-floor apartment. She had been shot once through her left eye. Unable to locate John Emil List, after police had entered his first-floor office they were in no doubt as to what had taken place and who had perpetrated this gruesome crime: List had left a five-page letter addressed to Pastor Rehwinkel, of his local Lutheran church, of which he was a devout member. The letter was dated 9 November 1971 – exactly four weeks previous – and was written in a matter-of-fact, detailed manner; in it, List took full responsibility for the murder of his entire family. He explained that he was facing bankruptcy and he had murdered his family in order to spare them (what he believed were) the sinful effects of a life of poverty – believing that they would all be in Heaven now. Two days after discovering the bodies, police found List's car at Kennedy International Airport. However, given that he had had a month's head start, for almost eighteen years the letter List left was to be the last that was heard from him.

By 1988, authorities thought that John Emil List either had since acted as a model citizen, having never been entered into any police database, or was dead. At this time, *America's Most Wanted*, a nationally shown television programme dedicated to bringing fugitives to justice, had had many successes. New Jersey Police approached the producers, asking them to take on what would be the oldest case the programme had ever featured. They refused. After repeated requests and refusals, it took until April 1989 before *America's Most Wanted* agreed to take on the List case. Because of the age of the case, programme producers took the then unusual step of asking forensic artist Frank Bender to attempt to recreate a bust of the likeness of List as he would have appeared at that time. Consulting with forensic psychologist Richard Walter after the completion of the bust, Bender decided to add a pair of black, thick-rimmed glasses; for this simple addition, the pair were particularly praised. By the time the programme aired, John Emil List had changed his name to Robert 'Bob' Peter Clark, had been remarried in 1986, had lived in Denver, Colorado, and was now living in Richmond, Virginia, where he had a job at an accounting firm. List, a fan of the programme himself, had managed to catch the end of it. Another viewer was an old neighbour of 'Mr and Mrs Bob Clark' from Denver, Colorado, who recognised List and knew that the couple had recently moved to Richmond, Virginia. After the neighbour called the programme with the tip, on 1 June 1989 federal agents arrived at the 'Clark' home whilst List was at work. List's new wife, Delores Miller, did not believe that her husband was fugitive John List. She directed them to her husband's accounting office in order to clear the matter up, and it was here that John Emil List was finally arrested for the murder of his family. What had driven this average, devoutly religious, seemingly successful family man to undertake such a brutal, callous and shocking act?

On 29 June 1989, the now 63-year-old List was extradited from Virginia to New Jersey to face first-degree murder charges for the killing of his entire family. After his arrival, the state hired criminal psychiatrist Steven Simering to assess List's mental condition. After a four-hour interview, Simering was to say, 'He said, essentially, something that had to happen – it was unfortunate'. Simering was of the opinion that John List was suffering from an obsessive-compulsive personality disorder:

> This simply means that he is the kind of individual who doesn't feel problems, but rather represses problems and tends to deal with things in an emotionless, rather cold, clinical way … He did not have a major mental illness …

According to Simering, the carnage found at 431 Hillside Avenue, Westfield, New Jersey, was simply the result of the accumulated pressure of several 'disappointments' suffered by List throughout his life. In attempting to alleviate this pressure, List had decided upon this horrific solution. Addressing this, List was to say:

> I've been analysed by the psychiatrist as being that type of person – I get into a rut of rethinking the problem and never coming up with any new ideas and just coming back to the same solution that I came up with the first time.

John Emil List was born on 17 September 1925 in Bay City, Michigan. List's parents, John Frederick List and Alma List, were cousins – John Frederick was twenty-eight years older than his wife. Before their marriage, Alma had been a nurse; when her cousin became ill, Alma nursed him back to health. A short time later, in 1924, the couple married and within a year, their only child, John Emil List, was born. List's parents were devoted members of the local Lutheran church, where John Fredrick was both trustee and treasurer. An unpopular man in the community, he had a great dislike of children and this extended to his only son; his only acknowledgement of John's existence was to call him 'The Boy', basically shunning him. List's father took very little part in the raising of his child. List's mother, however, more than compensated for her husband's lack of paternal love, and doted on young John. Fearing neighbourhood children would open her son's eyes to a god-forsaken world, Alma spurned any friends that he might have made, cosseting her son in her own intimate, social circle within the Church. At the List family home, young John was not even allowed the privacy of his own bedroom, his parents having him sleep in the parlour, where his every move could be monitored. This became List's life throughout all of his years at high school.

After graduation, much to his mother's chagrin, he enlisted in the Army, fighting in Europe (possibly looked upon by List as a welcome break from his mother). Taking leave in 1944 to attend his father's funeral, List – it was noted by those present – never shed a single tear, seeming unmoved by the whole event. After the funeral, List went on to gain a Bachelor's degree in administration at college. Even whilst attending college, List's mother made her presence felt by visiting her son every week when Alma and John would attend church, have their meals together and read and discuss the Bible. Continuing at college and eventually gaining a Master's degree in accountancy, List became a lieutenant in the Army Reserve (once again, possibly to escape his mother more than anything else). After gaining his Master's degree, List found employment, though this was cut short when he was called up to serve in the Korean War.

When he was eventually stationed in Virginia, one night during the September of 1950, whilst at a bowling alley (possibly celebrating his 25th birthday), he met his future wife, Helen Taylor. Helen was a 24-year-old widow who already had a 9-year-old daughter, Brenda (who lived with the family for some time, moving on before the tragedy). Alma List strongly disapproved of the couple's burgeoning relationship – a disapproval that would remain until both their untimely deaths in 1971. Within two months of their first meeting, John Emil List married Helen Taylor on 1 December 1951 at a Lutheran church in Baltimore, Maryland. During their short courtship, Helen had told List that she was pregnant.

Steven Simering noted that the first of the 'disappointments' List might have suffered leading up to the 1971 tragedy appears to have been what List considered to be his forced marriage to Helen. Upon telling List that she was pregnant, List had vowed to marry her. The day before the wedding, she announced that she was not pregnant; she had been mistaken. Despite this, List went ahead with the wedding. According to Simering, 'years later he was resentful about his impression that she, perhaps, had misled him as a way of getting him to marry her'. It was not long before the couple started their own family, Patricia, John and Frederick being born within four years of each other. By all accounts, List was an attentive father: 'From what others told me, I did a fairly good job: I certainly loved them all.'

By 1958, with a young family to raise, John List began a series of accounting jobs that brought little success, the family (often including List's mother) having to move home constantly whilst List found work. Simering says that this was not due to poor work performance, but rather through List's personality. The year of 1965, however, brought List some success; when he was hired by the First National Bank of New Jersey as a vice-president, his career seemed to have, at long last, been heading in the right direction. On the strength of this, the Lists bought one of the largest, most prestigious houses in an affluent suburb of New Jersey – a nineteen-room, Victorian mansion in Westfield. This, according to Simering, was another huge disappointment in List's life: not truly wanting to move into such a big house – feeling he was forced into this by his wife and the demands of his growing family – he borrowed money from his mother and invited her to live with them. Once the family were settled, the pressures continued to escalate. Having married at age 16, Helen had contracted syphilis from her previous husband before he had left to serve in the Second World War. Killed in combat, he never returned. Penicillin being reserved for military use only, doctors undertook a failed attempt at curing Helen by infecting her with malaria, and now Helen's condition was worsening; her advanced syphilitic condition had progressed into dementia. Half-blind and drinking heavily, she rarely spoke to her husband. The List children were showing no interest in the Lutheran Church (for which their father had become a Sunday school teacher). List's eldest child, Patricia, was smoking cannabis and dabbled in witchcraft. These pressures were only exacerbated by the presence of Alma, List's overbearing mother.

List owed $11,000 on three unpaid mortgages he had taken out on the family home; in order to pay the ever-mounting bills he had begun stealing money from a joint bank account owned by his mother and himself. In 1969, List lost his job as vice-president of the First National Bank of New Jersey and began selling life insurance. Eventually, this too failed and List became unemployed once again. Author Timothy Benford believes that this was the breaking point: 'From that point on, I think is when the downfall really began; that's when he started realising he was not a success, he was failing to provide for his family and the problems kept mounting.' List himself confirms this: 'I guess I was sorta beaten down from the feelings that I had had, and I was ashamed to let anybody know.' Desperate to maintain the illusion of success and maintain his pride, List hid his jobless condition from his family and his neighbours; each morning he would don his suit, drive to the train station and take the train a few stops down the line and remain there until it was time to return. Beleaguered by his problems, List began to look upon his family as an added weight. In explaining List's reluctance to turn to his family for help at this point, Steven Simering says, 'This was a man who was deeply repressed; a guy who had always kept his emotions to himself. From the time he was a small boy he kinda sucked it up and buried it.' By 1971, List was facing bankruptcy: for this proud, deeply religious man, his world had fallen apart and he began to contemplate his options. Simering says of the effects this had upon List:

> Mr List was not aware of the degree of his anger and his resentment: he was resentful of his mother for years and years; he was resentful of his wife from the time she had tricked him into marrying her, he believed; and he was resentful of his children for all kinds of reasons that many of us resent teenagers who can be a pain in the rear end.

Constrained by the doctrines of his religious beliefs, he ruled out suicide, believing it to be a mortal sin. List explained, 'I felt that if you committed suicide you would automatically go to hell.' Another option was to simply turn his back on the family – pack his bags, jump on a train and never look back; once again, his pride and his strong Lutheran upbringing forbade this. Fearing his family would become destitute and be forced to turn to the welfare state, poverty being a sin that would lead them to lose their eternal souls and be damned, List also quickly discounted this option. After several weeks of contemplation, in his own words John List's final solution was that 'if I would kill them that would save them from any problems … I felt that, even though I killed the family, I could still get forgiveness, eventually, from God.' Having made up his mind, on the morning of Tuesday 7 November 1971, John Emil List had dressed and, as he usually would, had gone downstairs to have breakfast with his three children: 'I tried not to act any different than I ordinarily would – so they wouldn't be suspicious.' After the children had left for school, List went out to his garage and readied two pistols, one that had belonged to his father, the other a souvenir from his army service in the Second World War. In the meantime, his wife, Helen, had awoken and was in the kitchen having a morning coffee: 'I came back in, said a few words to Helen and went into the front room; then I came around back and shot her in the head.' List then climbed the stairs to his mother's third-floor apartment, where she was having breakfast:

> She got over and greeted me and gave me a kiss, and she said 'What was that noise?' Now, at that point, I felt like a Judas – having kissed her too; and I said 'Oh it must

have been some noise out the back, that's why I came up.' She started going into the attic area, and as she got to the doorway, I killed her.

List had shot her once through her left eye. After cleaning up the kitchen, he dragged Helen's body into the little-used ballroom. Writing letters to his children's schools explaining that they would be absent for a while as they were going on a trip, he drove to the bank and withdrew $2,000 from the account he shared with his mother, then called at the post office to post the school letters and stop mail to the house. Returning home, List made a sandwich and waited for his children to arrive home:

> I don't believe that while I was eating – especially at lunchtime – that I had any feelings of, 'no, I should stop and not go any farther with this'; I just felt that once I had started it was incumbent upon me to kill all of the children so that not even one of them would remain and suffer the trauma that they would go through knowing that the rest of the family had been killed.

The first of List's children to arrive home was his 16-year-old daughter, Patricia. As she entered the kitchen, her father snuck up behind her and shot her through the back of the head. Moving her to the ballroom, he laid her on a sleeping bag close to her mother. Next to arrive was his youngest child, 13-year-old Frederick. Once again, List shot him through the back of the head and laid him on a sleeping bag in the ballroom next to his sister. List then left the house and went to pick up 15-year-old John from school: 'He had a soccer game; so I went over and watched the soccer game: he seemed to be playing a good game and enjoying himself – then we came home together in the car.' As father and son walked through the kitchen, List shot John through the back of the head: 'All of the others just dropped: finally they were dead. John, I don't know whether it was a muscle reaction that caused him to jerk around a little bit – but then I shot several more times' – ten in all. As with the others, John was placed in the ballroom on a sleeping bag, beside his brother and sister: 'That was the one thing I was trying to prevent; their feeling any wounds or suffering at the last moment. How compassionate, huh!'

List's method of execution appears to have been reminiscent of execution-style killing he may have experienced during his service in the Second World War; List had seen heavy combat during the final weeks of the war whilst serving in Germany. Finally, it was over. His final solution had been carried out: 'I think after I had shot John and cleaned up, I felt such a measure of relief that this plot that I had was carried out without being interrupted. I, more or less, relaxed after that.' John List sat at the table in the kitchen for another meal: 'Having been in combat, we were out killing and fighting and then we'd come in and have something to eat. I think that's what allowed me to eat peacefully in the room that I had killed my family.' After his meal, List went to bed.

The following morning, after turning down the thermostats to 50 degrees to slow down the decomposition of the bodies, turning on all the lights in the house and tuning the radio to his favourite radio station, List sat down in his office to write the five-page letter to his pastor. A month later, when this letter would be found, List was 2,000 miles away in Denver, Colorado: 'I just thought I would like to see the mountains and relax a little bit because I had been under a lot of strain.' Steven Simering explains:

> He enjoyed his life in Denver; it was a fresh start for him in every sense of the word. Remember, his problem was he was overburdened – he had been a failure in every way; he saw his family as a burden, not a source of support. They were all gone – poof – and he was free.

After almost two weeks, List's trial ended on 11 April 1990; the following day, after nine hours of deliberation, the jury found List guilty of five counts of murder in the first degree. As the crimes were committed in 1971, before the death penalty was reinstated in New Jersey, John Emil List was sentenced to five consecutive life terms. He died on 21 March 2008 whilst in custody at Trenton Hospital, New Jersey, from complications arising from pneumonia. He was buried next to his mother in Frankenmuth, Michigan.

John Emil List was not a career criminal, nor was he a serial killer in the accepted sense of the term; he was no John Wayne Gacy, Ted Bundy or Jeffrey Dahmer. What truly makes this case so horrific and enigmatic is the fact that it appears to have been perpetrated by a man who, in shunning confrontation and having no ability to take charge of his own circumstances, had simply reached breaking point – a place most of us have been at some point in our lives. In reviewing what appeared to him to be his limited options, the solution he settled upon, extreme as it was, was a solution nonetheless. Not only when this point of desperation was reached, but also during the time he had settled upon his diabolical 'final solution', he displayed no outwardly visible signs of stress or emotion. Whilst carrying out this horrific task, List appears to have treated it as one would treat any DIY household job: prepare the tools you might need, prepare the materials to be used, complete each stage, clear away any mess to be ready for the next stage. One can also see, in having a meal and retiring to bed once the whole 'job' had been completed, List found a sense of solace; the burden he was carrying had been lifted. In relocating himself 2,000 miles away from the source of his pain and in changing his identity, List provided himself with the simple solution he had craved for many years – a chance to start his life over again, and get it right.

Could the insight into this extreme, horrific case also provide us with William Herbert Wallace's motivation for bringing about the murder of his own wife? Both List and Wallace appear to share emotional as well as personal parallels: as a Stoic, Wallace too was disposed to keep his feelings and emotions under strict control, restricting his passions, regarding them as a distraction. Another stoical trait displayed by Wallace was a psychological independence from a society he deemed disruptive and unreasonable. Effectively, in the words of Steven Simering in relation to John List's obsessive-compulsive personality disorder,

> he is the kind of individual who doesn't feel problems, but rather represses problems and tends to deal with things in an emotionless, rather cold, clinical way … This was a man who was deeply repressed; a guy who had always kept his emotions to himself.

Could Wallace also have been suffering from a similar obsessive-compulsive personality disorder? Did Wallace, like List, feel as though he too had a string of mounting 'disappointments' throughout his life? In the draft copy of 'The Man They Did Not Hang', the *John Bull* series of articles proofed by Wallace and published under his name in 1932, he lists five of these disappointments as 'condemned to death': stricken with typhoid fever at the age of ten; two bouts of serious kidney trouble during his stay in Calcutta; four operations on his kidneys by a German doctor in China; and having his left kidney removed in Guy's Hospital, London. Upon his return to England, these disappointments continued. Because of his ailing condition, Wallace was unable to work for over eighteen months. When he did find work in taking up his old position at Messrs Whiteway, Laidlaw & Company in Manchester, this too proved too arduous and he was forced to leave. Like John List, whatever aspirations Wallace had, they were constantly being dashed. Shortly after his appointment as agent for the Ripon division of the Liberal Party, he met and married Julia. As has been shown, at the time of the couple's marriage, Julia had, at the very least, greatly exaggerated her age by deducting sixteen years, with the strong possibility that she had also lied about her parentage and the place of her birth. If Wallace had found this out, he may have felt he had married a 53-year-old stranger. At 53, Julia was way beyond childbearing age and almost old enough to be his mother; should Wallace have been hoping to start a family of his own, little would he have known at the time, but even this dream would have been dashed. If this was the case, and he had somehow found out Julia's deception, he, like List, may have felt he had been duped into marriage and greatly resented Julia. This could have been where the couple's apparent 'disappointment' with their lives together had stemmed from. Shortly after their marriage, at the beginning of the First World War, Wallace's faith in politics waned. As he put it:

> The war crashing into our quiet lives brought politics with a bang to the ground – indeed the party system for the nonce became a dead letter, and I was once again thrown on my beam ends.

Even Wallace's attempts to join the forces – a total of six times – were dashed because of his 'inefficient kidney' and he was found unsuitable. The mores of the time being what they were, coupled with Wallace's stoicism and reticence to deal with conflict, had the Wallaces' relationship become simply one of endurance? Given that added into this mixture were Wallace's possible unseemly acquaintance with Parry and Marsden and the knowledge of his imminent mortality, Wallace, like List, may have been an emotional dam waiting to burst. Like List, whilst yearning to begin his life over, he might well have been satisfied to spend what time he had left in relative peace and tranquillity.

At 29 Wolverton Street, in looking at the crime scene itself, I do not think any present-day detective of any accomplishment would doubt that this was a crime of passion – a passion of such degree that the intensity of the attack could only have been carried out with extreme emotion. This usually denotes a personal association between victim and assailant. As will be shown, the perpetrator of this crime did not only render the crushing blows that killed Julia Wallace, he also had to physically move Julia's lifeless body across the room – something Wallace was assuredly incapable of due to his long-term kidney problem which, as we have seen, had been escalating to such a degree that only six months previously he had had to undergo a stay in hospital. In several witness statements, comments concerning Wallace's frailty are liberally scattered. Amy Wallace: 'Mr Wallace was however not a strong man, and relied upon his wife a great deal to look after him.' Edwin Herbert Wallace: 'My aunt rather objected to him being up in the back room, as she said it was too cold and damp for him, as he was not strong, and she had to go to a great deal of trouble to look after him … I should say that neither he nor my aunt were very strong in health.' Florence Sarah Johnston: 'They were delicate and the winter months tried them very much.' James Caird: 'in July or August of last year, I was there, and Mr Wallace was very anxious to accompany her on the violin, but she said "No, Herbert; you're not strong; you'll only upset yourself if you play" … He was rather a highly-strung man, and was also in poor health … The accused was not a strong man. He was a delicate man I should say.'

The passion exercised in this murderous act stemmed, most likely, from jealousy, hatred – or fear. If jealousy, this would have had to have come from the person inflicting the damage and, as we have seen, this could not have been Wallace. If Julia had had a jealous lover, would not the damage have been inflicted upon the person he hated most – Wallace himself? Both Julia and Wallace were well known to be very private people, tending, for the most part, to keep themselves to themselves. By all accounts, those that knew Julia either liked her or had no feeling one way or the other. There is certainly no evidence that what few friends they had hated her enough to want to murder her in such a brutal fashion. The only option we are left with is fear: surely Julia could not have instilled so much fear in anybody to have forced them to have committed such a terrible crime?

At the time of the murder, it was revealed that the Wallaces were not, by any stretch of the imagination, affluent. After a lifetime's work, Wallace had only £150 in his bank account; Julia had £90. Giving evidence at Wallace's trial, during a cross-examination by Roland Oliver, Wallace's Superintendent at the Prudential, Joseph Crewe, stated that Wallace's accounts were and always had been in good order:

> *How long have you known Mr Wallace?* 12 years and a few months.
> *What is your opinion of his character?* An absolute gentleman in every respect.
> *Have you ever seen any sign of violence or ill temper about him?* None whatever.
> *Scrupulously honest?* Absolutely.
> *What about his accounts, were they always in order?* Always to a penny.
> *There was no question of his ever being wrong in his accounts?* None whatever.

This shows that Wallace could not have secreted a cache of money away through the embezzlement of his Prudential collection money. If Wallace had orchestrated Julia's murder and had managed to find either a willing or an unwilling 'accomplice', how could he have found the funds needed to pay for this most terrible of crimes? With no funds available, what did Wallace possess that would have induced someone to commit murder? Motive can easily be translated as 'benefit'. Who would possibly have benefited (besides Wallace), and in what way, from Julia's murder? Why would he have displayed so much emotion in his sustained and frenzied attack upon a lone, defenceless woman?

11

A Little Knowledge Goes a Long Way

As mentioned previously, at the time of Julia Wallace's murder, Joseph Caleb Marsden was a clerk employed by Bernard Murphy & Son, commission agents at 2 Kings Road, Tranmere, Wirral, Cheshire. However, Marsden was more than a simple 'bookie's clerk'. Marsden was married on 7 June 1932 at St Mary's church, Edge Hill, Liverpool, to Sylvia Alberta Taylor, daughter of the then deceased William John Taylor, a printer's manager, and Mary Jane Little. Not unlike Julia's marriage to Wallace, despite Marsden having three surviving siblings, two of whom were still residing in Liverpool (his older sister, Bessie Arnold, having moved to Hunter, New South Wales, Australia in 1919, shortly after her marriage to Harold McGrath), his older brother Harold Egbert and his younger sister Constance Irene (then married to assurance superintendent George Arthur Bertram Jones), both the best man and the bridesmaid at his wedding were his wife's siblings – Reginald William Taylor, her older brother, and Doris May Murphy, her older sister. At the time of Marsden's marriage, Doris May Taylor was married to Thomas Richard Murphy, the only son of Bernard Murphy – the founder of the very company Marsden was working for. On the day Marsden married Sylvia Alberta Taylor, Thomas Richard Murphy became his brother-in-law.

Bernard Murphy had his roots in Ireland. His grandfather, Bernard (1811), was born in Armagh, County Armagh; his grandmother, Margaret Phillips (1811) and his father, also named Bernard (the couple's only child, born 1841), were born in Ballymote, County Sligo. By the early 1860s, Bernard's grandfather having died, his grandmother and his father had arrived in Liverpool (along with his great uncle, John Phillips) and had set up business as fishmongers at Bispham Street, off Dale Street. During the autumn of 1861, Bernard's father married his mother, Elizabeth Brennan, in Birkenhead. Bernard, the first of three children, was born in Liverpool in 1864. Having eschewed the family's fish-selling business, the young Bernard became a corn miller. During the summer of 1898, he married Ellen Brereton, daughter of joiner Thomas Brereton and Louisa Jane Trelford.

At the time of Joseph Caleb Marsden's birth (1900), Bernard Murphy, his wife Ellen and their one-year-old son Thomas Richard were living at 48 Whittier Street, Toxteth Park, Liverpool, and were self-sufficient – Bernard having already become a bookmaker around the time of his son's birth. Around 1916, the business going so well, the family, now including five daughters (Ellen Elizabeth, Annie May, Agnes Louise, Elsie Victoria and Florence Lilian), moved house 'over the water' from Liverpool to a more prestigious residence in Birkenhead Road, Greater Meols, Wirral, Cheshire, which he named 'Glentworth'. On 28 March 1923,

Thomas Richard Murphy married Doris May Taylor at St Cyprian church, Edge Hill, Liverpool; Doris's bridesmaid was her only sister, Sylvia Alberta Taylor. By this time Bernard Murphy's enterprise had gone from strength to strength and, upon his death on 14 April 1924, only a year after his son's wedding, Bernard Murphy's estate was worth over £51,000 (the modern-day equivalent of over £2.5 million), to be divided equally between his wife and his only son, Thomas Richard – by this time living with his wife at 'Canterbury', Upton Road, Moreton, Wirral. At the time of Julia's death, Marsden was already working for his future brother-in-law and engaged to Sylvia; he may possibly have gained his position at Bernard Murphy & Son through his relationship with Sylvia Alberta Taylor.

In the strife-torn Britain of the 1930s – where, by March 1931, 2.5 million people were unemployed and the Labour government were spending more in payments to the unemployed than they were receiving in National Insurance contributions – if motive were needed for murder, what stronger motive can there have been than the possibility of someone demolishing what looked to be an extremely bright future by causing you not only to lose your job and your future wife, but also the acquaintance of a millionaire. Could Wallace have possibly known something about Joseph Caleb Marsden that, if revealed, would most assuredly have caused his fiancée to break off the engagement and, therefore, not only abruptly end any thoughts of future happiness with his future wife, but also put an end to any hope of future financial security through his association with the wealthy Thomas Richard Murphy?

Using the evidence already presented, might a possible reason for any hold Wallace may have had over both Parry and Marsden have already presented itself? Could it be possible that, sometime after the end of 1928, after Parry had brought Marsden to 29 Wolverton Street to apparently assist Wallace with his collections, Julia had been paying the cash-strapped men for sex? After all, she had grossly lied about her age and personal circumstances in order to marry a man almost young enough to be her son. Why should she not still enjoy the attention of younger men? It must also be remembered that, at this time (1928), Julia was purporting to be 51 years of age and not the 67 years of age she would have actually been. Could this possibly have been the principal reason Wallace could not risk taking out a divorce petition and risk the possibility of Julia revealing the whole sordid affair in court? In spite of popular conjecture that Julia may have been a prostitute, could it be that it was not she who had been prostituting herself at all? Julia knew her true age; by all accounts, she was not so well preserved as to fool herself into believing she would be attractive enough to deserve the attentions of young men in their twenties and thirties. She has been constantly described as 'old-fashioned'. Could this scenario also explain the strange underwear worn by Julia on the night of her murder and observed by Sergeant Harry Bailey when he had to take her body to the Princes Dock Morgue. As Goodman wrote:

> The underskirt, which was obviously home-made, was fashioned from a length of woollen material only slightly lighter in weight than the skirt itself ... The corsets were frayed and loose fitting, and it seemed to Bailey that they had been worn, not for support, but simply as a means of suspending the stockings. What at first sight appeared to be a small patch on the side of the corsets turned out to be a pocket

containing a one-pound note and a ten-shilling note. The oddest of all Mrs Wallace's odd undergarments was the last to be taken from the body – an unhemmed square of white flannel, folded into a triangle and pinned in the position of a diaper.

Regarding first the money in Julia's corset, this money, as was found, would have had to have been notes because with the body in certain positions, coins would have rolled out. During the sexual act, Marsden or Parry could easily recover the notes 'covertly'. Could this have been Julia's 'old-fashioned', polite way of not embarrassing the young men by handing them the cash face-to-face after the 'services' had been provided? Or, equally, of preserving some semblance of her own dignity? As we know from Professor MacFall's observations at the autopsy, Julia had not had sex that night; hence, the money was still in her corset.

Regarding the 'diaper', Julia was not known to have been incontinent. In fact, one of the symptoms of her condition as described by MacFall, 'Typical constipation bowel' (possibly Ogilvie's Syndrome), would have been constipation. In describing her uterus as 'clean', this would (along with her age) rule out menstruation. The diaper could simply have been used for practicality and comfort – easily slipped off before sex and, once the act was completed, easily slipped back on to act as a convenient method of post-coital hygiene, then simply thrown away in a bin. Could this 'unhemmed square of white flannel' have been cut from the bottom sheet of the bed from the front bedroom – stripped off the bed only that day? As can clearly be seen in the photograph of the Wallaces' kitchen, a pair of scissors is lying on top of what appear to be pieces of the white bed sheet. Might Julia, expecting the charlady, Sarah Jane Draper, to call the following morning, have been cutting the sheet up to use as cloths – and used one as a diaper? If she was in constant need of such an article, what had she been using previously? Surely, she cannot have been cutting up linen bed sheets on a regular basis. What could have prompted her to utilise this remnant material as underwear for that particular day? After receipt of Bailey's report concerning his observations of Julia's unconventional underwear, the next obvious step would have been to ask Wallace about them should they have any bearing on the case. From all the statements, trial transcripts and the many other hundreds of documents inspected by this author, it is plain that this question was never asked nor answered. If this had occurred, Wallace may simply have denied any knowledge of his wife's dressing habits.

During the meeting with Parry in 1966, Goodman noted that Parry had described Wallace as a '"very strange man" and implied that he was sexually odd'. If true, could he have been referring to the fact that Wallace may have known about Julia's liaisons with Marsden and himself? The most common sexual problem found in men with kidney failure is erectile dysfunction – impotence. This can cause much frustration when the sex drive itself is unimpaired. Add to this Wallace's possible inability to have undertaken the physical exertion that sexual congress with his wife would have required, and could Wallace have been party to these liaisons – in a voyeuristic capacity? As stated previously, during Wallace's illness at the end of 1928, when Parry and Marsden 'assisted' him with his collections, Wallace said of Parry:

While he was doing my work in December 1928 he called very frequently to see me about business, and he was well acquainted with our domestic arrangements. He had been in the parlour and kitchen frequently and had been upstairs in the middle bedroom a number of times to see me while I was in bed.

Wallace had said of Marsden, 'While he was working for me, he often came to my house to see me on business. He also knew the interior arrangements of my house.' Had Marsden also had to visit Wallace in the middle bedroom on a number of occasions whilst he was ill in bed? It would appear highly unlikely that it should take two young, fit men to do the same work as one invalided man. Parry, contrary to Wallace, had stated that he had been to Wallace's house on only two occasions during this time to pay in the premiums he had collected and had made no mention of Marsden. This would seem a more likely occurrence for the transaction of the business to hand. But why the disparity in the two statements regarding the frequency of both Parry's and Marsden's presence at the house? Why had Parry not mentioned Marsden's involvement? It has to be remembered that Parry, as has been shown, was a man constantly in search of money. Marsden was introduced by Parry to Wallace because 'He was an agent for the Prudential Company for two or three years and had left before he did my work. I gave him the job because he was out of work.' Marsden was another man in search of money. If the money found in Julia's corsets (£1 10s) was payment for sexual 'services', in modern-day terms this would have been equivalent to over £70. This was risk-free – more than enough reason for two men in desperate times to participate in such an undertaking, no matter how unsavoury the task. Could this have been the actual reason Parry introduced Marsden to Wallace? Had Marsden voiced his desperation to Parry, Parry then pointing him in the direction of some easy money?

If, as I have discussed, Wallace, wanted to rid himself of Julia and was desperate to get his final years on a more tenable track, had news of Marsden's engagement, forthcoming marriage and close association with millionaire Thomas Richard Murphy – possibly relayed to him by either Parry or Marsden himself – inspired him to formulate a plan by which these objectives could be achieved? Upon obtaining this information, Wallace would have realised that he now had at his disposal the very tools that would enable him to gain the serenity he yearned for – Marsden's fear of exposure and ridicule. Could Wallace have turned Joseph Caleb Marsden's momentous occasion of good fortune and future happiness against him in a despicable, abhorrent, self-centred plan to dispose of what he considered to be an encumbrance and an embarrassment – his own wife?

No remuneration would be necessary. Marsden's payment would be Wallace's silence. He might then have begun to piece together a plan to dispose of Julia, not only using the assistance of Parry and Marsden – but also Julia herself. Could this have been why, in his second statement, Wallace dissociates himself almost completely from Marsden? Could the statement, 'I do not know if he is working now and I do not know anything about his private affairs' actually be Wallace's way of dispelling any doubts as to his guilt should police eventually discover Marsden and Parry's complicity in the murder – Marsden then revealing that Wallace had blackmailed him into his involvement due to his activities with Julia and Wallace's threat to expose him to his fiancée and thus quash any plans for marriage and a future relationship with Thomas Richard Murphy? If all went to plan, he would be rid of his wife and have been able to carry on his work and follow his pursuits in quiet equanimity until he died.

Treated as the unfortunate, grieving husband by his friends and neighbours, Wallace might simply have remained at Wolverton Street – he could hardly have known of the financial benefits the slaying of his wife would eventually bring. On 2 June 1931, Wallace received a cheque for £300 from Allied Newspapers after filing a lawsuit against them for libel. On 14 July, he received a cheque for £200 from 'the newspapers in respect of the libels'. On 19 May 1932, Wallace issued a writ against Wyman & Sons Limited, the publishers of a nationally distributed monthly detective magazine, *True Detective Mysteries*. The writ stated that within their December 1931 issue (vol. 16, no. 3), in an article named 'The Crime at 29 Wolverton Street', Wallace had been portrayed as being guilty of the murder of Julia and, as such, had been 'greatly prejudiced and injured in his credit and reputation and been brought into public scandal, hatred and contempt'. The total amount of compensation for this action, though undisclosed, had to have been considerable. What we can be sure of is that Wallace received at least £500 (a modern-day equivalent of over £26,500) in compensation for these libel actions – possibly twice that amount if we include the compensation received from Wyman & Sons Limited.

At this point, the question could be raised as to why it could not have been Julia who was blackmailing Parry and Marsden. In this case, one must ask oneself what benefit would Julia have hoped to have gained. Whatever benefit she might have gained would have paled into insignificance if either Parry or Marsden exposed her: it would be her name that would be plastered all over the newspapers. There was the chance that the reporters would then dig too deeply and uncover her true age and background. After Wallace's inevitable success in any divorce proceedings, it would be Julia who would have to live the rest of her life being pointed at in the street, whispered about in the shops and the subject of constant neighbourhood gossip. For these reasons, it is highly unlikely that a threat of blackmail would have ever been issued by Julia.

Likewise, the question might be raised, was it both Wallace *and* Julia who were blackmailing Parry and Marsden? Once again, the facts do not bear this out. The wealth of inconsistencies in Wallace's actions and statements point to Wallace's complicity in Julia's murder, not least the fact that Wallace never simply said, 'It was Richard Gordon Parry and Joseph Caleb Marsden who committed this murder, and here are the reasons why' (of course he would have omitted the fact that he and Julia had been blackmailing them). If, indeed, Parry and Marsden had been blackmailed into committing Julia's murder, there could have been only one person responsible – William Herbert Wallace.

Wallace makes two interesting entries in his diary during January 1931. On Sunday the 4th, he comments, 'Work out some definite scheme of study of properly planned and rigorously adhered to each particular difficulty consistently tackled and overcome.' Could this cryptic entry be referring to the fact that Wallace had finally perfected his plan to have Julia murdered? Could this have been when Wallace approached Marsden and blackmailed him into murdering Julia? Ten days later, on Wednesday the 14th, he wrote, 'Reading very interesting book by J Lays published in 1889.' Finding this a strange way to reference a book one had enjoyed (surely you would simply note the author and title), I undertook research to find out exactly what the title and subject of this book was. According to the British Library and the Bodleian Library (which retain copies of every book published since 1610), no book could be found that had been published by a 'J Lays' in 1889 or any other year. In fact, despite my investigating of national and international databases (COPAC and WorldCat), no author of that name could be found. One could quite easily allow the imagination to run wild and ponder whether this had been a cryptic message from Wallace to himself – an anagram, 'J Lays' = 'Slay J'. If we treat the '1889' as a time, this would have been 18.89, resolved to 19.29: 'Slay J, 7.29 p.m.' Could this have been the approximate time Marsden had said he would murder Julia Wallace? The fact of the matter is that this was a reference to a book and an author that appear never to have existed.

The Detail

The simplest way for Wallace to have put his plan into action would have been to approach Parry and Marsden and cast his line, telling them of his intention to divorce Julia on the grounds of adultery and reveal the entire, sordid goings on, dragging their names through the courts by naming them as co-respondents. Taking the bait, and fearing it would not only taint their names, cast ridicule upon their families, but also put an end to Marsden's relationship with his fiancée, Marsden would have pleaded with Wallace not to name him. Reeling them in, Wallace would tell them that, thanks to them, his life with Julia was over and he wanted rid of her: if he could not divorce her, the only other way was to kill her. In that way, all their problems would be solved – and he had a foolproof plan. It would be up to them, if they wanted to go ahead with it, to contact him, possibly through Parry. If not, he would see them in court. After mulling it over for some time, Parry and Marsden would have contacted Wallace and the plan would have been put into action. An initial, secret meeting between Marsden, Parry and Wallace would have had to have been set up. Marsden would be the weapon Wallace would wield in order to dispose of his wife; Parry would be used as the intermediary between Marsden and Julia, and would then act as getaway driver. Julia herself would even play a vital role in this diabolical scheme. In arranging for such a 'delicate' liaison to take place between Marsden and herself, Julia would not only welcome her murderer into her home, she would also not have confided to anybody that the meeting was to take place.

At the meeting, Wallace would lay the plan before the two men. The phone call to the Chess Club would have to be made when James Caird was not there (he knew Wallace's address) and when Wallace had already left the house en route to the Chess Club around 7.15 p.m. Working for a betting office, Marsden may not have ended his day until sometime between 7 and 7.30 p.m. (possibly later); he could not make the call. Wallace had to be seen to arrive at the Chess Club at a time that would not have allowed him to make the call. Parry, in his statement, had said that on the night of the murder he had 'finished business about 5.30 p.m.'. In his botched statement to police regarding the night of the telephone call to the City Café he stated that he had driven Lily Lloyd to her home, also at 5.30 p.m. This has to mean that it was usual for Parry to have left work prior to 5.30 p.m. If this was his usual habit, on the night of 19 January this would have given him sufficient time to be able to make the phone call at 7.15 p.m.

However, there could be a problem. As stated previously, for several weeks prior to 17 November 1930, the Mersey Amateur Dramatic Society, of which Parry was a member, had been holding rehearsals at the City Café every Tuesday and Thursday; during these rehearsals, whilst the cast were going through their lines, every person present in the café, including waitress Gladys Harley and club captain Samuel Beattie, could not have helped hearing Parry's voice. Would his voice be recognised? The staff of the Anfield Telephone Exchange would not have been a problem. As far as Parry would have been concerned, nobody there would have known him and, besides, they would have received hundreds of calls a day. Who would have been able to distinguish his real voice amongst all of these? Parry would have known that when the phone rang in the café, it would most likely be Gladys Harley who picked it up. In her statement to Hector Munro, she states that 'usually when there is a call I answer it in the first place'. This being the case, Parry would have had no choice but to have disguised his voice when calling the City Café to minimise the chance of his own voice being recognised; hence the disparity in the descriptions of Qualtrough's voice from the various respondents. Parry would have been the ideal candidate to have made the Qualtrough telephone call. He had the acting skills required to disguise his voice. The phone call would have to be made by Parry.

A name and a fake address for the caller would be needed in order to pass it on to whomever answered the telephone. Wallace had to have already decided on Menlove Gardens East, as this then allowed him to call in to see his Prudential Superintendent, Joseph Crewe, who could then concretely establish his alibi for the time of the murder. However, a name would be needed. A name that could easily be remembered. A name for the murderer. After some discussion, Marsden may have offered 'Qualtrough': the name of one of his clients from when he was with the Prudential many years before. With it being so long since Marsden was with the Prudential (over three years), who would ever associate it with him? It was therefore agreed that the mystery caller would be Mr R. M. Qualtrough of 25 Menlove Gardens East. They would now need a reason for him to have called. It would have to be a good enough reason, with a good enough commission to make it worthwhile for an insurance agent to travel all the way to Mossley Hill in the hope of securing his custom. Parry may have suggested the 21st birthday endowment policy; it may have already been on his mind due to the fact that Lily Lloyd's friend, Leslie Williamson, was about to have a 21st birthday. As a man who was on the constant lookout for money and who was always 'looking for business', Parry may have already suggested this to Leslie Williamson's mother, hoping for the ample commission it would bring. These details having been agreed upon, there was one thing left to do – after Parry had made the phone call, he would then have to see Julia and tell her that Marsden wished to see her the following night. According to a letter sent to Hector Munro by Wallace's brother Joseph, on 20 April 1931, just two days before Wallace's trial at the Assizes, 'I called on Dr Curwen at Priory Road, Anfield, this evening … As a matter of fact Mrs Wallace called on Dr Curwen the night before the murder to pay a bill.' In his four statements to police, two statements to Hector Munro and his testimony at the committal trial, Wallace made no reference to this event at all. In all cases, he simply implies that when he left the house on 19 January, he left Julia alone in the house tending to her cold, and that was where he expected she was the whole night. However, it was not until after his brother had sent the letter to Hector Munro, on Friday 24 April, the third day of Wallace's trial at the Assizes, whilst being questioned by Roland Oliver, that Wallace was to finally reveal this important piece of information:

Was your wife a delicate woman? Yes, I think one could say that.

Do you know when she last saw the doctor? I am not sure whether it was the same morning or the day previous.

I am told it was the 19th. What was that for, do you know? She had had a bad cough over the weekend and had not slept very well at night and she complained about it and I said, 'Slip along to the doctor; he will know what to give you and that will put you right'.

According to Wallace, Julia went to see Dr Curwen at some time during the daytime solely for much-needed medical care. According to Joseph's letter, Dr Curwen had made no mention of her attending his surgery with an ailment. He simply said she called there that night to pay a bill. Wallace attempted to explain Julia's reason for visiting the doctor by saying, 'She had a bad cough over the weekend and hadn't slept very well at night'. Yet, if she was so in need of medical attention, why had she not gone during the Monday morning or afternoon? If, however, she went for the singular purpose of paying a bill, she could have done this any day of the week and, once again, any time of the day. Why that particular night?

Dr Curwen's surgery was at 111 Priory Road. En route to the surgery, Julia would have to have walked past the telephone kiosk 'Anfield 1627' where the Qualtrough call was made. This was directly opposite Priory Road. Could this have been the true importance of the position of the phone kiosk and not the fact that it was 400 yards from the Wallaces' home? Has the true significance of why Qualtrough made his telephone call to the Chess Club from this particular phone box been lost in the fact that it happened to be 400 yards from Wolverton Street? Could Julia have been enticed to pay the doctor's bill that night by Wallace and left the house with him when he left at around 7.15 p.m? As he made his way to Belmont Road (in the opposite direction) and on to the Chess Club, was she on her way to Dr Curwen's surgery? If this is the case, why had Wallace not walked part of the way with his wife, leaving her at the corner of Priory Road as he crossed to catch his tram on the corner of Lower Breck Road and Townsend Avenue? As Julia was either going to or coming from the surgery, whilst still in the phone kiosk, Parry could easily have seen her, waylaid her and told her about the rendezvous with Marsden. If this was the case, how could Parry have known Julia would be walking past the call box at this time – unless Wallace had told him that this is what he would entice her to do. Might this have been the parameter that had changed once the police, on 22 January, had managed to trace the call to City Café as having been placed from Anfield 1627 at 7.15 p.m? Had Parry been arrested upon suspicion of committing the murder and the call not been traced, if he told police that he had made the call from this location because Wallace had manoeuvred Julia to be walking past the call box in order for him to pass on the message that Marsden would be calling the following night, it could be strongly argued that the call could have been made from anywhere in Liverpool and that Parry was lying in order to implicate Wallace. If the police knew for certain where the call originated, Parry's assertions would have been a lot more convincing – and damning.

Parry had a car – so he could have made the telephone call to the Chess Club from anywhere he happened to be at that particular time. To maintain a valid alibi, would it not have been simpler for him to have gone to the Lloyds' house after work (5.30 p.m.), waited until Lily's student had arrived (around 7.10 p.m.), made the excuse he was popping out to the post office on Maiden Lane to get a paper and some cigarettes, and made the phone call from any phone box on the way? In returning to the Lloyds' house after having placed the call, he could have stayed there all night. Instead, the telephone call was placed 400 yards away from Wallace's house and, more importantly, on Julia's route to and from Dr Curwen's surgery. Why else would Parry have gone out of his way to have been in that area at that time? According to Lily Lloyd's statement regarding Parry's visit to her home on the night of 19 January, she states that he had called at 'about 7.35 p.m.'. If Parry had made the phone call to the City Café, according to the log of the call taken by Annie Robertson at the Anfield Telephone Exchange, he had been connected at 7.20 p.m. If we assume the conversation with Gladys Harley and Samuel Beattie had taken about five minutes, he would have finished the call at around 7.25 p.m. – this gave him approximately ten minutes to see Julia, convey the message and proceed in his car to Lily Lloyd's house. If Julia had left the house with Wallace at around 7.15 p.m. and had spoken with Parry at around 7.25 p.m., this would show that Julia had not gone to Dr Curwen's surgery for a consultation; she had simply dropped in to pay a bill. Had she been at the surgery for a consultation, in waiting her turn in the waiting room, then having the consultation, this would have taken considerably longer. On the day of the murder, Amy Wallace, Julia's sister-in-law, had visited her during that afternoon. According to Amy Wallace's statement, she stated that she had enquired after Julia's cold, asked her out to a pantomime that coming Friday, and Julia had told her of Wallace's meeting with 'someone in the Calderstones district'. She does not mention anything about Julia telling her that she had been to see her doctor the previous night, or that she was expecting anyone at the house that night. If Julia was expecting Marsden to call, why had she not told Amy? If Marsden was to call that night, it had to have been a clandestine meeting. As a clandestine meeting, it also had to have been suspicious.

Upon being told of Marsden's wish to call to the house, as far as Julia would have been concerned, that would have been impossible – Wallace would be home. Parry may have told her to wait in the entry at the back of the house; Marsden would be there at some time between 7.30 and 8.30 p.m. (his intention being murder, he would not want to enter the house via the front door). If she was not there, he would know that Wallace was home. In this way, Wallace assumed, because of her cold, she would be wearing her mackintosh – a vital piece of equipment in the murder plan. On the night of the murder, two things would have to be accomplished: Julia must be murdered and, in order for it to look like a robbery gone wrong, Marsden would have to take the cash box (which would have been emptied by Wallace previously) in which Wallace stored his Prudential collection money from the top of the bookshelves and throw it to the ground.

Date of Death

The time and date of the murder now had to be set: it would have to be the day after a Chess Club meeting when Wallace would have received the message from Qualtrough: a Tuesday or a Friday. Either of these days would, most likely, have suited Wallace or Parry – each was able, during the course of the night, to manufacture their own alibis. Marsden, however, would have a problem: he would not be seen to be anywhere at the time of the murder. His ideal alibi would be to have been in company at the time of the murder – an impossibility. Instead, the best he could hope for would have been to have been in company until the last moment before he had to make his way to Wolverton Street, then to have been in transit to somewhere else, arriving at his destination in good time in order to make it appear he had not had the time to commit the murder. To this end, another birthday was to occur at this time – not a 21st birthday, but a birthday on the 21st: Thomas Richard Murphy's 32nd birthday was on 21 January 1931.

In his meeting with Goodman and Whittington Egan, in 1966, was this, in fact, the birthday party Parry was alluding to? As Goodman noted, 'The police ... were satisfied of his innocence of the Wallace murder when he was able to produce some people with whom he had spent the night 'arranging a birthday celebration.' This, of course, was another lie; it was not what he had said in his statement to police. He had spent three hours, between 5.30 and 8.30 p.m. at 43 Knoclaid Road with Mrs Brine. Had he forgotten? Was he worried that if he attempted to remember his alibi, filled with lies as it was, he would implicate himself and, instead, had referred to an event he knew to be true – the birthday party of Thomas Richard Murphy? If a party had been held, it would have been held on Wednesday 21 January. Preparations might well have been going on for it at Thomas Richard Murphy's mother's house, 'Glentworth', Greater Meols, Wirral, on the Tuesday night. Could this have been the actual birthday celebration that was being arranged that Parry was referring to, and not that of Leslie Williamson? Could arrangements for Thomas Richard Murphy's birthday party have been Marsden's chosen alibi and the very reason why Julia was murdered on the night of 20 January 1931 and no other? If this was the case, besides being the only person of the three (Wallace, Parry and Marsden) who had a personal connection to one of the Qualtroughs of Liverpool and had a lot to lose should anything untoward or sordid be revealed at this crucial stage in his life, Joseph Caleb Marsden was the only one of the three who would legitimately have been involved in preparations for what would have been an elaborate birthday celebration the day following Julia's murder.

In the only piece of evidence we have as to Joseph Caleb Marsden's whereabouts on the night of 20 January, he had apparently stated that he was 'in bed with Flu'. No corroboration for this has been found. Whose house was he in? What was he doing the rest of that day? Why had police not gone into as much detail with Marsden's statement as they had done with Parry's? In questioning Marsden, the police would have asked his whereabouts at the time of the murder – between 6 and 6.45 p.m. as far as they were concerned. In telling them he was 'in bed with Flu', this would imply that Marsden had not been to work that day. As an unwilling assassin, his nerves and emotions would have been wrought; he could not have attended work that day. If you were the perpetrator of a preconceived and deliberate murder, in manufacturing an alibi, the path of least resistance would be to avoid as much unnecessary complication as you possibly could. The busier your day, the longer your statement would have to be. The more people involved in making statements to corroborate that statement, the greater the chance of your statement falling apart.

Method in the Madness – and the Mayhem

On the night of Monday 19 January 1931, William Herbert Wallace returned from his night at the Chess Club. Settling down to supper, he told Julia of the telephone message from the mysterious Mr Qualtrough, explaining that if it was business to do with Mr Qualtrough's daughter's 21st birthday, it could mean an endowment policy, which could give a good return in commission for them. He would tell her that the appointment was at 7.30 p.m. the following night, so he would have to leave around 6.45 p.m. in order to give him enough time to find the house. With the appointment being at 7.30 p.m., the negotiations might take around half an hour to three-quarters of an hour to complete. He would, hopefully, be back home sometime around 9.00 p.m. Julia now knew that it would be safe to meet with Marsden that following night.

On Tuesday 20 January 1931, after Wallace had gone on his morning rounds, Julia, for some reason, felt the need to remove the bottom sheet of the bed in the front bedroom. Why did she feel it needed removing now? According to the record, the last time the bed had been slept in was in June 1929 when Amy Wallace had stayed there for a fortnight after returning to England. In her statement concerning the relationship between the Wallaces, Mrs Wilson (Matron of the Police Remand Home at the time), who attended Wallace when he had pneumonia for three weeks in 1923, stated that 'During her husband's illness she [Julia] slept on the sofa in the kitchen although the front bedroom was vacant, and was much more convenient to the room occupied by her husband.' It would appear that Julia herself never slept in the room, it only being used to store her clothes, hats and handbags. At some time during the day, Julia went out to buy the scones for Wallace's tea. It may have been during this shopping trip she that she withdrew the £1 10s found in the pocket of her corsets from her Post Office savings account. Between 5 and 5.30 p.m., Parry left work and went straight to Mrs Brine's house at 43 Knoclaid Road, arriving there at around 5.30 p.m. At 6.45 p.m., Wallace duly left for his rendezvous with Mr Qualtrough.

Feigning illness (though the heavy, awful burden of what the night was to bring and the awful deed he would be forced to commit had to have be playing upon his tormented mind for some time), Marsden may have taken that day off work and either remained at 24 Adelaide Road or, concerned that his tortured demeanour would be only too obvious to his parents and cause too many questions to be asked, had already made his way to 'Glentworth', Mrs Murphy's house, in order to sort out arrangements for her son's birthday the following day. At some time between 7 and 7.30 p.m., he would have begun to make his way to Wolverton Street. Had he been at Adelaide Road, he could have left his home and gone to nearby Edge Hill railway station, only ten minutes away. From here, he was able to board a train that would take him directly to Breck Road station via the Edge Hill and Bootle branch line of the LM&S Railway – ten minutes' walk from Wolverton Street. Had he been at 'Glentworth', it would have been a simple walk of only yards to Meols station to catch a train on the Wirral Line to Birkenhead station, where he would change on to the Mersey Railway main line that would take him under the River Mersey to Central station (a journey he would have had to undertake every day on his way home from work). After a very short walk from Central station to Lime Street station, once again using the LM&S Railway, he would have made his way to Breck Road station – and on to Wolverton Street.

From the evidence, it would appear that had this liaison with Marsden occurred, it could not be construed as a meeting of two lovers and was purely a business arrangement. We should note the response of Sergeant Harry Bailey when questioned by junior prosecuting counsel Leslie Walsh:

There is one point I missed. Could you say, was Mrs Wallace very well dressed? I should say she was poorly dressed, homemade clothing.

If we add to this the fact that the kitchen table was still cluttered from earlier in the day, it is plain to see that Julia had made no attempt to prepare either herself or the house, as one might expect had this meeting been with a young lover. However, it would appear, when Marsden arrived, Julia *was* expecting him.

When Marsden arrived at the house, he either encountered Julia (who may have hurriedly donned Wallace's mackintosh instead of her own to protect her from the chill of the night air) in the entry at the back of Wolverton Street or, knowing Wallace was not at home, had entered the backyard, where Julia was waiting for him. Either way, when Marsden entered the house, Julia, if she was wearing any mackintosh at all, was not wearing her own. After ushering Marsden through the darkened kitchen and hallway, the pair entered the parlour. Julia having prepared the room earlier in expectation of her visitor, the gaslights were already lit, and the fire was burning. As Julia approached the fire, one of two circumstances may have arisen: had she been wearing Wallace's mackintosh, Marsden had politely offered to help her off with the coat. Turning her back on him, Marsden held the lapels of the coat from behind as Julia extracted herself from it then immediately threw it over her head. In this way, the inside of the mackintosh would be toward her. Alternately, had she not been wearing the mackintosh, upon following Julia into the parlour, Marsden had reached across the hallway and lifted Wallace's mackintosh from off the peg. As Julia approached the warmth of the fire, Marsden was already lurching toward her with the mackintosh spread wide, like bat wings, the inside of the coat toward her.

Forcing the mackintosh over Julia's head performs three functions: it prevents Julia's arms from flailing about and knocking any of the ornaments dotted around the room onto the floor, smashing and alerting the Johnstons next door; it stifles any sound that Julia might make; and it contains the inevitable surge of blood from the initial attack. Either way, once Julia is contained, Marsden forces her down toward the cushion of the two-seater settee. Falling across the fender of the gas fire, the left side of Julia's skirt, just under the placquet, comes into contact with the removable cover of the fire directly underneath the fireclay, as she receives a small bruise to her left upper arm (as found by Professor MacFall during his post-mortem examination) from the ball-headed rail support on the fender.

If we combine two statements concerning the burns found on Julia's skirt, it can be seen that the fire had to have been lit for some time previous to the arrival of her 'guest'. As City Analyst William Henry Roberts noted, 'At the bottom of the placquet there were 3 recent horizontal burns, which could have been caused by contact with the hot fireclay of a gas fire such as was in the parlour at 29 Wolverton Street.' Detective Sergeant Harry Bailey remarked, 'At the mortuary, I saw the front of the skirt on the body [the skirt had been twisted around the body, the placquet having moved from the left side to the front] was partly burned ... but there were no signs of burning on the underskirt.'

If we examine the gas fire in the photograph of the parlour taken from the doorway, it can be seen that the height of the fireclay from the hearth would preclude the side of Julia's prone legs from being able to reach it. However, if the removable cover underneath the fireclay is examined, it can be seen that it appears to be adorned with three prominent vertical columns – one at either end and one at the centre. Given that the burns on Julia's skirt were described as horizontal to the placquet (parallel to the hem of the skirt), this would imply that with Julia lying down, whatever heat source had caused them was vertical. As the City Analyst did not give any indication as to the distance between each of these burns, might one or all three of these columns have been responsible for the burns upon Julia's skirt? If all three, then the burns would have been almost equidistant to each other. If only one, the burns may have been close together, indicating they had been caused as Julia had struggled against her attacker.

If we examine Bailey's statement, he notes that there were no signs of burning on Julia's underskirt; this would indicate that Julia's left thigh was against the hot fire cover only very briefly – only long enough to burn through the skirt and not the underskirt. This being the case, the fire cover had to have been *extremely* hot in order to cause so much damage in so short a time. The only conclusion that can be inferred from this is that the fire had to have been lit for quite some time before Julia was attacked – quite some time before Julia's 'guest' had entered the room. From the record, it has been indicated that the parlour was only used for the reception of guests and for the Wallaces' musical evenings – the couple 'living' in the kitchen. Also previously indicated, the fire in the kitchen had been left to burn itself out – indicating, that night, Julia had had no intention of remaining in the kitchen. This might be further endorsed by the fact that in the parlour photograph taken from the doorway, it can plainly be seen that the two cushions on the chaise longue are in such positions as to accommodate a person who would appear to have been lying down – or at least reclining. A visitor to the house would never surely take up such a position in front of their hosts. During their musical evenings, Wallace would be standing playing his violin as Julia sat at the piano. According to Wallace, there was no one expected to call that night, yet it would appear that Julia had readied the parlour and been waiting with a warm reception for somebody.

Marsden's swift attack being so close to the open fire, the flapping skirt of the mackintosh drapes across the almost-vertical scorching fireclay and catches alight. Pushing Julia's head down into the cushion on the two-seater settee, Marsden reaches for the iron bar standing at the right side of the fireplace. Noticing the burning mackintosh, he administers two rapid, heavy blows to Julia's head to quieten her. This smashes the 2-inch by 3-inch gash through Julia's skull, slicing through the meningeal artery: a gush of blood is sent surging into and down the right-hand side of the mackintosh, into the sleeve, reaching as far down as her skirt. Escaping spray crosses the violin case and splatters onto the walls around the settee. Dropping the bar, Marsden beats out the flaming mackintosh with his gloved hand and turns off the gas fire. The initial wound on Julia's head was to the left, and a vast amount of blood was found to be inside the mackintosh in and around the upper right sleeve, and over the front of Julia's skirt (in the City Analyst's opinion, the blood on the left of the mackintosh, which was only on the outside, was blood picked up from the floor). Julia's skirt was burned on her left-hand side, and the mackintosh on the right-hand side; this is consistent with the mackintosh having been covering Julia's body when it caught fire, causing burns to the left of Julia's skirt and those on the right-hand side of the mackintosh: the mackintosh had to have been covering Julia's body when she was struck.

Despite the severity of this initial attack, it would appear that Marsden was not satisfied that Julia was dead. The initial blows were inflicted to quieten her – but Marsden would have to undertake a more sustained attack. The corner of the room being very cramped, Marsden carefully lifts the mackintosh to see if the blood flow has ceased. Flakes of the burnt mackintosh adhering to his glove fall onto the cushion around Julia's head. In his report, the City Analyst stated that on the cushion, 'There were numerous small Human Blood Stains on one side, together with particles of the burnt Mackintosh.' The escaping blood now having lost its initial force, Marsden throws the blood-drenched mackintosh out of the way into the centre of the room in case he should get any blood on him. Pulling Julia's lifeless trunk away from the settee, he turns her toward the sideboard and drops her, face down, onto the floor. (According to Goodman, the neck of Julia's jumper was badly torn on the left-hand side; this may have been the moment this had occurred.) Her head resting on the left side, blood from the wound pools onto the floor close to the two-seater settee. The huge bloodstain on Julia's skirt presses against the centre of the hearthrug, causing the bloodstain that was described by Professor Roberts, whilst being questioned by Edward Hemmerde at Wallace's trial:

Where about were the stains? In the centre of the hearthrug.

Straddling Julia's body, Marsden rolls it over toward the door. This causes the stain in the centre of the hearthrug to smear, as further described by Professor Roberts during the same line of questioning:

Was there any blood on the cash box? There were other bloodstains on the hearthrug. I mention that because it has been suggested that anybody who had committed the murder if he had been the murderer might have stains on the feet. The foot could easily have been wiped on the hearthrug.
If anyone had bloodstains on the feet, they might have been wiped there? Yes.

Rolling her over again onto her back shifts the head further along the edge of the rug to the corner of the hearthrug opposite the door. Realising that the chair Julia used instead of a piano stool, tucked under the keyboard of the piano, was taking up valuable space for his final dreadful act, Marsden lifts it and places it in front of the sideboard. This delay creates the second pool of blood close to the corner of the hearthrug opposite the door. He then rolls Julia's body forward into the centre of the room, her body thus adopting the position in which she was originally found by Wallace and the Johnstons: on her side; her right arm hidden underneath her body, her left arm resting across her chest and feet on their sides, slightly apart, toes pointing to the window. During the process of rolling the body over the floor, Julia's skirt has twisted around, moving the placquet (and the burns) from her left hip around to the front.

The back of Julia's head is now facing the doorway. Marsden once again takes up the iron bar and, positioning himself in front of Julia's head, rains down two heavy blows to the back of the head. As the heavy bar hits the floor, two loud thumps fill the room. These would be heard by Mrs Johnston next door in her kitchen at No. 31:

> I did not hear any unusual noise in Wallace's house until about 8.25–8.30 p.m. I was then in my kitchen and I heard two thumps which I thought was my father in my front parlour taking off his boots.

To cushion the noise, Marsden reaches for the mackintosh, quickly folds it in half and pushes it close to Julia's head and right shoulder. Professor Roberts said that the mackintosh had been heavily bloodstained on both the inside and outside of the right-hand side, but only the outside of the left cuff and a large area near the left pocket were similarly stained. Could this suggest that in placing the mackintosh close to Julia's head, Marsden had folded it in half, placing the bottom left-hand portion on the floor in the pool of blood already exuded from Julia's head after the previous two blows? Kneeling in front of her head once again, Marsden grips the back of Julia's hair and pulls the head forward, towards him, to expose the back of the skull and to steady it. Not realising that she is wearing a chignon underneath her hair, he begins to rain down the final blows. As the iron bar rises and falls with tremendous force, blood is flicked from it high onto the walls, the piano and the doorway as bone and brain matter ooze out of the gaping fissure at the front of Julia's head and onto the carpet. In his autopsy report, Professor MacFall says of the wounds on the back of Julia's head, 'On the back of the head on the left side were ten diagonal, apparently, incised wounds.' This is consistent with the assailant being in front of Julia's head, and being right-handed; when crushing the back of her skull, the iron bar would have been sweeping down from right to left, hitting the left side of the skull at an angle. This is clearly displayed in the morgue photographs; the impact marks can clearly be seen running from the lower left side of Julia's neck, up towards the upper right side of her head. Despite the chignon underneath Julia's hair having detached itself as the head lurched further forward with each frenzied, crushing blow, Marsden holds on. By the time it is all over, the head having been forced so far forward by the impact of the iron bar, the chignon is clinging to the last strands of Julia's hair. At the committal trial, Professor MacFall described his observation of Julia's hair at the murder scene: 'The hair was disarranged and loose. It was drawn out, and a pad of hair was right away from the head and almost free from the rest of the hair.'

Commonly referred to as 'overkill', this type of needless, frenzied, sustained attack is often considered to be indicative of a crime of passion, invariably committed by somebody known to the victim. If one can believe that this terrible act was performed by a man who did not want to do this – by a man who, under normal circumstances, would never have contemplated such a hideous act, his mind had to have been filled with terror, horror, confusion, anguish and desperation. If Joseph Caleb Marsden had been forced into this unimaginable nightmare because, desperate for money, he had participated in sordid sexual encounters for payment and, on the cusp of a lifetime of happiness and the prospect of a secure financial future through his impending wedding, Wallace had placed an almost insurmountable barrier in front of him, could this have been where the 'passion' lay? As much as he would not have wanted to have carried out this grotesque deed, the survival of his future life would have been the compelling force that drove him on. Wallace gave this man no way out – except to kill Julia. Who could he have explained the whole sordid story to and be certain that his fiancée would never find out? He could not have told police, as no crime had yet been committed. What could they have done? As far as Marsden was concerned, Wallace could have then simply gone ahead with the divorce proceedings and all would have been lost.

The execution of this crime can be described as quick, quiet and controlled, as indicated by the crime-scene photographs and Superintendent Hubert Moore's comments upon the lack of displacement of any of the furniture and ornaments in the room. During the commission of the attack, it would appear that all precautions were taken to eliminate any possibility of sound penetrating the thin walls adjoining 31 Wolverton Street and alerting anybody who might be in the parlour of the neighbouring house. The mackintosh would stifle Julia's screams. The initial blows were struck whilst Julia's head lay on the cushion of the two-seater settee. The body was rolled over the floor, not dragged and dumped, whereby the point of impact (Julia's head) would be as far away from the shared wall as possible. And the final blows were struck with the mackintosh tucked close to the back of Julia's head in order to stifle the sound should the iron bar hit the floorboards. It is highly unlikely that any of these precautions would have occurred had this attack been unplanned and spontaneous. If the assailant's sole purpose in entering 29 Wolverton Street was to murder Julia Wallace, why had he not attacked her as soon as he had entered the kitchen through the back kitchen door? If, as stated previously, Mr and Mrs Johnston and their family used the kitchen at 31 Wolverton Street as their living room ('We were in our living room at the back of our house'), and Mrs Johnston's father, Arthur Mills, was incapacitated and living in the parlour, it would appear the murderer had to have been armed with this information and had either waited until Julia had taken him into the parlour, or suggested to Julia that they go into the parlour, in order to lessen the possibility of detection. Once in the parlour, the attacker would have had to have had knowledge of the arrangement of the furniture, and had the scene 'set' for his arrival (the iron bar readied at the side of the fire, the cushion on the two-seater settee). Wallace could supply the information concerning the living arrangements at No. 31 and set the scene. As Wallace had stated, Marsden had been in the parlour on numerous occasions, so he would know the placement of the furniture.

His gruesome task now over, Marsden takes one of Julia's mittens from the top of the sideboard and wipes most of the blood from the iron bar before pushing them into pockets in his overcoat. John Parkes described the bloodied glove he had taken out of Parry's car as follows: 'It was a thumb and all fingers. This part was all fingers and just a thumb.' John Parkes was describing a mitten. Surely, a thief – let alone a murderer – would not have chosen to wear a pair of mittens during the commission of his crime. Could Marsden have simply donned Julia's mittens after entering the house? Highly unlikely: Julia was approximately 5 feet tall, and of small frame. Marsden was described by Wallace as being 5 feet 6 or 7 inches tall. In the first instance, it is highly unlikely that Julia's gloves would have fitted him: had they done so, why had he not taken both mittens with him? According to police records, no damning fingerprints were to be found anywhere in the house; Marsden must surely have been wearing his own gloves before entering the house. If one looks closely at the right-hand end of the sideboard in the crime-scene photograph of the parlour taken from the window, there can be seen what appears to be the back of a single, fur-edged mitten. Could this be the remaining mitten, proving that Parkes did see the other one, soaked in blood in Parry's car? In relating the incident, Parkes claimed that Parry had said of the mitten, 'If police got that … that would hang me!' This can only pertain if the blood-soaked mitten, in coming into the possession of the police, could then be matched with the other taken from the crime scene. Did Parry know the other mitten was still to be found at 29 Wolverton Street?

Taking off his own bloody gloves to avoid leaving smears, Marsden made good his escape and left the parlour. Given the proof provided earlier regarding the blood clot on the toilet pan having possibly arrived there through the unprofessionalism of the investigation team (likewise the blood smears on the notes in the middle bedroom), and the disturbance in the front bedroom having been caused by Julia herself, we can be almost certain that Marsden never ventured upstairs. This crime had one purpose and one purpose only – to murder Julia Wallace.

With the carpet covered in pools of blood, Julia's body covering most of the available floor space and the room being so cramped, why would a man, so desperately avoiding any contact with blood, have dared to turn out the only available light source he had, and risk tripping over the body or stepping into the blood? We should note that the police and scientific experts could find no traces of blood (except the one single spot on the toilet pan and the smear on the banknotes in the middle bedroom) outside of the parlour. Not even footprints. To have accomplished this in total darkness would have been a minor miracle. Especially if one considers the extreme state of panic and anxiety Marsden had to have been experiencing. Marsden had to have left the gaslight in the parlour burning. Entering the darkened kitchen, every fibre of his being would be compelling him to leave that house. He may, however, have had one more task to fulfil before he left: he would have to make the murder look like a robbery. Either because he was behind schedule for his meeting with Wallace, the time now possibly being 8.30 p.m., or because of his utter panic, Marsden had failed to do this. Instead, he might have used a handkerchief or a towel in the back kitchen to open the door (hence there being no fingerprints on the lock) and ran from the house. If it had been he who had pulled the door off Wallace's photographic box or tampered with the cash box, there would most surely have been some traces of blood on either or both of them if he was wearing his gloves. If he was not wearing his gloves, he would not have risked leaving fingerprints on them.

Heading through the entry at the back of Wolverton Street, Marsden enters the entry into Richmond Park. On the opposite side of the road, he sees Wallace waiting anxiously in front of the entry at the side of the Parish Hall. Marsden approaches him and quickly reports on the night's events, telling him that the parlour light is still on and he has failed to take the cash box down from the bookshelves. As far as he is concerned, he never wants to hear from Wallace again.

As the men talk, unknown to them, Lily Hall, the young typist who knows Wallace, is walking home from work down Richmond Park to her home in Letchworth Street. She sees Wallace and Marsden in conversation:

> I came straight home along Richmond Park and as I was passing the entry leading from Richmond Park to the middle of Wolverton Street, I saw the man I know as Mr Wallace talking to another man I do not know. Mr Wallace had his face to me and the other man his back. They were standing on the pavement in Richmond Park opposite to the entry leading up by the side of the Parish Hall … Mr Wallace was wearing a trilby hat and a darkish overcoat when I saw him talking to the man in Richmond Park on Tuesday night. The man he was talking to was about 5ft 8ins and was wearing a cap and dark overcoat; he was of a stocky build.

Wallace described Parry as being 5 feet 10 inches tall, and Marsden as being 5 feet 6 or 7 inches tall. Also according to Lily Hall, the last thing she saw was one of the men going down the entry at the back of Wolverton Street, whilst the other walked down Richmond Park towards Breck Road. In the notes taken by Jonathan Goodman concerning his meeting with Parry in 1966, Goodman had questioned him regarding a statement given to him by Parry's father three days earlier, when John William Parry had said, 'He [Parry] was in Breck Road (close to Wolverton Street…) on the night of the murder having the batteries of his car recharged.' Parry simply told Goodman that he did not remember. Parry had a solid alibi for the night of the murder corroborated by two witnesses: Olivia Alberta Brine and Harold English Denison. He was with them from 5.30 p.m. until 8.30 p.m. at Mrs Brine's house. It would appear time had affected his memory of exactly what he had said in his police statement. If we assume this alibi to be nearer to the truth of the matter upon his leaving Mrs Brine's house, could it be that when Lily Hall saw Wallace's companion (Marsden) walk off towards Breck Road, he was indeed meeting up with Parry in the getaway car that was waiting, not in Breck Road, but at the corner of Breck Road and Lower Breck Road? As stated previously, this portion of Lower Breck Road (upon which the telephone kiosk, Anfield 1627, and the Cabbage Hall Cinema stood) had, before 1927, been named 'Rochester Road' and it was this name that was incorrectly used in all official reports and plans pertaining to the case. When Parry had told his father he had been in Breck Road fixing his car, might he have actually meant he was on the corner of Breck Road and Lower Breck Road – near to the Cabbage Hall Cinema? In a statement given to Hector Munro, a Mrs Anne Jane Parsons stated:

> On Tuesday the 20th January 1931. I was walking up Hanwell Street about 8 o'clock in the evening; I think it was nearer 8.15. I was going to a meeting. I noticed a man running down Hanwell Street towards Lower Breck Road. He was followed by another man close behind him who was also running. They were running very fast. I cannot say what they were like. I did not take much notice of them. They only aroused my attention from the fact that they were running so fast.

The top of Hanwell Street opens out into Richmond Park, on the correct side of the road, and in the correct direction that the man seen talking to Wallace by Lily Hall had taken after the meeting between the two men had ended; the bottom of Hanwell Street comes out almost opposite the Cabbage Hall Cinema. After leaving Wallace, had Marsden then turned into Hanwell Street, where Parry was waiting to lead him straight to the waiting car? Were the pair then seen careering down the street (past Mrs Parsons) on their way to Parry's car, parked near the Cabbage Hall Cinema? In John Parkes's statement, he says that Parry had told him that 'he had dropped the bar down a grid outside a doctor's house in Priory Road'. The Cabbage Hall Cinema was close to the corner of Breck Road and Lower Breck Road – opposite Priory Road.

Next door but one to the Cabbage Hall Cinema was Dr Dunlop's surgery, where John Sharp Johnston had attempted to seek medical assistance before going on to Anfield police station to report Julia's murder. In the statement given by Mrs Ada Cook concerning Parry's parents going to see her father and begging him to smuggle their son out of the country, she said, 'I heard, I don't know where from, that the murder implement was dropped down a grid near the Clubmoor [cinema] where Lily worked.' Could this actually have been outside the Cabbage Hall Cinema? In both statements, we have a common factor – the bar was dropped down a grid, in one outside a doctor's surgery, in the other outside a cinema. In locating the grid outside the Cabbage Hall Cinema, we bring the two statements together in the one location: next door but one to the Cabbage Hall Cinema was Dr Dunlop's surgery. As further corroboration of this, a note contained within the Merseyside Police files states, 'Seen: Mrs Smith, next door to Dr Dunlop saw one of the men.' 'Mrs Smith' was Jane Smith, who lived at 'Windermere House' along with an Isabella Bain Hewson – the house between the Cabbage Hall Cinema and Dr Dunlop's surgery. According to this brief note, she had seen 'one of the men', implying she had witnessed there being more than one man, but she had only seen one of them. Could these men have been Richard Gordon Parry and Joseph Caleb Marsden?

Upon reaching Parry's car, whilst Parry had got into the driver's seat to start the engine, had Marsden put the iron bar down a grid outside both the Cabbage Hall Cinema *and* Dr Dunlop's surgery (thus vindicating both Mrs Cook's and John Parkes's statements) and Mrs Smith had seen him before he had got into the passenger seat before the car sped off down Lower Breck Road towards West Derby Road and Hignett's bicycle shop in order for Parry (according to his statement) to pick up his accumulator battery?

Having returned to Wolverton Street via the entry in Richmond Park, Wallace began traversing the entries between the front door and the back door. This served two purposes; it would be the natural thing to do in such a situation until you then knocked on a neighbour's door, raised the alarm, and had a spectator to witness your entry into the house. It would also give Marsden and Parry time to make their getaway before the police became involved. By this time, Marsden and Parry would have been well on their way down Lower Breck Road, heading toward West Derby Road. Having previously prepared this stage of his alibi by placing an accumulator battery at Hignett's shop in order for it to be charged, Parry was on his way to pick it up.

Having been told that the scene had not been set for the 'robbery gone wrong' motive and the gaslight was still lit in the parlour, Wallace having left the Johnstons by the backyard door, entered the house. Besides lighting the gaslights in the kitchen, not wanting to have his own fresh fingerprints on the cash box and knowing the door to the photographic equipment box had previously been broken and temporarily repaired, he quickly ripped half the door off and placed it on the floor. Digging into his own pocket, he placed the loose change onto the floor. After putting the latch on the front door in order to back up his story that he had tried his key in the lock earlier and was unable to gain entry and – still needing to give Marsden and Parry time to get out of the area – ignoring the light in the parlour, he searched the house as he would have done if it had been in total darkness. When he finally entered the parlour, he made a quick reconnaissance and then went out to fetch the Johnstons.

In the meantime, Parry and Marsden had arrived outside Hignett's electrical and bicycle shop in West Derby Road. Walter Hignett's shop was at 513 West Derby Road – next door to the entrance to Tuebrook railway station. Upon leaving the car, Marsden realised that Julia's blood-soaked mitten was still in his pocket and shoved it in the glove box, telling Parry to get rid of it. Knowing that Marsden would need to change his overcoat, Parry might have brought this with him in a holdall. After changing and tidying himself up, as Parry went into the shop to collect his accumulator battery, Marsden would have slipped into the station to await the arrival of a train that would take him to Lime Street station. Alighting at Lime Street station, it would be only a very short walk for Marsden to Central station, where he could then catch a train on the Mersey Railway main line under the River Mersey – a journey he had to have undertaken every day on his way to work at Bernard Murphy & Son. This would take him to Birkenhead Park station, Wirral, Cheshire. Changing trains onto the Wirral line, he would alight at Meols station – yards from 'Glentworth', Mrs Murphy's house – where he then assisted in the preparations for Thomas Richard Murphy's birthday party the following night. As he would have been undoubtedly shaken (possibly in shock) after the night's events, it is unlikely that he would have wanted to return to Liverpool that night (if he wanted to return ever again); and so, feigning illness, he may have spent the whole night at 'Glentworth'.

After leaving Hignett's shop, Parry stated that he had called into Mrs Williamson's house at 49 Lisburn Lane for ten minutes. Might this have been to enable him to freshen himself up and calm his nerves? As shown previously, there was no love lost between the Williamsons and Richard Gordon Parry. How could he be sure Annie Williamson would allow him into the house? In his conversation with Roger Wilkes during the Radio City phone-in after the airing of *Who Killed Julia?*, Leslie Williamson had said:

On the week of the murder, I was at home, on leave from sea ... he [Parry] called at our house ... about four or five o'clock or something like that, one evening, and I answered the door. He wanted to see my mother – my mother was a music teacher, and she had a pupil in at the time, and it was a sacrilege to break into the lesson ... he was most adamant ... he got in through the vestibule ... and he wanted to see my mother about a song: he wanted some music. Well this is funny... Anyway, he did see my mother; my mother came out after I'd asked her, and I can always remember them going to the music stool and asking the student to get up off the music stool, and he chose a song out of this particular stool.

In obtaining the sheet music, was this Parry, once again, preparing his alibi for the night of Julia's murder? Was the loaning of the sheet music simply a ruse to gain him access to 49 Lisburn Lane after dropping off Marsden and leaving Hignett's shop? In maintaining his alibi, Parry had had no time to dispose of the glove, so had left it in the glove box of the car and continued on to Lily Lloyd's house. After leaving Lily Lloyd's house, not wanting to touch the glove and needing to get the car cleaned of all incriminating evidence, he decided to take it to Atkinson's garage and have John Parkes hose the whole thing down – including the glove. John Parkes stated:

> I got the glove out because I'd of saturated the glove if I'd of squirted on it – and then, I didn't squirt on it. And I pulled it out and Parry snatched it out of me hand and he said to me, 'If the police got that … that would hang me!' And I realized then, he wanted me to swill the box out and the glove and all – but I didn't – I got the glove out before I started that. It was a thumb and all fingers. This part was all fingers and just a thumb – and I think it had a – I think it had – I'm not sure now – I think it had a little tear in it – I think it had a little tear in the glove.

Life Goes On

During 1933, just a year after his wedding, and the same year as Wallace's death, Marsden, despite his menial position as a bookie's clerk, managed to buy a recently built house in the middle-class Liverpool suburb of Childwall, at 26 Rudston Road (ironically, living at 33 Rudston Road were Elizabeth Warburton (née Qualtrough) and her sons, Thomas Qualtrough Warburton and Harry Qualtrough Warburton). At that time, these houses were offered at a starting price of £675 (a modern-day equivalent of around £32,300). Here the couple remained for only four years until 1937. By this time, Thomas Richard Murphy and his wife, Doris, had moved from their home in Upton Road, Moreton, and relocated to Birkenhead Road, Meols – close to his mother's house, 'Glentworth'. Thomas named their new home 'Dorimur' after his wife. However, by 1937 both Thomas's wife and his mother had died. Doris May Murphy died on 17 November 1936 when complications arose after having her gallbladder removed. She was only 37 years of age and left five children behind. Joseph Caleb Marsden, present at the death, registered it the same day. On 13 January 1937, Thomas Richard Murphy sailed from Southampton on the SS *Berengaria* for a nine-day break in New York, staying at the Pennsylvania Hotel. On 5 February, he returned to Southampton on the RMS *Aquitania*. The following month, on 22 March 1937, his mother, Mrs Ellen Murphy, died. It was during 1937 that Joseph Caleb Marsden and his wife left Rudston Road, and moved into Dorimur with Thomas Richard Murphy. At this time, all of Murphy's sisters were married except for his youngest sister, Florence Lilian, who was still living at Glentworth. Why had she not moved in with him? Instead, Florence Lilian (then 24 years old) moved out of Glentworth and bought a house at 31 Sandringham Avenue, Meols, half a mile from Dorimur. The bond between Marsden and Murphy had to have been close – possibly brotherly. During 1939, Florence Lilian Murphy left 31 Sandringham Avenue – and Mr and Mrs Joseph Caleb Marsden left Dorimur and moved in.

In 1941, Thomas Richard Murphy remarried in Southport, Lancashire; he and his new wife, Kathleen Douglas Hawthorn, were to have a son of their own. When Murphy died on

27 January 1962 (whilst still living at Dorimur), there were only two obituaries in the local press: one from his wife naming all of his children, including those of his previous marriage, and one from the Prince Arthur Lodge No. 1570 – a Liverpool-based Masonic Lodge of which he was a member. There was none from any of his sisters, nor any from his children from his marriage to Doris May Taylor. In Thomas Richard Murphy's will, all of his estate was divided between his wife and *their* only son. Not a single mention was made of any of his five previous children.

Why had his sisters and his children not put any obituaries in the local press upon the death of their brother and father? Why had he not included the children of his first marriage in his will? Had a cataclysmic event entered the family and torn it apart, the children relinquishing all ties with their father, their father relinquishing all ties with his children? Had Thomas Richard Murphy been ostracised by his family? If so, might this have been because Thomas Richard Murphy had not cared for his wife – or might even have been having an affair with Kathleen Douglas Hawthorn before or soon after her death? All indications are that this cannot be true. When Murphy moved to Birkenhead Road, he named the house 'Dorimur' in tribute to his wife. Upon her death, he erected a magnificent memorial stone to her memory that bears the epitaph 'SHE RADIATED HAPPINESS WHEREVER SHE WENT'. He married his second wife five years after Doris's death. Could this cataclysmic event have been his having some unwitting complicity in the brutal slaying of Julia Wallace? Could Thomas Richard Murphy have unknowingly assisted Joseph Caleb Marsden in the commission of Julia Wallace's murder by supplying him with the car used by Richard Gordon Parry, providing him with sanctuary and aiding him in the manufacture of his alibi?

The Marsdens were to remain at 31 Sandringham Avenue until their deaths. Joseph Caleb Marsden died on 27 June 1967 at the Cottage Hospital, Hoylake, Cheshire; Sylvia Alberta Marsden died on 8 February 1986 in Clatterbridge Hospital, Cheshire. In all the years that passed since the commission of this brutal crime, despite all of the press coverage, discussions, radio plays, books, and so on, Joseph Caleb Marsden never came forward to identify himself, prove his innocence and put an end to the speculation surrounding his involvement in the murder of Julia Wallace.

If Marsden was involved in Julia Wallace's murder, how would it have been possible for him to have remained anonymous for so long? Why had police not taken an official statement? The police obviously knew of his association with Wallace, Parry and Richard James Qualtrough – and yet, they appear to have done nothing at all to verify his whereabouts on the night of the telephone call and the murder. How can a major suspect in a murder case disappear so efficiently?

12

It's Not What You Know …

As mentioned previously, Joseph Caleb Marsden's aunt, Alice Gertrude Marsden, was married to Robert Duckworth,[10] a member of the Liverpool City Police Force. Duckworth, however, was no ordinary beat-walking constable.

Robert Duckworth's career in the Liverpool Police Force was both colourful and notable. One newspaper described his capabilities as equalling those of the contemporary, fictional detective Sherlock Holmes. After he joined Liverpool Police in 1889, one of Duckworth's earliest cases involved a bank clerk who had absconded with around £2,000 of his employer's money. Duckworth, in searching the man's office, came across a manuscript in the drawer of his desk; it was a story the man had written and sent off to a magazine, which had rejected it. (The story concerned the commission of a crime, whereupon the perpetrator had absconded to London and laid low until things had quietened down. Hiring a clergyman's outfit, he quietly slipped out of the country.) Contacting the man through the personal column of a national newspaper (presumably by pretending to be the publisher who had turned down his manuscript), Duckworth learned that he was hiding out in Edinburgh. After contacting all of the clerical tailors in Edinburgh, he learned that an outfit had been ordered by a man fitting the description of the villain, who was soon apprehended.

Only four years after joining the force, in 1893 Duckworth was promoted to the Plain Clothes Detective Division and, in 1895, was involved in his biggest case to date. Known as the 'Redcross Street murder', it involved the murder of bookstall owner Edward Moyse. Living at 26 Redcross Street with 15-year-old John Needham, a young man who did odd jobs for him, he ran a bookstall at Mann Island, close to Liverpool's Pier Head. During the night of 18 February 1895, a one-time lodger at 26 Redcross Street, William Miller, broke into Moyse's house and, thinking he had a hidden cache of money, bludgeoned him to death in his bed with a poker. Not wanting to leave any witnesses, he then turned the poker on young Needham. Needham, however, managed to drag himself into the street and alerted passers-by. After recovering in hospital, Needham was able to provide police with a description of the assailant, which included the fact that he had a pronounced facial tic. Duckworth apparently remembered that a woman had complained to police that her husband, William Miller, had deserted her and ran away to America with another woman. Miller, however, had also deserted his lover and had returned to Liverpool with the woman hot on his heels. Once in Liverpool, the woman reported Miller to Liverpool Police for theft in America. Duckworth remembered that Miller, who worked on the Liverpool ferries, had a similar facial tic to the one described by Needham and this led to his downfall and eventual death at the hands of the hangman.

On 2 March 1897, Robert Duckworth married Alice Gertrude Marsden at Christ Church, Kensington, Liverpool. At the beginning of 1899, their first child, Robert, was born. During the August of 1899 Duckworth (now a Sub-Inspector) was sent across the Mersey to Seacombe to arrest a man named Alfred Marshall who, it had been alleged, had been stealing money from his employers, the Free Electric Wiring Company. After Duckworth had read him the warrant for his arrest, Marshall was allowed to go to the toilet, whereupon a bang was heard: Marshall had shot himself through the head and killed himself.

In January 1903, and now Detective Inspector, Duckworth was involved in dealing with murder and piracy on the high seas when he was arresting officer in a famous case of its time: the '*Veronica* murders'. The *Veronica* was a British barque carrying timber from Biloxi, Mississippi, to Montevideo, Uruguay. During the trip, it was claimed by the accused men, Otto Ernst Theodor Monsson (18), Gustav Rau, alias August Mailahn (28), and Willem Smith, alias Dirk Herlaar (30), that they not only suffered much physical abuse and intimidation, but also sexual harassment from officers and certain members of the crew – all under the indifferent eyes of their captain, Alexander Shaw. Whilst still at sea, the captain, the first mate, the second mate and four other crewmembers were brutally murdered and thrown overboard. In order to escape, the accused men had set the *Veronica* ablaze and put themselves and two other crewmembers – ship's cook Moses Thomas and sailor Heinrich Flohr – adrift in one of the lifeboats. The men were eventually picked up from Cajueira Island (owned by Liverpool ship owners, it was known as 'Ship Island'), off the Paranhyba River in South America by a passing steam ship, the SS *Brunswick*, on its way to Liverpool. During their passage, the cook gave them away and the men were brought to Liverpool and arrested by Duckworth on 28 January. At the end of the trial at the 1903 Spring Assizes held at St George's Hall, Liverpool, on 15 May 1903, after only twelve minutes, the jury found all three men guilty, sentencing them to hang, though a recommendation was given that Monsson be shown mercy on account of his age and previous good character.

At the beginning of 1904 Robert and Alice's second child, Alice, was born. By 1905, Duckworth was promoted once again – to Chief Detective Inspector.

By 1.30 p.m. on the afternoon of 27 August 1910, Liverpool's Pier Head had been besieged by masses of spectators. Here, Duckworth was to be seen on the promenade deck of the White Star liner *Magantic*, deep in conversation with another passenger. Via the White Star tender *Magnetic*, Duckworth had boarded the liner two or three hours earlier at the Mersey Bar in order to assist colleagues from London's Metropolitan Police to escort two very important passengers from Liverpool to London – Dr Hawley Harvey Crippen (travelling under the pseudonym 'Cyrus Field') and his lover, Ethel Le Neve (travelling as Miss J. Byrne). The passenger Duckworth was seen talking to was Inspector Walter Dew. The attention of the crowds having been diverted by the passengers disembarking on the main gangplank, a door had been opened in the side of the ship, a gangplank used for luggage quickly lowered and a disguised and handcuffed Crippen quickly ushered off by Dew and Duckworth. Le Neve having left the ship by the main gangplank earlier, the party, including Duckworth, were quickly ushered to Riverside station to a reserved saloon carriage in a boat train, which whisked them off to London at precisely 2.23 p.m.

On 11 December 1913, a sack was recovered in Liverpool from the Leeds and Liverpool Canal, in which were discovered the remains of 40-year-old Christina Catherine Bradfield, manageress at her brother's tarpaulin manufacturers, Messrs J. C. Bradfield & Co. of 86 Old Hall Street, Liverpool. She had been missing since the previous Wednesday, 10 December. This was another case involving Duckworth, this time as Detective Superintendent. The accused were two of the company's packers: 18-year-old Samuel Angeles Eltoft and 22-year-old George Ball, alias Sumner. On the evening of Wednesday 10 December, Eltoft claimed that at 7.15 p.m. he was in the company office with Sumner (Ball) when Miss Bradfield had told him he could go. As he left, Sumner asked him to wait outside for him. After waiting for half an hour, Sumner called him back into the shop, whereupon he pulled a tarpaulin-covered handcart into the street and asked Eltoft to take the cart to the canal while he locked up the shop. Sumner eventually caught up with Eltoft near to Leeds Street and took the cart himself. Asking what it was, Eltoft was told, 'It's a bag of rubbish.' After crossing halfway over a brickfield, Sumner tipped the bundle out of the cart, undid the tarpaulin, dragged the sack down to the canal and pushed it in. Sumner maintained that the crime was committed by a third person, 'a man with a brown moustache', who must have hidden himself inside the shop – appearing when he was there alone with Miss Bradfield. He said the man threatened him with a gun, struck Miss Bradfield on the head three times with a 'marlin spike' (a tool once used in any sort of rope work – a slender, cone-shaped iron rod, usually 6–12 inches long), stole her satchel (containing money) and ran off. He and Eltoft, scared in case they were blamed for the deed, tied up the body and threw it into the canal. At the end of the trial, the jury found Sumner guilty of the wilful murder of Christina Catherine Bradfield and sentenced him to death. Eltoft was acquitted of murder, but found guilty of being an accessory after the fact and sentenced to four years' penal servitude.

As can clearly be seen, Robert Duckworth's career was indeed both colourful and rewarding. On 13 February 1917, he was awarded the King's Police Medal; on 21 March 1917, he attended Buckingham Palace to receive the medal from King George V in person. Though publically announced as being awarded for 'displaying extraordinary tact and ability in the discharge of his duties', one newspaper, the *Liverpool Express*, on 22 March 1917 said:

> The coveted distinction was awarded to Superintendent Duckworth in connection, chiefly, it is understood, with certain confidential work of an important character which has been carried out under this able officer's direction during the period of the war.

On 3 June 1918, Duckworth received an MBE. That same year he retired from the Liverpool Police Force and, on 1 November, became Chief of Police for the London & South Western Railway Company (Southern Railways), succeeding Superintendent George Robinson, who retired at the end of October; it was a post Duckworth maintained for eighteen years. During January 1936, King Edward VIII appointed Duckworth a Serving Brother of the Venerable Order of St John of Jerusalem. In December of the same year, Duckworth retired. Returning to Liverpool around 1948, he and his wife moved into 137 King's Lane, Bebbington, Wirral. However, a case involving Duckworth never to figure in any litany of his accomplishments, found him in a courtroom once again – this time as defendant.

Welsh v. Duckworth and Others

On Friday 9 May 1902, an action brought before Mr Justice Wills (Sir Alfred Wills was the presiding judge at Oscar Wilde's retrial in May 1895, in which he sentenced Wilde to two years' hard labour) and a special jury at the Liverpool Spring Assizes, placed Duckworth and two high-ranking Liverpool police officers in the dock facing charges of conspiracy and false imprisonment. The plaintiff, William Patrick Welsh, a 34-year-old ex-Detective Sergeant, was claiming damages for the maltreatment he had suffered at the hands of Chief Superintendent Edwin Sperrin, third in command of the Liverpool Police after the Assistant Head Constable, Leonard Dunning; the Detective Chief Inspector of 'A' Division, Thomas Strettell; and Inspector Robert Duckworth of 'C' Division. There were also suggestions that the then Head Constable, Captain John William Nott Bower (Commissioner of London City Police at the time of the trial), was involved. Mr W. F. Taylor, KC, and Mr Frederick Arthur Greer were prosecuting on behalf of Welsh, with Mr Robert Alfred McCall, KC, and Mr Alexander Hyslop Maxwell (brother of the Chairman of the Liverpool Watch Committee, Alderman Maxwell Hyslop Maxwell) as defence counsel for Sperrin, Strettell and Duckworth.

The whole affair appears to have originated during 1892 and 1893, when Welsh was a constable whose beat included the Liverpool Docks. During that time, not only Sperrin and Strettell, but also Nott Bower's wife, Florence (née Harrison), were availing themselves of Welsh's convenient position. According to Welsh, he was receiving letters from both Sperrin and Strettell asking him to acquire goods for themselves and Mrs Nott Bower from the docks and bonded warehouses, including corn, cigars, tobacco, music books, scent and spirits.

Welsh had joined the Liverpool Police Force in 1884 and, according to the entries in his Good Conduct Book, had risen through the ranks from a fourth-class constable to a first-class Detective Sergeant by the November of 1900 with hardly a blemish on his record. However, things were about to change. Sometime around the Christmas of 1900, when, as a member of 'A' Division, stationed at Hatton Gardens, Liverpool, where he occupied a largely clerical position, rumours concerning Welsh's involvement with the thefts at the docks had been circulating throughout the station. Although a superior officer, Superintendent Tomlinson, was aware of the rumours, he did nothing about them until he was told that Welsh had been showing a letter around a public house. Written to Welsh by Sperrin on 21 December 1892, it asked Welsh to obtain cigars for him for Christmas. Tomlinson informed Nott Bower. During January 1901, Nott Bower transferred Welsh to 'C' Division, stationed at Upper Essex Street, Toxteth – Duckworth's Division. According to Nott Bower, in January 1901 he was reducing the strength of the Central Branch of the Detective Department and, as Welsh was the junior sergeant, he would have had to have placed him on plainclothes duty, which would have meant a reduction in wages. Not wanting to do this, and with a vacancy coming up in 'C' Division, Nott Bower transferred him there. Under cross-examination from the Crown Prosecutor, Nott Bower was asked if, at the time he had transferred Welsh, he had any suspicions as to his sanity; Nott Bower said he had had reservations about his sanity from about the time he had promoted him to first-class Detective Sergeant (24 November, 1900). Counsel was shocked. Apparently considering Welsh to be of unsound mind, not only had Nott Bower promoted him, but had transferred him into more active detective duty among the general public. Nott Bower argued that a Head Constable could not act upon suspicions alone and, therefore, had no choice. It could have been pointed out to him that it was well within his power to order Welsh before police doctors, as he had done at a later stage.

At 'C' Division, all went seemingly well for a while, then on 1 May 1901 Welsh was ordered to attend the May Day Parade. Unfortunately, due to his wife being extremely ill (Mrs Welsh had heart disease), he was unable to. That same day, Duckworth told Welsh that he was the only inspector who would accept him in his division because he was seen as a thief, having been stealing from the docks. Welsh told him if he had been stealing, he had only done it for the benefit of others and he had letters to prove it. On 6 May, Duckworth reported Welsh to Sperrin for non-attendance at the May Day Parade, intimating that he had smelled of stale beer, adding, 'In my opinion he required to be under more restraint than a detective can be.' On 9 May, Welsh was told to report to Sperrin's office in Dale Street. Upon entering the office, Sperrin was interested in anything but Welsh's non-attendance at the May Day Parade – he wanted to know about the letters. Showing Welsh a report headed 'Alleged Threat Against Members of the Force' that claimed Welsh had stated there was a lot he could reveal about the conduct of certain members of the police, had letters to prove it and, if need be, would use them, Sperrin wanted him to write a report detailing whether he had indeed made the statements, if the letters existed and, if so, who were they from and whether could they be produced. Sent to another office to make out the report, Welsh completed it stating that the allegation against him was 'unmistakably misconstrued'. Fearing fellow police officers would be sent to his home in his absence to retrieve the letters, he managed to slip out of the Detective Office, return home and hide them. Returning to the station, Welsh handed the report to Sperrin. Sperrin asked him for the letters, telling him to bring them to his house that night. Welsh said he would consider it, but never did. The following day, Welsh had to present himself before Nott Bower. No mention was made of the letters; instead, Welsh was taken to task regarding issues of discipline: drunkenness, disobedience, and so on. Referring to this meeting, Nott Bower said:

P S Welsh appeared before me, to answer the charges against him. I fully investigated all of them. Welsh practically admitted having taken too much drink; he gave explanations (not in my opinion satisfactory) as to the acts of disobedience; he stated he had no charges to make against anyone; he expressed regret for his conduct; and he asked for consideration. He never even suggested that he held letters which reflected upon anyone.

According to Nott Bower, Welsh was reprimanded and cautioned that any further incidents would result in his removal from the Detective Department altogether. Welsh, however, maintained that at that meeting Nott Bower was only interested in his absence from the May Day Parade. He denied having admitted any drunken bouts or that he had been reprimanded and threatened with removal from the Detective Department. In fact, he maintained that

Nott Bower had said he would be lenient and even complimented him upon having been a capable officer. Upon Welsh's leaving Nott Bower's office, both Sperrin and Duckworth were waiting for him. Sperrin took him into his office and showed him the report he had written the previous day. Telling Welsh he was not satisfied with it, he told him to include the line, 'I have made no charges against anyone, nor have I any to make.' Welsh refused. Sperrin told him it was an order from Nott Bower and he must do it. Reluctantly, Welsh complied, interlineating the sentence on the report.

Three months passed, then during August 1901 Sperrin sent another report he had received from Duckworth concerning Welsh to Nott Bower for having been absent from his home after 6 p.m. when supposedly ill and off-duty. Shortly after this, Duckworth submitted another report stating that Welsh appeared to have been so drunk whilst on duty at the police office he had suggested to him that, being incapable of carrying out his work properly, he had better sign off duty. Welsh had apparently refused, so Duckworth charged him with having been drinking. Having to confirm this officially, Duckworth sought the opinion of the Bridewell Keeper, who agreed Welsh had been drinking, but was fit enough for duty. Not satisfied, Duckworth then took him to a colleague, Inspector Kitchen, who judged him to be perfectly sober. On 24 September, Sperrin presented Nott Bower with another report from Duckworth concerning Welsh, this time for being generally inefficient as a detective and using insolent and insubordinate language to his inspector (Duckworth). Sperrin added to the report:

Inspector Duckworth says he is a most troublesome man, and he can do no good with him. He certainly is not fit for Divisional detective work, and his general conduct is such that in my opinion unfits him for the rank he holds.

The following day, Welsh was ordered to appear before Nott Bower once again. Arriving at the Central Office with both the Bridewell Keeper and Inspector Kitchen to corroborate his case, Welsh was met by Duckworth and Sperrin. Duckworth asked him to leave the force and take his pension – Welsh refused. 'Well you're fucking well mad,' Duckworth retorted, 'and I'll tell the Head Constable so.' With that, Duckworth and Sperrin marched into Nott Bower's office. It appears that due to the conversation the three men had – and not due to any official documentation – Nott Bower wrote a note upon Welsh's report stating:

Before dealing with this case, I should like to have the usual certificates from two medical officers as to this sergeant's mental fitness for police duty. He seems to have been long suffering from delusions as to persecutions, etc, etc.

As a consequence of this, Duckworth carried out the instruction and, on 2 October 1901, Welsh was examined by Police Surgeons Dawson and Lowndes. On the same day, they issued a certificate:

Police Sergeant 38H William Patrick Welsh was incapacitated for the performance of his duty as a police constable by reason of infirmity of mind, the particulars of the infirmity being Mental Delusions.

Upon seeing Strettell, Welsh asked him what was going on. Strettell told him he was to be pensioned off as suffering from delusions. That same day, Welsh sought out a solicitor, G. J. Lynskey. On 14 October 1901, the Finance Sub-Committee received a report from Nott Bower containing the certificate from Dawson and Lowndes, urging that Welsh should be pensioned off the force. Shortly after, Welsh appeared before the Finance Sub-Committee and, in what Nott Bower described as a 'rambling and confused manner', Welsh asked them to investigate his claims of misconduct by certain officers. According to Welsh, at that meeting, upon the insistence of Alderman Maxwell Hyslop Maxwell, Chairman of the Watch Committee, he was forced to tell them that not only was he asked to procure corn for Sperrin but also, through letters she would send to Strettell, for Nott Bower's wife, Mrs Margaret Nott Bower. Welsh was immediately sent out of the committee room and Strettell sent for. Upon being called back into the room, the committee blasted so many questions at Welsh he was unable to reply to them all in a coherent manner. During the trial, whilst being questioned by defence counsel, Nott Bower said he had asked Welsh if he had any complaints to make against anybody else. Welsh said he had: against Mrs Nott Bower for whom he had obtained corn. Defence asked Nott Bower if this was the first intimation he had had that his wife was connected with the procurement of corn from the docks. Nott Bower replied, 'I had no idea where she got her corn.'

However, much later in the trial a witness came forward, John Henry Leybourne, Chief Constable of Chester, in order to corroborate one of Strettell's statements concerning the receipt of letters from Mrs Nott Bower requesting corn. He could recall only that the incident had occurred sometime between 1893 and 1897 when he was a member of the Liverpool Detective Force under Strettell. Strettell had asked him to reply to a letter that had been sent by Mrs Nott Bower, to inform her that the corn had been ordered. After writing out the reply, Leybourne had observed to Strettell, 'What a very large hand Mrs Bower writes: it is a peculiar thing, Captain Nott Bower writes the same hand.'

In consideration of the claim for a pension, the Watch Committee postponed a decision on Welsh's case until Nott Bower had fully investigated the claims and Dawson and Lowndes had engaged the assistance of a medical expert. Nott Bower was requested to give Welsh a month's leave whilst his claims were investigated.

On 21 October 1901, Welsh was ordered to attend the Central Police Office. Upon his arrival, he was ordered to go into one of the rooms, whereupon Strettell said to him, 'Welsh, we are trying to get you your full pension. Mind you say that you have had a bad bit of the head when you go inside.' Once inside the room, Welsh was examined for over two hours by Dawson, Lowndes and Dr Joseph Wiglesworth, Medical Superintendent of Rainhill Asylum, Liverpool. Eventually they reached the conclusion that Welsh was in a *worse* condition than he was previously – and was, in fact, as reported in the *Liverpool Courier* on 10 May 1902, 'suffering from dangerous delusions of suspicion and persecution: they regarded him as insane, looked upon him as a man who might develop dangerous tendencies, and considered that he ought to be placed under care and control'. Upon issuing a certificate to this effect to Sperrin, Nott Bower left for home, where he was phoned by Sperrin. Nott Bower told him to arrest Welsh and take him to Smithdown Road Workhouse, where they had a padded cell. Under the provisions of the Lunacy Act (1890), Welsh was prevented from leaving the building and told that Strettell wanted to see him; he tried to leave once more and was stopped by another officer. Strettell told him he could not leave the building because the doctors had certified him as a dangerous lunatic and, taking him into an adjoining office, told him it was because he had said too much at his meeting with the pension committee.

'Didn't I tell the truth?' Welsh asked.

'Yes, I know you did,' said Strettell, 'but it didn't suit them. I know you are no more mad than I am. They are only heaping coals on their own fire. They will be sending me after you [to a lunatic asylum] in about a fortnight's time.'

Shortly after, Welsh was driven off in a taxicab to Smithdown Road Workhouse by Strettell and Duckworth.

Whilst Strettell took Welsh on to the workhouse, Duckworth went to the home of Dr David Smart, the workhouse's Visiting Medical Officer. (Upon being asked at the trial if he had ever had a case where an inspector had called to his house in reference to a man having been sent to the workhouse as insane before he had arrived there, Smart replied 'Never.') He told Smart that one of their detective officers had gone out of his mind, had been certified insane by police doctors and pronounced a dangerous lunatic by Dr Wiglesworth. Although Duckworth had no certificates with him, he told Smart that Welsh was suffering from delusions, was a dangerous lunatic and should be kept under constraint. At this point, the Master of the Workhouse phoned the doctor and told him he had a detective reported to have gone insane. He was in the charge of another detective, standing at the gate. A certificate had been produced but there was no order. What should he do? Smart told him to get one of the other doctors to see to Welsh, that he was a dangerous lunatic and to put him in a padded cell.

The following morning, Smart went to Smithdown Road Workhouse to question Welsh. Fearing Smart was another police doctor, Welsh refused to talk to him. Upon his return that afternoon, Smart was informed by an attendant of Welsh's mistake, whereupon Smart examined him. That evening, Welsh's solicitor, Mr G. J. Lynskey, arrived at the Smithdown Road Workhouse with Dr William Alexander (a visiting surgeon at the Liverpool Workhouse since 1872; all of the lunatics who passed through that establishment came under his supervision) to examine him. After half an hour alone in the padded room with Welsh, Alexander was of the opinion that Welsh was cool, collected and coherent, and his story was fairly consistent, except with regard to some letters; Lynskey then produced the letters. After the two doctors had read them, Smart apologised to Welsh for having him placed in a padded cell; however, due to the late hour, he would put him in a more comfortable side ward the next day. Soon after, Smart phoned Duckworth's house and left a message that he was to call to see him – no matter what time he arrived home. It was midnight before Duckworth arrived. Smart told him all that had gone on and that, unless he had more information, Welsh would have to be discharged. The following morning, Smart went to see Welsh. In the afternoon, he called Drs Dawson, Lowndes and Alexander, Mr Lynskey and Mr Stewart (a stipendiary magistrate) to the workhouse, where they discussed Welsh's position. Afterwards, Mr Stewart was taken down to see Welsh, whereupon they chatted for three quarters of an hour. On coming out of the ward, Stewart made a statement, whereby Welsh, now considered perfectly sane, was discharged immediately. On 14 November 1901, Alexander examined Welsh once more – and certified that he was not insane.

On 15 November, Nott Bower and Drs Dawson, Lowndes and Wiglesworth gathered at a meeting of the Watch Committee to discuss Welsh being pensioned off the force. Once again, the doctors issued certificates stating that Welsh was a dangerous lunatic, needing to be under care and constraint. He was pensioned off at £35 9s 1d per annum. Despite the mountain of evidence proving that Welsh was not a dangerous lunatic, Nott Bower seemed determined to have him incarcerated. On that same day, he wrote to the Clerk of Justices informing him that Dawson, Lowndes and Wiglesworth had certified Welsh as a dangerous lunatic and, as he was at that time living with his wife (Norah) and four children (Annie, 12; William, 7; Francis, 5; Norah, 2), with no other men present in the house (87 Fountains Road, Kirkdale), he did not think he could be regarded as being under proper care and control. The letter was sent via Strettell with an instruction to the Clerk of Justices that Strettell would relay the facts of the case on oath before one of the magistrates if need be, whereupon the magistrate would be able to take appropriate steps. Unfortunately, for Strettell, the appointed magistrate was Stewart. Having already given his opinion that Welsh was perfectly sane, the case was passed on to Mr Henry Peet, Justice of the Peace of Liverpool and one of the magistrates appointed under the Lunacy Act for Liverpool. Acting upon Strettell's evidence, Peet ordered Drs Bernard and Bickersteth, both of Rodney Street, to examine Welsh. Dr Bernard, Examiner for the Magistrate in Lunacy at the Liverpool Workhouse, came to the conclusion that he could not certify him of unsound mind and the only signs of persecution he detected in Welsh was that from Sperrin and Strettell. Dr Edward Robert Bickersteth examined Welsh and could not find any trace of him being a lunatic, let alone a dangerous lunatic. Peet himself had visited Welsh at his home and talked with him for over an hour and, in his own opinion, could detect no signs of insanity. On 22 November, Peet held an inquiry and the case was dismissed. At around this time, Welsh had decided to set up an appeal to gather funds to enable him to bring a court case against Sperrin, Strettell and Duckworth. After failing to have an appeal published in the local press, he turned to friends. Apparently, some of his friends promised him substantial amounts in order to carry on the action, but only if he withdrew the case from Lynskey. On 19 March 1902, Messrs Gradwell, Abercromby & Co. issued a writ against Sperrin, Strettell and Duckworth.

The trial had lasted seven days, and on 16 May 1902, during final speeches, defence counsel Mr McCall put it to the jury that Welsh had not brought the case before the court for redress for a wrong, but purely out of spite for the defendants and, with the subsequent press coverage, to incite in the general public of Liverpool a violent prejudice against the police. He went on to say that the charge of conspiracy brought by Welsh was a very grave and serious one and, therefore, overpowered any silly questions about breach of regulations.

Prosecution counsel Mr Greer, in his final speech, asked the jury to consider whether the defendants were responsible for incarcerating a perfectly sane and intelligent man in the lunatic ward of a workhouse and subsequently for his discharge from the police force with the ban of mental weakness being upon him for the rest of his life. He asked them to consider that the doctors who had certified Welsh as being insane had all been in contact with the police and had been receiving information from the police, whilst those who had declared him perfectly sane, and that there was no justification whatsoever for locking him up as a dangerous lunatic, had had no statements from the police at all.

In his summing up, Judge Wills declared that he had had no prior knowledge of what the case was about before it commenced as he was in the habit of not reading the pleadings. The case had given him the greatest anxiety and, indeed, the greatest pain; he was staggered at what he considered personal attacks made by the prosecution against Nott Bower, but was eased when Greer (during his final speech) intimated that he did not suggest that from the beginning to the end of the case there was anything that should reflect upon the personal honour of Nott Bower. As far as the case was concerned, Judge Wills informed the court that with the 1890 Lunacy Act being so open to interpretation, having puzzled more people than the Head Constable of Liverpool, he could see difficulties for the defendants. He referred to the fact that he had recently tried a similar case (Morris *v.* Atkins) and had put a construction on some of the sections of the 1890 Lunacy Act, the outcome of which was, after three weeks, still under consideration by the Court of Appeal. Considering the most important charge to be that of conspiracy 'to do one of the most wickedest things that could be imputed to a man of any sort', he particularly condemned Duckworth (as reported in the *Liverpool Courier* on 16 May 1902) for the role he played in the dealings

> without any motive the Judge could see, except the supposed incentive that he wished to please his superior officers. He had nothing to gain, nothing to fear. The letters did not affect him. His position in that respect was totally different from that of the other defendants.

At the end of the trial, the jury took just half an hour to reach their verdict: Sperrin, Strettell and Duckworth were found not guilty of conspiracy, but guilty of false imprisonment. Welsh was awarded £200 compensation (the equivalent of £18,000 today). However, Justice Wills gave a stay of judgment until 27 May, pending the judgment of the Court of Appeal on the Morris *v.* Atkins case. So much public interest had been shown in this particular case that the courtroom was filled to capacity every day of the trial. At the end of the trial, despite the rain, the plateau outside St George's Hall was crammed with thousands of people eagerly awaiting the verdict. As Welsh left the court and appeared on the steps of St George's Hall, great cheers rang out. He was whisked off the steps and held shoulder-high as the crowds carried on cheering and waving their hats in the air. He was eventually placed into a hansom cab, a path was cleared and he was rushed off into the city centre.

By 27 May, the judgment at the Court of Appeal for Morris *v.* Atkins had been decided in favour of the Police Authority on a technicality; consequently, Justice Wills found Sperrin, Strettell and Duckworth not guilty on both charges; Welsh thus lost the £200 compensation. If these attempts to certify Welsh as a dangerous lunatic had been successful, Sperrin, Strettell and Duckworth would not only have succeeded in tearing his family apart, but would also have forced him to have to endure the strict regimes and conditions prevalent in the asylums of the time, with no restriction as to his length of confinement. For a perfectly sane man, this would have been a living nightmare beyond endurance.

Throughout the whole of this trial, the judge, both counsels, and even Welsh himself, went to great pains to underline that, whatever was said, asked of or implied concerning Nott Bower or his wife should not be taken as an imputation upon the character, honesty or integrity of either. In effect, this then rendered Nott Bower's conduct and handling of Welsh's case, and his wife's acquisition of corn from Welsh, as being beyond reproach and well within the law.

On 16 June 1902, the Watch Committee were informed by the Town Clerk that Welsh had entered an appeal to overturn Justice Wills's recent verdict. Having funded Sperrin, Strettell and Duckworth's defence during the trial, the Watch Committee refused them any further financial assistance should an appeal be lodged. On 30 June 1902, the current Head Constable, Leonard Dunning, informed the Watch Committee that an ex-Superintendent of Liverpool Police, Mr Churchill (who was pensioned in the January of 1899), was actively helping Welsh's counsel and had recently published an appeal for funds to help Welsh take the case further. Telling the committee that Churchill's motive (once again) might have been born out of a personal animosity for Sperrin, Dunning added that he thought it a disgrace that a man who had held such a high rank had sided with Welsh – who was, in Dunning's opinion, a self-confessed thief and receiver of stolen goods. He asked the Watch Committee to put a stop on Churchill's pension. Unfortunately, it would appear that Welsh was unsuccessful in acquiring enough funds to continue with his appeal.

Regarding Nott Bower's move to London, during the Christmas of 1901, the Commissioner of London City Police, Lieutenant-Colonel Sir Henry Smith, retired and nineteen candidates vied for his office. One of them was Captain John William Nott Bower. On 21 March 1902 (two months before the commencement of the trial), he became Commissioner of the London City Police, Leonard Dunning becoming Head Constable of the Liverpool Police Force. To assist his candidacy, Nott Bower received high testimonials from, amongst others, the Lord Mayor of Liverpool, the Liverpool Watch Committee, Mr Justice Grantham – and Mr Justice Wills.

On 4 May, 1912, during the US Senate hearing on the sinking of the RMS *Titanic*, held at the Waldorf Astoria Hotel in Washington, Gilbert William Balfour, an inspector for the Marconi Company, was giving evidence regarding the response given by the RMS *Baltic* (the very ship on which Florence Sarah Johnston's father, Arthur Mills, was a bedroom steward) upon receiving a distress call from the sinking ship. Balfour was present in the radio room of the RMS *Baltic* when, at about 11.00 p.m. on 14 April 1912, she received the CQD call (the precursor to SOS) from the *Titanic*. Gilbert William Balfour was married (1901) to Letitia Edwina Sperrin – Chief Superintendent Edwin Sperrin's daughter.

After police had unexpectedly arrived at Marsden's home to take his statement and told him that Wallace had named him alongside Parry as potential suspects, had Marsden felt he had been set up? Fearing the worst, his nerves in tatters, had Marsden broken down and explained the whole sordid tale to his father? Had Marsden or his father contacted his uncle, Robert Duckworth, and told him the whole diabolical tale of his association with Julia, Wallace's blackmail threats, his fear of losing Sylvia and his new position in life? Had he shown his uncle enough remorse for him to have decided that Marsden was as much a victim of Wallace's self-centred, demented mind as Julia, and decided to send the evil genius to the gallows where he belonged? In this respect, Superintendent Hubert Moore would still get his man – and the acclaim he sought. Could it have been to protect the reputation of one of Britain's most accomplished, decorated and respected police officers that Marsden's name and anything that might reveal his name was airbrushed from the case? Might it have been as a personal favour to his wife's brother that Duckworth was somehow able to influence the ongoing investigation and have all references to Joseph Caleb Marsden removed from the police files? Might it have been a combination of both? Did this cover-up include disregarding Parry's incompetent alibi, should it prove so inadequate as to lead him into the dock, where he might reveal his association with Marsden? Does this account for the police's reluctance to pursue Wallace about where he had gone on the night of 22 January, after leaving the Detective Office at 9.40 p.m. and 'bumping' into Samuel Beattie at 10.20 p.m. at the tram stop in Lord Street and quizzing him over his recollection of the time of the Qualtrough telephone message? Could this be the reason why Joseph Caleb Marsden and Richard James Qualtrough's names and association were airbrushed from the case: official knowledge of either one leading to the other? If this was the case, would Robert Duckworth have gone so far as to knowingly send a man he *knew* to be totally innocent to the gallows – or had Marsden convinced him of Wallace's domination in the murder of his wife and the ruination of many other lives?

The problem police then faced was how to arrest Wallace for murder when he had a cast-iron alibi for both the night of the telephone call to the City Café and the night of the murder. If we scrutinise the case files, it is easily seen that the weakest point would be the testimony of milk boy Alan Close. If his statement regarding the time he saw Mrs Wallace could be changed to an earlier time, this would give a sufficiently arguable amount of time for Wallace to have murdered Julia and caught the tram at the junction of Smithdown Road and Lodge Lane at 7.06 p.m.

Roland Oliver, during his opening speech for the defence at the Assize trial, consistently voiced his opinion of the Liverpool Police Force's handling of the case and the methods they employed:

> Let me say now that this is what is sometimes called a police case. If there is one kind of crime that is an abomination to the police, it is an unsolved murder. Everybody attacks them if they cannot get a solution. They are apt to take a biased view of the case, and pursue it relentlessly.

In illustrating this 'relentless pursuit', Oliver pointed the jury towards the evidence given by milk boy Alan Close:

> It must have been a terrible shock to the police – that time of a quarter to seven. Quite obviously, in spite of what they had said, the police were suspicious of this man. The time of quarter to seven was a fatal time. If Close had delivered the milk at a quarter to seven, this man was clear. The argument of delivering the milk at 6.30 is, I suppose, that it would give sufficient time for this murder to have been committed. You have only Close's own word that he looked at the church clock. That is not what he said to the children the following evening.

Oliver then moved on to the police and prosecution reluctance to provide the defence with information and statements of witnesses the police had interviewed and were not calling at the trial:

Why would they not give us the names of the people whom they were not calling so that we could fill things up? They are all powerful, these people. They can comb out Liverpool. You heard the police superintendent say 'I sent out cars' etc. They could do anything they liked, but we, the defence, are wretchedly hampered. Again I ask, why were we not given these names? Is it that the police are afraid to help the defence? Why should they not call these people? … There is no reason why they have not been called, except that their evidence does not fit in with the police case … I comment upon this to show the attitude which has been shown in this case. So far from persisting, the police have done everything they can to throw ropes in front of this man, to prevent facts coming out.

He then condemned the police for drumming up evidence against Wallace:

Before the case comes here it goes before a magistrate to be tried in order that the accused might be able in good time to prepare his defence and to know what the case is against him is. Not one word was said at the police court in all this great mass of depositions about Wallace's demeanour being unnaturally calm or about him being very cool and collected. That has all been thought of since. I wonder whose brain devised it? A very subtle form of attack this, all thought of since the police court. Do you think the police do not know the value of that sort of evidence? What is the excuse for not giving it before?

Oliver even went as far as chiding the prosecution for playing the police's game:

There are some things the Recorder said which struck me at the time, as showing he had been very curiously instructed by the police. Of course, my learned friend only says what is given to him to say.

In two letters written to Hector Munro by Mrs Charlotte Elizabeth Disberry on 28 April 1931, and by her husband, William Edward Disberry, on 29 April 1931, the couple underline the deep corruption within the Liverpool Police of the time. Mrs Disberry argued:

You were quite right in censuring the police re their procedure and conduct in the case. Our Police Force in Liverpool is far from what it should be, it is corrupt, and consequently is inefficient. I happen to know through my own husband's service in the Force, and when any one endeavours to bring matters to the notice of those who could bring about a clearer administration of justice, it is suppressed … *I know that there is a very grave state of gross corruption in our City Police, which strongly effects efficiency of same, and it is very necessary to bring pressure on the Home Office to intervene. It is not my husband's fault that this has not been done.*

Mr Disberry then supports his wife's opinions:

[On] the question of corruption in the Liverpool City Police, which Mrs Disberry has mentioned, can we possibly have an efficient Force when promotions are paid for, Etc?, and especially when those in authority take no notice. In fighting my case with the Local Authority here, I informed no other than a Member of the Watch Committee, and Chairman of a Sub-Committee at that. Some time ago, when I was dealing with the Home Office, I mentioned the fact of gross corruption here, but I rather think that it went no further than one of the Permanent Officials ... in any case I am going to see the corruption question through, at whatever cost to me or mine.

At the time of writing, William Edward Disberry was a costing-clerk. However, as a one-time police constable, he had been dismissed from the Liverpool City Police Force during the police strike of August 1919. Jonathan Goodman was to say of this event:

The City Police Force, which was known to a good many local people as 'The Jiggery Pokery Brigade', was in very poor shape indeed.

The reason could be traced back to the police strike of 1919, which was precipitated by the progress of the Police Bill through Parliament. Under the terms of this Bill, the Police Union, organized and controlled by the police themselves, was to be abolished, and a new Union, the Police Federation, formed with officials appointed by the Chief Commissioner. The Police Union called for a nation-wide strike of its members in protest against 'this perversion of democratic principles'. Throughout most of the country the call went unheeded; only two cities, London and Liverpool, were affected to any great extent.

In Liverpool more than half the members of the police force went on strike.

In the climate of post-war hopelessness and despair, the Liverpool police strike created a situation that was conducive to anarchy. Men who had been unemployed since demobilization were soon prowling the streets, forming themselves into gangs, breaking into shops and private houses, and looting anything they could lay their hands on. At night candles lit street corners where men gambled with the loot of the day. The Lord Mayor appealed for law and order, for volunteers, for special constables to report for duty; troops were called in to patrol the worst-hit areas of Scotland Road and Byrom Street; a battleship and two destroyers steamed into the Mersey to protect the docks.

The Watch Committee issued a statement saying that all strikers would be dismissed from the force, and none would be reinstated. This caused a few of the strikers to return to duty; but 951 members of a force of 1,874 remained on strike and were dismissed.

Recruitment began. Advertisements appeared in the local papers offering commencing wages of seventy shillings a week, uniform, pension, good opportunities for advancement. There was no shortage of applicants; there was not time for the recruiting officers to take up references. Within a fortnight over 500 men were sworn into the Liverpool City Police Force. Some of these new constables were of excellent character; others were not. More than a few of them found themselves in the distinctly odd position of having to patrol the streets where, a few days before, they had engaged in looting and gambling.

There had been a certain amount of corruption within the police force before the strike, but now it increased: a few nasty sores became a rash. The force became overstocked with dishonest policemen – 'bent Jacks' – some of them only slightly bent, but a lot of them bent almost double. In at least one division a Chicago-style protection racket was organised. Some members of the force took up house-breaking, either as spare-time occupations or to ease the monotony of long spells on duty. This often led to situations wherein the criminals investigated their own crimes. Needless to say, they never solved them.

Forty-eight of the dismissed strikers were sergeants; many others had passed examinations and were waiting for their promotions to be authorized. So the strike created a shortage of officer material, and men were promoted to positions they were unqualified to fill.

Some members of the force, trying to justify their ranks by large numbers of arrests, used decidedly unconventional methods in the investigation of crime. Results were what counted. On the few occasions when an officer was reprimanded for overzealous conduct he generally pleaded that he was fighting fire with fire. A lot of innocent people were burned by these counter-arson activities. The overzealous conduct was ascribed to a genuine but misplaced desire to combat crime; in fact, crime was simply being used as an excuse for making arrests, and the kudos attached to these arrests was being used as an aid to the retention and pursuit of power.

By 1931 much of the Liverpool City Police Force was hardly up to the task of dealing with parking offences, let alone a full-scale murder investigation.

Could this have been what Mr and Mrs Disberry were alluding to in their letter to Munro?

As for the inept, juvenile, malingerer Richard Gordon Parry, the perpetual 'accident waiting to happen', every step would have to be taken to keep him out of the dock – even going as far as impressing upon him that if he ever breathed a word of what had happened that cold, January night in 1931, the full force of the law would land on his doorstep and they would make sure that he would be charged with Julia's murder. I believe, had Duckworth been involved, Parry's biggest threat was from the police. This would be an ongoing threat that would last every day of his life. In the end, though, Parry most likely came to enjoy the notoriety and attention paid to him by authors and press, safe in the knowledge that, when all is said and done, he had not murdered Julia Wallace.

I have previously indicated that Robert and Alice Gertrude Duckworth had two children, Robert and Alice. At the beginning of 1927, when their father was Chief of Police for the Southern Railways, Alice married Cyril Arthur Hicks in Wandsworth, London, and in 1930 Robert married Nellie Dorothy Carling in Brentford, London. At the beginning of the Second World War, Robert Duckworth Jr was an agent for the Cunard shipping line. On 18 February 1942, as an 'Army Officer', he arrived in New York on the SS *Ville de Tamatave* on a diplomatic mission, his destination being the British Military Authority based at 25 Broadway – the magnificent Cunard Building. Named as his next-of-kin, his wife, Nellie, and his eight-year-old son, Robert, were living at 11 Netherpark Avenue, Thornliebank, Glasgow, where he was to return when his mission was over. However, on 9 June 1948, he boarded the SS *Queen Elizabeth* bound for America as 'Ship Owner's Representative'; and this time his stay was permanent. His destination was San Francisco, and he was on his way to visit a friend, 'D. Cowie, c/o G.Vermillion, 1745 Pacific Ave'. Although described as married, he gave his next-of-kin not as his wife, or even his parents, but as his sister, Alice Hicks, then living at the picturesque village of Perrotts Brook, Cirencester, Gloucestershire.

On 6 November that same year, the RMS *Mauretania* left Southampton on its way to New York with a passenger list that included both Nellie Dorothy Duckworth and her then 14-year-old son, Robert. Their final destination was to be the Gotham Hotel, 835 Turk Street, San Francisco − one mile from Pacific Avenue. However, when the *Mauretania* made a stop at Halifax, Nova Scotia, Canada, it was noted that both Mrs Duckworth and her son 'Did Not Embark'. From the record, it would appear that Robert Duckworth Jr had left England for good in 1948 and, in describing his next-of-kin as his sister, had relinquished all ties with his wife, his son and both of his parents. Was Nellie Duckworth on her way to San Francisco that winter of 1948 with hopes of reconciliation with her husband? If so, she never made it. Robert Duckworth Jr died in San Francisco in August 1977.

In his doorstep conversation with Jonathan Goodman and Richard Whittington Egan in 1966, 'Parry claimed that John Rowland's agent called to see him, circa 1958–1959, when Rowland was writing his book on the Wallace case, and that he was promised money − but got nothing. Incidentally, he thought Rowland's book poor.' John Rowland's book, *The Wallace Case*, was in fact published by Carroll & Nicholson in 1949; this being the case (and Parry was not lying to Goodman in order to squeeze money out of him), Parry had to have been approached during Rowland's researches for the book, possibly in 1947 or 1948. Had Parry panicked and contacted Marsden to tell him of the encounter? Had Marsden then approached Robert Duckworth about the impending book and somehow his son had found out about his father's involvement? Distraught, had he told his sister and fled the country?

Alice Gertrude (Marsden) Duckworth died on 7 September 1958, aged 86, at 137 King's Lane, Bebington, Wirral, Cheshire. Her only obituary simply states that she was the 'Dear Wife of Robert Duckworth'. Robert Duckworth, MBE, died on 18 June 1960, aged 94, also at 137 King's Lane. His only obituary simply states he was 'formerly of Liverpool CID and Chief of Southern Railway Police' and 'Husband of the late Alice Gertrude Duckworth'. In both obituaries, there is no mention whatsoever of either of their children. Like Thomas Richard Murphy, there were no obituaries placed from both the couple's siblings or children. Had a rift also entered the Duckworth family that was so hugely devastating it not only drove Duckworth's children to deny the existence of their parents, the parents to deny the existence of their children, but also drove their son to relinquish all contact with his own wife and son and take refuge over 8,000 miles away? Could this rift have been the fact that their father had a hand in diverting the course of justice away from the possible brutal killer of a frail old woman, the killer being their own cousin, Joseph Caleb Marsden?

Devil in the Detail?

Had William Herbert Wallace, faced with his own impending death, attempted to regain some semblance of control over his ebbing life by formulating a horrifically ingenious plan to dispose of his burdensome wife? If this is the case, had he not only left behind the brutally battered body of his wife Julia, but also, in procuring the assistance of two desperate young men to use as the very tools of that destruction – Joseph Caleb Marsden and Richard Gordon Parry – left a trail of shattered and broken lives and families? Was William Herbert Wallace the real devil in the detail?

Far from being the 'perfect murder', the 'nonpareil of all murder mysteries' and 'Unbeatable', this case has been strewn with both incriminating evidence and proofs of the perpetrators from the outset. Had it not been for one very important fact (possibly unknown to Wallace) – Joseph Caleb Marsden's uncle, Robert Duckworth, was once a very high-ranking, highly decorated and influential member of the Liverpool Police Force – this case would have been solved within days of its perpetration. In fact, as has been shown, within five days of the start of the police investigation, all of the culprits had already been rounded up and enough evidence had been gained to build a case against them.

As the Right Honourable Justice Wright so eloquently stated at the beginning of this book:

> A man cannot be convicted of any crime, least of all murder, merely on probabilities, unless they are so strong as to amount to a reasonable certainty. If you have other possibilities, a jury would not and I believe ought not, to come to the conclusion that the charge is established.

Are we now able to say, with the weight of evidence presented in this book, that the brutal killers of Julia Wallace have at long last, been found? William Herbert Wallace – the troubled mastermind behind the murder of his wife. Joseph Caleb Marsden – the brutal, if reluctant, instrument of Julia's death. And Richard Gordon Parry – the accomplice, aiding and abetting the commission of this dreadful crime? The verdict is up to you – the jury.

Edgar Lustgarten, in his foreword to Jonathan Goodman's book *The Killing of Julia Wallace*, said, 'I have always hoped that someone – analytical, literate, really steeped in the facts (both central and peripheral) – would produce what could be deemed a scriptural Book of Wallace.' My greatest hope is that, at the very least, I have contributed towards that. To echo Roger Wilkes's sentiments at the close of his radio programme *Who Killed Julia?*, 'I have done what I can and, sadly and uneasily, once again, the case must rest.'

Notes

1. James Caird was born on 23 May 1879 at 96 Salisbury Road, Everton, Liverpool. The second son of six boys – Robert Nisbet (1876, Scotland), James (1879), John William (1881), Lionel Gordon (1884), Albert Victor (1887) and Arthur Ogilvy (1888) – born to builder James Caird (born 1850 in South Muir, Forfar, Scotland) and Sophia Campbell (born 1853, also in Scotland), James was married to Mary Gamwell (born 11 October 1888), the youngest daughter of five children – Charles (1881), Harry (1885), Edith (1887), Mary (1888) and Frank (1891) – born to one-time cobbler, then clockmaker Charles Gamwell (born in 1857 in Pocklington, Yorkshire) and Mary Thompson (born 1859 in Sefton, Liverpool). James and Mary were married at All Saints church, Stoneycroft in June 1910; shortly after their marriage, James left the family home at 13 Argyle Street, Anfield and the couple moved into their (then recently built) first home at 3 Letchworth Street, Anfield; whilst living here, the couple were to have three children: Charles Gamwell (1912), Kenneth Campbell (1916) and Mary (1923). At the time of his marriage, James and his brother, John William, had already gone into partnership and opened their own shop – J. & J. W. Caird, Grocers – at 113 Stanley Road, Liverpool. This partnership was to continue until John William left to run his own enterprise at 114 Cherry Lane, Walton. At the time of Julia's murder, James Caird was still providing groceries to his customers at 113 Stanley Road. James Caird's nephew, Colin Caird, born 1906 (son of Robert Nisbet Caird and Emily Craig Collins), was an apprentice to one of Liverpool's foremost masons, Herbert Tyson Smith, for four years. An artist of incredible precision and creativity, Colin Caird's work can still be see today on edifices such as the Martin's Bank building, both Liverpool Mersey Tunnel shafts, the Dock entrance to the Mersey Tunnel, many buildings in Manchester and Preston, and Stormont Castle in Ireland, where he worked for five years. After Colin's death, his son Alastair published a book of his father's poetry, *Colin Caird: Selected Poems* (1985), written by his father whilst working away from home. James Caird died in 1969 in Greenwich, London; his wife died in Greenwich in 1973. Colin Caird died in West Derby, Liverpool, in 1982.

2. Evan Reginald Lloyd's family stemmed from Wrexham in Denbighshire, North Wales, where Lily's great-grandfather, John Lloyd, was a printer. After marrying, John and his wife Susanna moved to Mold, Flintshire, North Wales, where Lily's grandfather, Ebenezer Lloyd, was born in 1836, the middle child of five children: John (1833), William Walter (1834), Ebenezer (1836), Hugh Owen (1841) and Susanna (1843). By the late 1840s, the family

had arrived in Liverpool and were living at 17 Queen Ann Street. During the summer of 1858, Ebenezer, now a printer's compositor, married Susan Amelia Moss in Newport, Monmouthshire. Returning to Liverpool that same year, they had their first of eight children: Susanna Maria (1858), William Henry (1861), Kenrick Morton (1863), John Edward (1867), George Henry (1869), Charles (1874), Evan Reginald (1876, Lily Lloyd's father) and Lilian (1880).

From as far back as the beginning of the seventeenth century, the Hewitts, Lily Lloyd's mother's family, had lived in Birmingham. On 12 September 1742, Lily's great-great-great-great-grandfather, Thomas Hewitt, moved to Rugby, Warwickshire, and married Sarah Mansfield. By 27 December 1840, the Hewitts had arrived in Liverpool; Lily's great-grandfather, Edward Hewitt, a master tailor, married her grandmother, Ellen Ward, at St Nicholas' church, Chapel Street, Liverpool, and the couple had five children: William Edward (1842), John Ward (1844), Thomas Alexander (1846), Henry Frederick (1851) and Jane McWilliam (1862). In 1871, Thomas Alexander Hewitt, by now a tailor himself, was married to Sarah Evans at St Michael's church, Toxteth Park, Liverpool: Lily Lloyd's mother was the youngest of their three children, Thomas (1872), Rosalie Rene (1873) and Josephine Ward (1876). At the beginning of the 1900s, Josephine Ward Hewitt was a domestic servant at Fairlawn House, Bankfield Road, West Derby, Liverpool; Evan Reginald Lloyd was an insurance office clerk, living with his parents at 273 Lower Breck Road, Liverpool – close to Wolverton Street.

3. At the beginning of the eighteenth century, as with most of the area surrounding Blackburn, Lancashire, Over Darwen's relied on a cottage industry producing textiles that were sold on to the surrounding villages and towns. As the century progressed, so did technology; the supremacy of the machine became more and more prevalent, bringing with it the subjugation of the master weavers and dramatic socio-economic and cultural changes. Outcompeted by mills with enormous output and low costs of manufactured materials, the cottage industries fell into dramatic decline. The surrounding populace, in desperation, were forced from their villages into the mills and the substandard housing adjoining them, having to endure long, back-breaking hours in noisy, often dangerous conditions for a pittance in recompense – barely enough (and more than often, not enough) to provide anything like a decent standard of living. One of these families was the Marsdens: James Marsden, his wife Ellen Polettet and their seven children. During the 1780s two of their sons – their second child, James, born in 1756, and their youngest, Joseph, born in 1769, both brushmakers – decided there were better prospects to be had elsewhere, and so joined the ever-increasing mass migration of people travelling from all over the kingdom to take advantage of the rapidly increasing prosperity of the major cities.

The brushmaker's craft has a long and far-flung history, reaching beyond the Romans, the Greeks and the Egyptians and to practically every inhabited corner of the planet. The heart of the manufacturing process was the 'panshop': four 'panhands' working around a 'panframe', a large, circular, heavy wooden table with a cauldron of hot tar simmering at its centre. To begin the process, the stocks of the brushes and brooms would be drilled on a hand lathe worked by a treadle – each hole would be drilled at a slightly different angle to the next. The stock was then held in the panframe whilst the hair bristles were drawn from a 'drawboard', parted (to prevent their natural curvature forcing them into one direction), the root end dipped in tar and tied with twine. The 'knot', as the bundle was now called, would be dipped once more and inserted, very precisely, into the stock before the tar cooled. The panhand would then have to 'get the bend' of the bristles by ensuring that each successive knot of bristles inserted into the stock kept its natural bend, running in the correct direction at each part of the stock. Different sizes of brush and broom required different numbers of knots; generally, during the nineteenth century, the average rate of pay for a panhand was a penny per twenty knots, and a good-sized broom could be as large as ninety knots.

As brushmakers, James and Joseph would, most likely, have been members of the Society of Journeymen Brushmakers; formed in the early eighteenth century to ensure the well-being of its members, it was, for all intents and purposes, a trade union – though, trade unions being banned at the time, its members would never have admitted so openly. When times became hard and work became scarce, those members of the Society that were able-bodied would be sent on 'the Tramp'. A brushmaker would be issued with a certificate to prove his craftsmanship, an official book called a 'blank', and a small sum of money. A route would be determined to take the journeyman (invariably on foot) across country from branch clubhouse to branch clubhouse in the hope of him finding employment; typically, these clubhouses were usually found in taverns or inns. Upon his arrival at a clubhouse, the journeyman would be given food and lodgings at a much-reduced rate and be introduced to the local society secretary. If employment could not be found, the branch secretary would sign the journeyman's blank book to show that no employment could be gained at that stop on his journey, give him another small amount of money and forward him on to the next branch clubhouse on his route. If James and Joseph Marsden had been sent on the Tramp, upon their arrival in Liverpool, they may have had to report to the now demolished Stag's Head Inn, Duncan Street, which was a one-time Society of Journeymen Brushmakers branch clubhouse; the fact that they remained in Liverpool implies that, after leaving Blackburn, they at last found much-needed employment.

During the summer of 1786, James (despite being a Nonconformist) married Hannah Young at St Nicholas's church, Chapel Street, Liverpool and, by 1798, his brushmaking enterprise was up and running with a shop at 6 Cable Street, off Castle Street, which at that time was close to the resplendent St George's church – now the location of the Queen Elizabeth II Law Courts. By 1807, James's income had to have been sufficient enough for him to send his fifth child, John Astley Marsden (born 1793), to the newly founded Mill Hill Protestant Dissenters' Grammar School in London, where he became one of the first twenty or so pupils to be educated there. James's fourth child, Joseph, appears to have been the first of the brothers to have established himself as a commercial brushmaker after his father. Married to Frances Allen in 1812, Joseph in 1814 had his own premises at 14 Kitchen Street, Toxteth Park. For the following ten or so years, he had shops at various locations around the Toxteth Park area of Liverpool, including 89 Pitt Street, 91 Pitt Street, 30 Park Lane and 77 Dale Street. In 1825 both his older brother James and his younger brother John Astley joined their father in what had now become the family business, with premises at 62 Cable Street, 50 Bold Street, 1 Love Lane and 32 Park Lane. By far the most successful of James's sons who followed their father into the brushmaking trade was John Astley Marsden. His brushmaking skills enabled him to purchase 'Marine Villa', a turreted, castellated mansion in Liscard, Wirral, where he lived with his wife, Anna Maria Singleton, and his nine children. In 1842, John Astley Marsden founded the Liscard Independent Church, then situated on Rake Lane, at a cost of £1,200, with a further refurbishment the following year costing £800. Such was his prominence in the area, the house became variously known as 'Brush Castle', 'Marsden's Folly' and 'Marsden Castle' before eventually being known as 'Liscard Castle'. Ultimately, after becoming run-down and overgrown, it was demolished in 1902. For some time, the road on which it stood was renamed Marsden Lane after him; it is now called Seaview Road.

Joseph Marsden's brushmaking enterprise continued unabated until around 1827, when, described as a 'Gentleman', he became clerk to St George's church, Everton. In September 1832, he suffered two major blows. On the 23rd, his oldest son, Caleb, died at the tragically young age of only 18 due to what was described as a 'rupture' – possibly a ruptured spleen, where the abdominal cavity fills with blood; this most painful condition can result in shock and, ultimately, death. The following day, his wife Frances died. Over the following years, until his own death on 17 December 1853, he became clerk to Holy Trinity church, St Anne Street, and occasionally dabbled in organ playing and teaching music.

4. John Sharp Johnston was born at 12 Rose Street, Birkenhead, Cheshire in 1879. He was the middle child, and only son, of shipwright Robert Pearson Johnston (born in 1851 in Maryport, Cumbria) and Mary Russell Sharp (born in 1854 in Maryport). After their marriage in 1876 in Cockermouth, Cumbria, Robert and Mary Johnston moved to Birkenhead, where their first child, Mary Frances, was born in 1877 – soon to be followed by John Sharp then Jane Hall in 1886.

Florence Sarah Mills was born at 212 Claughton Road, Birkenhead, in 1880; she was the eldest child of coach smith Arthur Mills, born in Birkenhead in 1857 (youngest son of coachbuilder John Mills, of Milnthorpe, Westmoreland, and Sarah Newport of Barrow in Cheshire) and Mary Elizabeth Cartwright, born in Birkenhead in 1858 (eldest child of warehouseman John Cartwright from Repton in Shropshire, and Mary Ann Tunstall from London). In 1889, when the couple's only other child, Frederick Arthur Mills, was born, Arthur had become a ship's steward, working almost exclusively for the White Star Line's RMS *Baltic* as a bedroom steward. In 1901, his wife Mary died whilst living at 27 Beechwood Avenue, Wallasey, Cheshire. Being away at sea for much of the time, Arthur sent his children to stay with his older brother George Mills and his family, who were living at 7 Sutton Street, Tuebrook, Liverpool – close to St John the Baptist church; it was here, in 1902, that John Sharp Johnston married Florence Sarah Mills. During this same year, Arthur Mills married again, to Agnes Lucy Kermode, the couple moving into 31 Wolverton Street shortly after their marriage.

5. Mary Ann Blackwell, an elementary schoolmistress, had married William Dartmouth Sykes, an elementary schoolmaster from Linthwaite, Yorkshire, in 1885. That same year, the couple had moved to Norfolk. William Dartmouth Sykes died in 1913, leaving three children, Percy (1886), Reginald (1890) and Dorothy (1896).

6. Horace Willows Skelsey, born in 1872 in Thorne, West Riding, Yorkshire, had arrived in Halifax, Nova Scotia, Canada on 16 March 1890. By the April of the following year, he had established himself as a farm labourer in Selkirk, Manitoba. By the June of 1900, Horace had moved on to Mason County, Washington, USA. Having lived with her sister and her brother-in-law, Mary Ann and William Dartmouth Sykes, at their schoolhouse in Norfolk for over ten years, Ellen Maud had become an elementary school teacher. On 16 October 1902, she left Liverpool on board the SS *Tunisian*, arriving in Montreal, Canada, on 25 October; her destination was Seattle, Washington, USA. The following year, she had met and married Horace and had the first of their two children, Edmund Ernest (1903) and Horace Joseph (1907).

7. Sarah Jane Spenley was born in Toxteth Park, Liverpool, in 1882, the fourth child and second daughter of William Spenley, a bus driver (eventually a tram driver) from Foxholes, Yorkshire, and Sarah Jane Gordon, from County Wicklow, Ireland. Moving from Foxholes after the birth of their first child, John William (1873), the couple arrived in West Derby, Liverpool, sometime during 1874, in time for the birth of their second child, Mary Edith. Three more children were soon to follow: Robert Botterill (1879), Sarah Jane (1882) and Henry Gordon (1884) (Henry was to become a private in the 1st/10th King's Liverpool Regiment, and was killed in action in Calais on 24 April 1918, leaving a widow). On 26 April 1908, Sarah Jane married James Draper, a labourer from Toxteth Park.

8. Frederick William Jenkinson was born in Dalton-in-Furness in 1881, the second son – James Wilson (1877), Catherine Amalie (1878), Frederick William (1881), Thomas Walter (1882), Lillie Gertrude (1887) and George Herbert (1895) – of Thomas Jenkinson, an iron miner, born in 1851 in Marown, Isle of Man, and Margaret Cretney, born in 1852, also in Marown, Isle of Man, the youngest daughter – James (1836), Thomas (1841), Ceaser (1847), Catherine (1848), Ann (1850), Margaret (1852) and Phillip (1855) – of agricultural labourer James Cretney and Catherine Kelly. Soon after their marriage, in 1875, Thomas Jenkinson and Margaret Cretney moved to Whitehaven, Cumbria, where their first child, James Wilson, was born. That same year, the family moved to Dalton-in-Furness.

At the time of the Wallaces' arrival at 151 Chapel Street, Dalton-in-Furness, Frederick William Jenkinson was around 10 years old and living at off Chapel Street at 26 Cleater Street, next door to his future wife, Alice Ann Williams, who lived at No. 28. Also born in 1881, Alice was the oldest child – Alice Ann (1881), John James (1887) and William Harry (1888) – of James Williams, an iron miner, born in 1857 in Devon, and Elizabeth Benson, born in 1862 in Cartmel, Cumbria, daughter of John Benson, an iron miner, and Ann Kendall. It would be here that long-lasting friendships would form between the Wallaces, the Jenkinsons and the Blackwells. Frederick and Alice were to marry in 1908 after Frederick had completed his studies at teacher training college. Arriving in Liverpool a fully fledged teacher at the beginning of 1909, the couple moved into 50 Guernsey Road, Stoneycroft. The following year, Frederick and Alice's first child, Fred Wilson, was born. After their move to 112 Moscow Drive, in 1913, their daughter Stella May was born in 1915. Frederic William Jenkinson died in Liverpool in 1958; his wife Alice died in Birkenhead, Cheshire, in 1974.

9. William Brine was born in Sherborne in Dorset in 1870 (he may have been a direct descendant of James Brine of 'Tolpuddle Martyrs' fame) and led somewhat of a nomadic early life, spending most of it in service; it was whilst he was a footman at the beautiful Rydal Hall estate in Westmoreland that he met and married Grace Anne Sproat at the beginning of 1892. The couple moved, almost immediately, to Ellesmere in Shropshire, where they had the first of their four children – James Frederick, born on 18 May 1892, and Percy Alexander, born on 3 July 1894. Within five years, the family had move to Blyth, Nottinghamshire, where in 1899 Grace gave birth to their third child, William Reginald, who would die aged 19 whilst serving in France as a private in the 1st Battalion, King's Shropshire Light Infantry during the First World War. Shortly after moving into 18 Leyfield Road, West Derby, Liverpool, the couple's final child was born, Dorothy Evelyn. At this time, William was described as a 'butler'. At around 1905, the family moved once again, to 59 Bonsall Road, West Derby; it was whilst living here that William changed his profession and became a ship's steward – his eldest son, James Frederick, followed in his father's footsteps when he was 18. After another move to 11 Rosthwaite Road, West Derby, the family moved into 21 Auburn Road, West Derby, in 1912. Percy Alexander Brine's life, however, is somewhat more chequered. Sometime around 1917, when only 23, Percy appears to have relocated to America and not only changed his name to 'William Percy Brine', but also changed the year of his birth from 1894 to 1892. Here, he married and, in February 1918, his wife Bridget gave birth to their first child, William. Living at 2535 Church Avenue, Kings, Brooklyn, New York, Percy was working as a motorman, driving the car trains on the elevated railway from the Flatbush depot of the Brooklyn Rapid Transit Company. By 1928, Percy was living at 93 West 53rd Street, Bayonne, New Jersey. He died in Bayonne in 1972. Up until the year of Julia's murder, William Brine senior had remained at 21 Auburn Road; as with James and his wife, his daughter Dorothy had lived there with her husband, Thomas Wilkinson Stewart, from the time of their marriage on 19 April 1924 (between 1924 and 1929 when James, wife Olivia and daughter Savona moved to Knoclaid Road, this must have been a very cramped house). Grace Anne Brine died on 5 January 1926, her body being interred in her childhood home of Ambleside, Westmoreland. Sometime during 1931, shortly after Julia's murder, the Brines left 21 Auburn Road. William became a permanent member of the crew (as bathroom steward) on the American steamship *California* running between New York and San Francisco; whilst with the company he named, as his next of kin, his son, 'Percy: 93, West 53rd Street, Bayonne, New Jersey'. As far as the records have shown, both William and Percy Brine never returned to England again. There appears, however, to have been some link to Ireland: in 1932, Percy's son William made a trip there, seemingly alone. Again, in August 1954 and July 1956, Percy made trips there himself – under his real name, Percy A. Brine. James Frederick Brine died in Liverpool in 1958; Percy Alexander Brine died in Bayonne, New Jersey, in 1972; Olivia Alberta Brine died in Liverpool in 1975; and Savona (née Brine) Chilcott died in Denbighshire, North Wales, in 1998.

10. The history of the Duckworth family reaches far back into the history of the Liverpool building trade – possibly reaching as far back as the building of Liverpool's first dock in 1715. The first definite appearance of Robert Duckworth's ancestry appears in 1792, when

his great-grandfather, bricklayer John Duckworth, married his great-grandmother, Mary Metcalf, on 12 August at St Nicholas's church, Chapel Street, Liverpool. Of their seven children, the four boys – William (1793), John (1799), Jonathan (1806) and Robert (1808) – were all to take up the hod and trowel. On 10 November 1834, his other brothers having previously married, Robert married Margaret Webb at St John's church, Old Haymarket, Liverpool (originally standing on the site of St George's Hall, Lime Street). Of their two children, John (1836) and William (1840), only William was to survive. Their older brothers William and John having branched out on their own, Jonathan and Robert Duckworth combined their skills and established their own building and contracting enterprise, J. & R. Duckworth, with premises at 49 Prince Edwin Street, Liverpool. In 1845 Robert's wife died and, on 27 October 1847 he married again at St Augustine's church, Everton, Liverpool: Eliza Worsley was a milliner, born in Parr, St Helens, Lancashire; ten years his junior, she had been living in Prince Edwin Street since the early 1840s. By 1851, their building venture having gone from strength to strength, Jonathan and Robert were employing a labour force of sixty men. An interesting note on the Duckworths' oldest brother, William (by this time describing himself as an architect and surveyor), is that on Sunday 1 May 1859, after returning home from a church service with his second wife, Margaret Hammond, he found that his 18-year-old stepdaughter, Isabella Emily Hammond, had failed to do the housework: this chore was usually taken up on alternate Sundays by Isabella and her younger sister Margaret (also William's stepdaughter). Unfortunately, whilst Mr and Mrs Duckworth were at chapel, a relative of the family, newly married, arrived with her husband and the girls were disposed to entertain them. Upon the return of the girls' parents, the guests had left and the housework was yet to be done. William took great offence at this and, despite his own assertion that he was 'the kindest of stepfathers ever in the country', he called Isabella a 'pig' and kicked her in the groin. He and his wife then went into the parlour and sang a hymn. After that, William found Isabella in the kitchen and told her, 'You pig; you shall leave my house. I'll have nothing more to do with you', and was on his way upstairs to gather up her belongings when his wife begged him, 'Do let this holy day go over, and we will turn her out tomorrow'; turning to her daughter she advised her to 'go on the town' to earn her living (i.e. become a prostitute). Her injury causing her great pain, Isabella took a summons out on William: on 16 May 1859, Mr Dixon, the presiding magistrate, addressing the court, said, 'Whatever the defendant's idea might have been of his right to chastise the girl, it was a cowardly act for any man to take the means of correction which he had done.' Addressing Duckworth, he said, 'This is one of the most gross outrages which ever could be brought before the court. For a man in your position of life to go and attack a girl in this way is a disgrace.' Duckworth was ordered to pay £5 plus costs or go to gaol for two months. Not having any money with him and not wanting to spend time in gaol, Duckworth sent his wife from the courtroom with his pocket watch: after she had managed to pawn it, she returned and paid off the fine.

At the beginning of the 1860s, Robert's son by his first wife, William, seemed to have wanted little to do with the building trade, instead becoming a pawnbroker's assistant for John Harris Gibson, a master pawnbroker from Ireland who ran a shop at 1 Ford Street, Vauxhall, Liverpool. On 15 October 1865, he married Eliza Ann Rothwell, daughter of pub landlord William Rothwell and Hannah Jones. William Rothwell had been landlord of the Royal Oak public house in Great Nelson Street, Liverpool, since 1860; Great Nelson Street being almost a continuation of Prince Edwin Street, it is very likely that the Royal Oak public house had been a destination for the Duckworths and their workers at the end of their working day. William Rothwell's wife having died in 1859, Eliza Ann was working with her father, and it is more than likely that this is where the relationship between William and Eliza originated. In February 1867, their first child, Robert, was born. That same year, William managed to open his own pawnbroker's business at 17 Springfield Street, Liverpool. During the brief three years the family resided here, the couple had two more children, Jonathan (1868) and Benjamin (1870). William's venture seeming to have failed, about 1870 the family were forced to vacate the property in Springfield Street, and move into a boarding house in Eldon Place – along with four other families. Unfortunately, Benjamin must have been a very sickly child; unable to be baptised during the months that followed his birth, he was eventually baptised on 9 October 1872 – the same day as his burial service. It would appear, however, that things did not get much better for William and his family; struggling to find work, around the end of the 1870s, the family, now augmented with the birth of two more sons – William (1874) and Osborne (1876) – moved to Sutton, St Helens, Lancashire, where William became a glass bleacher at the Nuttall & Co. glassworks. Robert, at this time 14 years old, became an apprentice baker, whilst Jonathan became an apprentice painter. Remaining here until the mid–1880s, William and Eliza had two daughters, Maria Hannah (1880) and Eliza Ann (1883), before their return to Liverpool. Once home, the family moved into 28 Martensen Street, Kensington, Liverpool, where William became a warehouseman. In 1889, Robert Duckworth, then aged 22, joined the Liverpool Police Force – a choice of vocation that was eventually to prove popular with all of the Duckworth brothers.

Select Bibliography

Books

Bridges, Yseult. *Two Studies in Crime*: Hutchinson, 1959.

Goodman, Jonathan. *The Killing of Julia Wallace*: George G. Harrap & Co. Ltd, 1969.

Hussey, Robert. *Murderer Scot-Free*: David & Charles, 1972.

Murphy, James. *The Murder of Julia Wallace*: Bluecoat Press, 2001.

Rowlands, John. *The Wallace Case*: Carroll & Nicholson, 1949.

Sayers, Dorothy L. 'The Murder of Julia Wallace' in *The Anatomy of Murder*: The Bodley Head, 1936.

Waterhouse, Richard. *The Insurance Man: A Real-life Whodunit Reconsidered*: Leyburn Designs (Publishing), 1994.

Wilkes, Roger. *Wallace: The Final Verdict*: The Bodley Head, 1984.

Newspapers

Aldershot News.

Empire News.

Liverpool Daily Post.

Liverpool Courier.

Liverpool Echo.

Liverpool Evening Express.

Other Sources

Assize Trial Transcript.

Documents held by Cheshire Record Office.

Documents held by Hill Dickinson LLP.

Documents held by Liverpool Record Office.

Documents held by Merseyside Police.

Who Killed Julia? Radio City documentary, produced by Wally Scott, researched by Roger Wilkes and Mike T. Green, written and presented by Roger Wilkes, 1981.

Acknowledgements

The writing of this book could never have been accomplished without the assistance and indulgence of many people and organisations; to those I have omitted, please accept my apologies and deepest gratitude.

A huge thank you goes to Roger Wilkes, who offered not only materials from his own archives and gave up his valuable time to read my manuscript, but maintained much interest and support throughout my endeavour. I owe an enormous debt of gratitude to Hill Dickinson LLP for not only accommodating me and allowing me unprecedented access to the wealth of original documentation contained in Hector Munro's Wallace Case archive, but also for their generosity in furnishing me with their permission to publish original documentation from this material. Likewise, I owe an enormous debt of gratitude to Kate McNicol and Merseyside Police for their more than generous support; not only in accommodating me and furnishing me with all of the remaining Wallace Case Police Files, but also for their overwhelming generosity in granting me permission to publish both original documentation and sensitive pictures. I would like to thank Richard Whittington Egan, Mike Macilwee, Mike T. Green and Paul Francis Williams for their support in giving up their valuable time to read and assess my manuscript. My warm, heartfelt thanks go to Wendy and Russell Johnston, Phil Mann and Donald Munro for their interest, encouragement and support – but most of all, for their friendship. A huge debt of gratitude is extended to the Jonathan Goodman Estate, Tom Brady, Jennifer Dunthorne, I. D. Fryer, Alastair Caird, Ann Williams, Kath Flynn, Pauline Truesdale, Tom Slemen, Tim Costello and Tony Swarbrick for their extremely generous and valuable contributions.

I should like to make it clear that my criticism of individuals within the Liverpool City Police Force at the time of Julia Wallace's murder does not apply to the force as a whole, or reflect upon the professionalism and integrity of the present-day Merseyside Police Force or any individual member within it.

Index